THE MOTHER OF ALL DILEMMAS

DREAMS OF MOTHERHOOD AND THE
INTERNSHIP THAT CHANGED EVERYTHING

KATHLEEN GUTHRIE WOODS

STEEL ROSE PRESS

Cover Design by BookCoverZone.

Photo courtesy of Jacob Guthmore.

Published by Steel Rose Press, Santa Rosa, CA.

The Mother of All Dilemmas: Dreams of Motherhood and the Internship That Changed Everything / Kathleen Guthrie Woods – 1st ed.

Library of Congress Control Number: 2021912179

ISBN: 978-1-7373048-0-7 (ebook)

ISBN: 978-1-7373048-1-4 (print)

————

Author's Note: Some names and/or identities have been changed, and some stories have been combined, to protect individuals' privacy.

For Jake

PROLOGUE

"*Y*ou really should have kids, you know."

I stood in the parking lot as my blood beat its way to the dangerous staccato that precedes a panic attack. I held my breath in a vice grip, afraid that if I let go, I'd unleash a primal scream. Regrets and frustrations, dreams deferred and lost, all that I'd been stuffing down for decades came roaring to the surface, while time and place froze around me. Everything I'd been denying about my not-quite-okay life came before me in a moment of excruciatingly painful clarity.

"You really should have kids, you know," he said to me.

"You." You—and you alone—really should have kids.

At 38, I wasn't married, I wasn't a mother, I wasn't fully a woman. I was nothing, and nothing I would remain, because Mr. Not-Quite-Right—the man who knew me best, my on-again, off-again, charming and frustrating, fiercely supportive and emotionally distant boyfriend of two-plus years—was not going to help me realize my dreams for a family. There was no "we" in his pronouncement about my future.

His offhand editorial was a compliment, really, based on a scene he had witnessed minutes earlier, as well as similarly intimate and recurring scenes in our past. While he shopped for a gizmo for his computer, debating the pros and cons of various models with a clerk, I settled on a stool in the store's showroom and fiddled with an online chess game. I sensed a presence, and out the corner of my eye spied a little boy, probably about six years old, observing me.

"Do you know how to play chess?" I asked.

He shook his head and a thick curtain of brown bangs fell before his eyes.

"Would you like to learn with me?"

Without making direct eye contact, he nodded, then with the back of his hand, nudged those soft bangs out of his face and stepped closer.

I talked to him about pawns and kings, sharing my limited knowledge of the game, while he eased in closer to the computer screen and to me. A hand on my knee, a lean against my outer thigh. The computer beat us without mercy, but we remained optimistic and hit "Replay" until...

"Time to go, buddy!" a dad called from the distance, and my little mate hopped off with a quiet "Thank you!" before I fully registered he had made his way into sitting on my lap.

Lately, and more and more frequently, children not unlike this sweet sprite cozied up to me in unexpected public places. There was the inconsolable infant who was passed around a group until she curled into my shoulder and fell into a peaceful sleep. An antsy toddler seemed determined to disrupt everyone with his pacing and chatter until I claimed his attention with a game I made up on the spot. I relished my roles as the fun aunt and the cool neighbor who was always up for a game of catch with the little kids in my life. My spirit quickened around children as I engaged with them, fascinated by their personalities, intellects, and unique observations.

I really should have kids.

And, oh sweet God, time was running out for me.

I'd been a good girl, I'd been playing by the rules; this wasn't supposed to be my fate. I had been waiting for the right partner, while hoping Mr. Not-Quite-Right would change, hoping I could inspire him to change to fit the pretty pictures in my head of perfect family life and my perfectly outlined Plan A.

Mr. Not-Quite-Right had tried.

"Let's just go to Vegas," he'd said.

"Let's just have a baby. I know it's what you want," he'd said.

"I want to make you happy," he'd said.

"No," I'd said. "But thank you."

For I knew. I knew our relationship wasn't right, and I knew I needed more. It didn't *feel* right. I wanted more for him, too, more of what he wanted for himself, and though I couldn't articulate what I thought he needed, I was certain I wasn't it.

Still, I'd lacked the courage to break free to find my elusive "it," to take the risk that I could find something—and someone —better. I was stuck in a killer cycle of "this is good enough," that place where women find themselves marrying for security or companionship or money or babies or prestige, or the coveted "Mrs." that confirms to outsiders *She must be worth loving*, then not much later finding themselves in divorce court wondering, *What the hell was I thinking?!?*

Meanwhile, everyone—my friends, family, doctors, celebrities—were telling me I should

BE A MOTHER!

Everything in society, my society in the early years of the 21st century, demonstrated to me

Womanhood means *Motherhood*.

No pressure.

My 40th birthday—with the irritating tick-tocking of my

biological clock and an epic case of baby lust—was less than 24 months away, and time was not my ally. There was so much I wanted: the miracle of pregnancy and birth, the passing on of holiday traditions, sugar-fueled birthday parties, family road trips across our great state, handmade Halloween costumes and forts made out of pillows, back-to-school nights and beach bonfires, cuddles and kisses. I longed for the struggles and challenges of parenting that pay off like no other achievement when you realize you've contributed a good human to the world. It was no longer enough for me that I had succeeded in my career. I wanted a successful *life* experience. I wanted to be a whole person, a fully expressed woman. I wanted to be the recipient of real love and God's blessings. I wanted to matter. And that, to me, meant having kids.

You really should have kids, you know.

I wanted to hate Mr. Not-Quite-Right, to blame him for everything that hadn't worked out for me. But in that moment in the parking lot, when he slammed the car door shut and revved the engine to snap me out of my internal hell, I knew that he had given me a gift. He released me from my fog, my patience, my denial, and lit a fire of passion under me. He set me free to pursue my dreams, because...

I love kids. I would be a wonderful mother. I should be a mother.

That morning I slid out of the passenger seat of his car and into the driver's seat of my own life, no longer okay with letting life happen to me. I turned my anger and angst into a fuel that would help me bravely face my fears, stare down any regrets, claim my power, and begin making some bold decisions about the life-altering choices I was finally confronting.

––––––

From my earliest days when I cuddled my favorite doll, Mary, I'd known that I wanted to bear and raise my own children, to follow in my mom's footsteps as my own family's Chief Nurturer. It was what I was supposed to do, it was expected of me, and I also yearned to experience the joys of parenting that my own mother and father modeled. As a single adult woman, I longed to express my gift for nurturing beyond the limitations of my circle of friends and Mr. Not-Quite-Right. I wanted to curl into a nest with flesh of my own making, not just that of the children of my friends and siblings. I wanted to be recognized as an adult, not just an old maid who couldn't settle down, take responsibility, commit. For too long I had waited in the wings as my closest friends went through pregnancy and into motherhood. I lived vicariously, certain that I would get my membership card in the mommy club soon, that I would join their ranks as a contributing grownup. I wanted to please, for once, my parents by following their examples and living up to their expectations of a good daughter.

But having been through my share of not-great relationships in my 20s and 30s, I knew for sure that I didn't want to get into co-parenting with someone who was not spouse-worthy, and my options were limited. And this wasn't 1950, or even 1970. This was a new millennium when women were better positioned to make choices for themselves about career, family, and self-fulfillment. We were told we had the right and the abilities to create and realize self-empowerment; we could Have It All. What I wanted most was to decide my own path, to get everything I wanted and needed, to live a fully realized life in my time and society, to be recognized for my contributions.

You really should have kids, you know.

Yes, I know I should, dammit!

Mr. Not-Quite-Right was not The One, not My One. I was no longer going to wait around for a man to give me the keys to my future, to give me a magical kiss and make all my dreams come true. So, following an amicable parting, I hitched up my big-girl breeches, ditched Plan A, and started exploring an option that was unimaginable to my mom's generation: becoming a single mother with the aid of donor sperm.

This would be my Plan B, and with an ounce of confidence, I felt ready(ish) to commit to seeing it through.

I embarked on a journey that day in the parking lot, one that would force me to deeply examine the expectations I'd long held about family, confront the realities of having and raising a child on my own, and wrestle with redefining my self-worth. Amidst embarrassing missteps, absurdly hilarious ah-hahs, and the heart-expanding and heart-crushing revelations that helped me evaluate what was the right path for me, I formulated plans, observed friends, listened to my heart, and struggled to decide for myself: *Could I do this, all on my own? Did I really want to?*

As I pooled my resources and set my mind to "getting it done!", I found myself in a scary vacuum. *How do I make a big life decision like this without knowing what it's really like? How do I know if real life will give me the fulfillment I long for?*

This is the story of how subsequent events and decisions formed my evolution from desperate, disempowered single woman to whole woman of my own design and definition. It wasn't a straight or smooth path. I thought I knew the route and final destination, but I was in for many surprises. Some came from unexpected mentors, opportunities, chance encounters and conversations, challenges, cathartic meltdowns, and leaps of faith. Some came from friends who candidly shared their stories from different perspectives of the motherhood discussion, and others came from strangers who opened up to me and trusted me with their confessions. I had to have faith that my teachers and my answers would come.

I hoped and prayed I wouldn't have regrets. I hoped to prove that my life was not an utter, shameful waste. Over time, I grew stronger, more conscious, and better able to make the choices that were and are right for me. I won't promise that I have all the answers, but I hope that by sharing my story, I will empower you as you find the courage to face your own crises of faith and life-defining dilemmas.

You really should have kids, you know.

It was time to determine for myself if that was true.

"Motherhood is as hard and as rewarding as everyone says. If it's something you really want, spending time with your child will not be a burden at all."

—*Valerie, Mara's mom*

"I cannot imagine what life would be like without my son. If everything else comes crashing down, I know that the one significant thing I've done in my life is to be a mom to somebody."

—*Liz, Dylan's mom*

1

TO BE—OR NOT TO BE—A (SINGLE) MOMMY

*A*lthough there are photographs of me gingerly holding each of my newborn siblings, I was too young (three years old when Carrie arrived, then four and a half for Kevin) to imprint the memories of my mother's pregnancies or what it was like to welcome a baby into the house. My first truly cognizant understanding of the baby-making process happened when I was maybe eight, and a family friend, pregnant with her third child, came for a visit. It looked like she had stuffed a basketball in her very tight T-shirt. "Would you like to touch it?" she asked. *Sure, okay.* It felt taut and firm, kind of like how it would feel if she had an actual basketball under her shirt. But then that ball moved. *Wowzer!* I snatched my hand back and about jumped out of my sandals, much to the delight of my mother and her friend, who coaxed me back for more. It was electric, it was magic! And then something, a tiny elbow or foot, jabbed the smooth surface as if it wanted to tear its way out. No kidding: There was a *person* in there.

While I wasn't all that keen on my inklings of how that little person would get out of there, I knew I wanted what our friend had. From that day forward, I had a desire and expectation for motherhood that imbued every fiber of my being. Evolution, natural selection, biological urge, maternal instinct.... I never thought to analyze what caused me to feel this way, it just...was. When I asked my closest girlfriends about it, they had felt the same way. "I knew since I was five that I wanted to be a mom," Joanna said. "Two kids—one boy, one girl—and a picket fence," Jill said, when I asked her to describe her dreams of adulthood.

Why did I want to be a mother? I honestly couldn't answer that because I never thought to question the desire. I just did. It's what women wanted. My own mother said her years of being home with us three as we were growing up were the happiest period and role of her life. It's what my sister and friends wanted, so, of course, I wanted it too. I longed to experience the rites of passage that I was told to expect. Having someone fall in love with me, ask for my hand in marriage, the wedding and all its celebratory events. Then, when the time was right, oh, God, the quickening, the expanding belly, the first kicks, the changes that occur as the most magical of machines, my own body, created from a few cells a whole new being. I wanted to experience a deep connection with a child— my child—starting with the creating and giving of life, followed by that special love that mothers bragged about to us still-single and childless gals, all that "I never knew love until I was a mother" stuff. I wanted the answers to the mysteries implied when people said "You'll understand when you're a parent," and I looked forward to bedtime stories, trips to Disneyland, Little League games, family picnics, board games, holidays, and the triumph of raising a good human. I imagined a mini-me with a unique personality, and I daydreamed how this fabulous creature would make me glow with pride whenever someone said to him or her, "You're just like your mother."

Along with any inborn biological inclinations and genetically wired baby lust, I also have to acknowledge that external pressures to conform played a role in my pursuit of motherhood. Everywhere I looked, I saw mommydom. News of a celebrity's engagement ring was quickly followed by speculation of a "baby bump." Actresses were photographed carrying their designer-clothed toddlers around town, as if they were the season's hottest accessory. The reality TV lineup was packed with shows about families with multiples, families with many, and families trying to conceive more. Even news headlines led off with "a mother of three..." versus "a woman was brutally murdered in her home...". I started to wonder...no, I began to *fear* that the only way I would have any value in society was by becoming a mother.

Was my life meaningless? I already felt I'd been on hold for my real life to begin, but geez. How was I going to fill this void?

"You really should be a mom," said my friend Rachel.

Dammit. I was so tired of hearing this and experiencing the waves of stress, guilt, desire, and shame that came with it. I just wanted to get on with the life I was told I should have.

Having celebrated the births of my friends' many children, I thought I was ready to embrace the changes to my family dynamics when my first niece arrived when I was 34. But as my sisters-in-law and sister, Carrie, and joined the mommies club, I found myself quietly disappearing into the background as they—and a growing number of my girlfriends—closed ranks at get-togethers to discuss childcare stories. Teething, sleepless nights, vaccinations, preschool options—all were important conversations, in which they were each able to feel supported, understood, and appreciated.

And I was envious. I longed to join in, but I had nothing legitimate to contribute, and I certainly wasn't so selfish that I would barge in and try to change the topic to something about my work or my busy schedule or my sometimes-entertaining adventures in dating. Still, behind my "I'm okay!" smile, it hurt to feel excluded, shunned, and silently branded as unworthy to participate at "family" events at church, in my community, in my own family. I was too much of a grownup to sit at the kids' table, but not yet mature enough to have earned a place at the parents' table. I spent holiday dinners in an awkward, yucky limbo.

One Christmas, I traveled from my home in Southern California to Northern California to be with my immediate family, with a reserved spot on Carrie's futon. But shortly after my arrival, Carrie departed to drive a couple of hours away to be with her partner's family. In my rental car, I drove about 30 minutes to join my brother, Kevin, his wife, Molly, and their guests for Christmas Eve dinner and festivities. After I helped Molly tuck their young girls into bed, Kevin pulled me aside and asked, "Can you come late tomorrow morning? We want to have some family time."

I understood his request on an intellectual level. They had just hosted an elaborate holiday feast for a large group of family and friends, would host a similar gathering the next day, and just wanted a few hours of quiet time together, to discover the booty from Santa, to hang out in their pj's and sip hot cocoa.

But *family time?*

What am *I*?

"Of course," I said graciously, fighting to hold back the tears that were welling up inside me and stifle the scream that threatened to escape through my pores. My heart was breaking as the reality sunk in that I had outgrown my original nuclear family, that I was not a part of this family, that I was not a part of any family.

I drove back to an empty house, where I was a guest. I occupied the remaining hours that night watching TV and trying to read a book, and resisted the temptation to drink myself to sleep on cheap red wine. I finally depressed myself to sleep.

On Christmas morning, I bundled up and went for a two-hour walk around the unfamiliar neighborhood. I breathed in the scents of fires burning in hearths. I caught glimpses of family members starting breakfast and feast preparations in softly lit kitchens. I listened to the quiet of the street as I wandered the blocks alone, separated from all the activity going on inside each home, and longed to be part of some family holiday tradition of togetherness. It killed the time. It killed a part of me.

"Never again," I vowed to myself. Never again would I allow myself to be so alone and so horribly vulnerable to heartbreak. I felt compelled to create my own solution by creating my own family, and I was starting to sense it wouldn't look anything like the dreams I had carried for so long.

———

Funny things started to happen to me as I zoomed through my 30s toward 40. Suddenly, all the time I thought I had to manifest Plan A—find a great guy, fall in love, and plan a life—disappeared in a poof. The biological clock I never heard ticking before was pointed out by...

Friends: "My mom said to tell you to hurry up because pretty doesn't last." *What?*

My mother: "I want to set you up with the nephew of my tennis partner's dentist's wife." Me: "Okaaaay. What's he like?" Mom: "You're both single." *Sigh....*

My gynecologist: "You really should have had children sooner." Me, as I hopped off the exam table: "Well, let me go home and fire up my time machine and I'll get back to you." *Really? Not helpful!*

I told myself I wasn't desperate, that I was instead merely

eager to get on with creating my own family and living the life I'd been programmed to expect. But when I did manage to meet an interesting guy with potential, I caught myself doing new math in my head: *If we date for 6 months, get engaged at Christmas, hold a June wedding and get pregnant on the honeymoon, I'll have my first baby before I'm 40 and can cram in a second child while I'm still 42.* What the fruitcake?! This was so backwards! Mother Nature was forcing me to find a fertile daddy before I could fully evaluate whether or not I was ready for the long haul of matrimony with a particular individual, or if we were even compatible. I found myself thinking about whether or not a guy was daddy material—stable career, from a close family, wants to settle down and raise offspring—versus who would make the best partner for me, that "great guy" I wanted. Perfect Dating Guy might be the one who loves to travel, likes to take risks, is creative and a tad dangerous. Not the best attributes for the role of Perfect Daddy I was trying to cast. Besides, I still thought of myself (for the most part) as a savvy woman who was willing to wait for the right Mr. Right, not just a uterus that was shopping for complementary DNA. I wanted the full package of relationship, partnership, and true, passionate companion.

I told myself I had to face my fears and allow myself to envision my future as a continuation of my present: single, childfree. I knew I had to start exploring the possibility that if I decided *not* to become a mom, I would somehow be okay going through life without ever experiencing the unique bond of unconditional love a mother shares with her child. That I wouldn't have regrets even though I'd miss things I'd looked forward to experiencing, like that sweet moment when a baby looks up, recognizes his mother, and breaks into a wiggly, room-filling grin. I needed to explore the possibility that I had wasted most of my childhood and all of my adult life waiting, longing, and planning for something I ultimately couldn't have.

Brutal! I had to search within myself to determine if I would be content with being the favorite aunt, and I had to strengthen my emotional armor so that I didn't seethe with resentment and jealousy every time Mother's Day rolled around. I needed to redefine my identity, reinvent my future, and refuse the label of lonely and bitter spinster. Therefore, I had to find meaning in my life, to create value in and for myself, so that I did not become more invisible and insignificant over time.

Denial was so much easier.

Instead of bravely counteracting my fears, I embarked on a new course of action. There had to be a way to get my dream, even part of my dream. I had been 38 when Mr. Not-Quite-Right steered me toward my new course. Since that day when I had gritted my teeth and begrudgingly accepted that the window for Plan A (going the traditional route of getting married and making babies the old-fashioned way) had closed, I steeled myself to look beyond the limitations of my fantasy world and embrace a new goal I could break down into clearly defined steps and bring to fruition. Plan B: I could become a mother on my own...with a donor daddy.

Whew! Deep breath. Shake off that weight of doubt. This was good. Progress! I was in a good place. Not frantic yet, but I was motivated to charge forward. I knew if I waited much longer, I risked being a medical experiment. I didn't want to endure fertility treatments, nor did I want to be the woman my kid's friends mistook for his grandmother. It was time to educate myself, build my support system, and knock myself up.

2

BEST NOT-GETTING-LAID PLANS

*O*kay. What did I need to do to get myself knocked up?

My friend Joanna had gone the sperm bank route 10 years earlier, when she was in her late 30s. An exam had revealed severe endometriosis, and Joanna's doctor gave her the "now or never" spiel. So—solo—she shopped the reputable agencies, found a hunky, handsome, and intelligent donor, placed the order, got pregnant, and delivered a healthy baby boy. David grew to be a tall, smart, and engaging teenager, and Joanna eventually married a man she met through friends at church who had three children from a previous marriage. Joanna created her family. She would be my role model, and I knew I could call on her for support.

With that success story in mind, I visited my friend Cori. Cori not only was a doctor of Chinese medicine, she also had her two kids in her late 30s. I figured she'd be a wealth of information. She was encouraging as she helped me lay out a regimen for getting my body ready. I cut out sushi, fried foods, and alcohol. I purchased a basal thermometer and drew charts to track my ovulation cycle. I made certain my daily vitamins contained the recommended increased amount of folic acid, and I added more lamb to my diet. I wanted my system to be ready to go on command as soon as I found Donor Right.

There was one particularly awkward experience during a lunch break when I was working onsite with a big client, when a coworker and I popped into the market to pick up a few supplies before heading back to the office.

"Oh, CONGRATULATIONS!" the female checker said to me in a voice loud enough to attract other customers' attention. "You're PREGNANT!"

"Uh...no...," I said in a very tiny voice, hoping the floor would open up and allow me to escape through the basement.

"What happy, happy news!" she said, holding aloft my supersize jar of prenatal vitamins.

"You're pregnant?!" my coworker asked, looking at me sideways as the gears went to work in her brain. "But I didn't think you were, like, even seriously dating any...."

"Not! No. Thank you." *Oh my God.*

I grabbed my bag, grabbed my coworker, and skedaddled out of there.

"You're...?"

"No," I said, sucking in a deep breath then responding in a rapid stream of explanations I hoped would shut down any further discussion. "Just planning ahead, trying to take care of myself and getting my body ready for when the time does come. Haven't made any big plans beyond that." I touched her arm and pleaded with her with my eyes. "Please don't say anything to anyone."

"Okay," she said, and gave me a conspiratorial smile. "But let me know."

I took several more deep breaths, hoping to calm my racing heart and cool my face from beet red to healthy glow. Clearly, I was not ready to handle the encounters coming my way, and I was going to have to get more comfortable responding to intrusive questions stat if I was going to be publicly single and pregnant with a baby of unknown origins. Maybe I'd practice out loud in front of my bathroom mirror, like I did when I worked on incorporating new affirmations. (*I am a strong, independent woman*). "Hi! I am having a baby on my own!" (*My body is a vessel of love.*) "Yep, excited about being a mom!" (*Everyone supports my highest good.*) "There is no 'father' and it's none of your f-ing business!" Oof. I had my work cut out for me.

Meanwhile, I made a list of the things I wanted to do before my time and attention was fully devoted to growing and raising my little one. Novels I wanted to read and movies I wanted to see. I booked long overdue vacations to Italy and France. I expanded my list of clients and built a solid foundation for my business. I adopted Beau, a one-year-old yellow Labrador Retriever, who some friends said would provide great training for caring for a future child, and others swore would attract eligible men. I started checking to-dos off my list while I prepared myself physically and mentally. I was on a mission and time was critical!

In six months, I told myself, if I hadn't met anyone special (i.e., daddy material, because—let's be honest—I hadn't 100 percent given up on that option), then I would start researching donor organizations.

Those six months sped by in a flurry of travel, movie nights, new work commitments, dog walks, and ovulation trackings, so I gave myself another six.

During that time, I told a few close friends about my plans. Paula, who was married and finally pregnant with her first child after going through fertility treatments, was thrilled. "You will be a *great* mother! This is wonderful news!" Gretchen, one of my best friends and a stay-at-home mother with three girls, made a commitment to coach me through labor. "I'll even go to Lamaze classes with you!" she promised. And Michael, a single gay man I'd grown close to at a former job, swore in a text message he would be "the best uncle in the world!" I was buoyed by the offers of support for me and my child-to-be.

But a little voice kept poking holes in my picture-perfect bubble, nagging me, distracting me with glimmers of reality. Michael had promised to meet me for dinner once a month, yet because of our busy careers, it had been three years since I'd last seen him in person. Gretchen lived more than an hour's drive from me, and she could barely keep up with her own kids' schedules. Paula and her husband were exploring the possibility of adopting other children, in case they weren't able to get pregnant a second time. They all had full lives with overwhelming obligations and responsibilities. I found it difficult to believe they could add my future family's needs to their own. I couldn't reasonably expect them to help me when the baby was colicky or to offer me a break so I could catch up on work. Expecting consistent support from my own existing family was equally unrealistic, as my aging parents were an hour away by car, and my siblings were an hour away by plane.

After the initial excitement of my kid's first few weeks, I couldn't really count on anyone to stick around to change poopy diapers when I was out-of-my-mind exhausted. The possibility of my getting sick, being sentenced to bed rest, and having no one else to rely on for childcare and financial support was terrifying. I had a one-bedroom apartment and a career as a freelance writer in a temperamental industry. As a single gal, this freedom was stimulating, exciting, motivating; as a potential mommy, the lack of stability and security posed serious risks. I faced potential money woes, healthcare needs, lack of social life, reduced living conditions. Being a parent demands incredible sacrifice; being a single parent demands the usual sacrifices without the safety nets that come with a family unit.

Furthermore, I had to ask myself *why* I wanted a child, *if* I could support that child, *how* I would fend for myself and that child. If I chose the single mother route, I needed to be ready to assume every responsibility, for I wouldn't have the luxury of being able to fall back on a partner who could provide physical, emotional, and financial support. The more I explored my concerns, the scarier reality looked.

I toyed with the fantasy that I could win big in the state lottery and be set for life, but while money could afford me day care, school tuitions, and a roof over our heads, I'd still lack the emotional connections I craved for myself. I needed to know who I was going to call when my child said his first word, took his first step, and performed his first drum solo on my pots and pans. In my mind, I felt I'd be missing a key piece of life experience if I had no one with whom to share these things. No partner, no family, certainly no village. I was on my own.

I know many people who have turned out just fine after growing up in single-parent households. My father was one of them; his father passed away when my dad was 11 and his sister was seven, and their mom raised them on her own while working as a fourth grade teacher. It wasn't glamorous, they struggled financially, but they made it work. I also have friends who grew up with single moms after their parents divorced, but even then, there were two incomes and shared parenting. I respect and admire the people who make single parent/single income households work, but I couldn't imagine choosing that path.

Then again, that's not quite right. I could imagine choosing it, with confidence and happy anticipation, if—big *if*—I had the foundation to support that choice. I live in a remarkable time in history when women—and men—really can make their own choices about parenthood. Come to think of it, one of the most joyous celebrations I've ever attended was a welcoming party as a social worker handed a baby boy over to my friend Phillip, a big-hearted, generous, hardworking, single gay man. "You would be a great dad," his friends had long said to him, so he, too, took a nontraditional route to building a family: He became a father with the assistance and generosity of a surrogate. If he could do it, well.... My friend and his son just might be the first two members of my new village.

When I shared some of my concerns with my friend Alicia, whose baby had just moved past the toddler stage, she encouraged me to proceed. "When I look back at pictures of him, I just can't stand it," she said. "He was so cute and so smiley; he is still such a sweet boy. And those precious years when they are so excited about everything and they're such little love bugs—you really do yearn for that."

I yearned for that. Oh, how I yearned for that.

"I do know that becoming a single parent was not really an option for me in terms of economics. I also remember long ago taking a walk and hearing the piercing cry of an infant and knowing in my heart that that was not a sound that I would want to face day after day on my own."

—Alicia, who thought she'd aged out of motherhood until she reconnected with a former boyfriend, married, and got pregnant with her first child at 41

3

MILESTONES & MIRACLES

*a*nd then I turned 40. That magical number. If I were in a Hollywood movie, I'd play the grandmother. In the year leading up to my own milestone day, my mailbox was flooded with invitations to surprise big birthday parties for friends, hosted by their loving spouses. I felt so alone. Not only would I be going to those parties solo, I faced hosting my own party for my own Big Birthday, if I could muster up the courage to do it. It felt like less of a celebration and more like another mark of my failings. While many of my friends knew that I wanted to have a man in my life, few knew of my desire to have a child. Since I hadn't yet fully confirmed my plans with myself, I had only confided in a handful of close friends. Furthermore, I hadn't mentioned any of this to my mom.

I knew she wanted to be helpful. And I knew I wanted to give her the gift of being a grandmother to my children. I thought back to a Christmas pageant I'd attended with friends, to see their adorable six-year-old perform in his debut role as "Nonspeaking Shepherd." As I craned my neck to watch the procession of children come from the back of the cathedral, I caught sight of two women in the pew behind me, a woman about my age, and an older version of her, who I assumed was her mother. I watched the electrified moment as they spotted a tiny girl dressed as an angel, with a gold tinsel halo slightly askew. The child beamed and waved shyly when she noticed the women waving at her, and as they turned back to the front, the older women squeezed the hand of her daughter and they exchanged a look with flushed faces and quivering smiles. They both had tears in their eyes, and so did I. I so wanted to give this to my own mother. I felt guilty that she was attending bridal and baby showers, lavishing gifts upon the daughters of friends, while I had denied her her own day in the Mother-of-the-Bride spotlight and grandmotherly bragging rights. Yes, she had received this from my siblings, but I remained the great disappointment.

Right. So beyond the internal pressures and the external pressures, there were the parental pressures. That inelegant mix of guilt and shame and disappointment that came from not graduating my parents into grandparents. Since I hadn't confided in my mother yet, I certainly wasn't going to start now and quite potentially set her up for more disappointment. I couldn't bear to risk telling her about my rather extraordinary Plan B, then have it fall through, or worse, chicken out and once again fail to meet her expectations for me. I was on my own, and time was of the essence.

———

On the north side of 40, conscious of my eggs' shelf life nearing expiration, I had to decide if—for real—becoming a mom with donor sperm was something I could do and wanted to do. But as I approached each self-imposed deadline to take the leap, I knew in my heart I wasn't ready to progress to the next step. I didn't want to have a baby for all the wrong reasons: to fit in, to create my sense of worth based on being someone's mother, to please my parents. I didn't want to rush into something I would later regret.

The rational half of my brain told me I needed to research the actual dollar costs of acquiring donor sperm, as well as learn about the physical process, so that I could schedule work commitments and maternity leave, create to-do lists, and prepare for, well, every possible scenario.

I bit the bullet and googled "how to get pregnant." Item number one read "how to get pregnant with a boy." I assumed the answer would be your basic birds 'n' bees, so was a little shocked when the post instead offered tips on how to create a male baby. (Have sex closer to ovulation because male sperm die off faster and female sperm have better odds due to their persistence.) Interesting, but not what I needed.

Next up were scary warnings for women ages 35 to 39. The odds were not in my favor, as there was no mention of women 40 and beyond.

Finally I searched for "how to get pregnant as a single woman." A long list of articles popped up, with topics ranging from the cost of fertility treatments (save to read later), to how to choose a donor (ask for his medical records to make sure he's disease-free—yikes), instructions for at-home insemination (save for later), and effects of stress on fertility (well, *now* I'm stressed!).

I logged off and checked in with my mind and heart. Rational, emotional, rational, emotional. *Tick tock.* I wasn't ready to take the next step. My heart wanted the end result of a beautiful baby, but my head was chickening out of working out the finer details, the nuts and bolts, of taking this mostly (to me) uncharted course. I couldn't even get curious about looking at donors' bios or start imagining the attributes of my designer child. Honestly, I didn't want to admit that I was giving up on

Fate, Love, and my fairy-tale ending. I couldn't face that buying sperm and inseminating myself (gack!) was my last and final option. There was no romance in that scenario! Quite simply, I hadn't yet hit my rock bottom of running out of time, facing a deadline, and having to pull a plug on a choice. What awaited me at the other side of that choice? Would I make the "right" choice? Committing to an unknown future, without a team to guide me or even a partner to journey with me, scared me, and I wasn't yet motivated or inspired *enough* to embrace the path ahead as a solo adventurer.

Which left me feeling frustrated and disappointed in myself. I had been a risk-taker in the past—quitting a draining job before I had a more fulfilling one to go to, giving notice on an apartment while trusting the right new home would open up in time—but they were always calculated risks. In each case I knew my resources and my limitations, and was confident I would ultimately land on my feet.

I knew I had to face the realities of being a single mother before I committed myself fully. What tugged at my mind was recognizing that, while I'd always *expected* to have a family life, I'd never considered whether I really *wanted* it—wanted it enough to embrace all the challenges along with the loveliness. I had only one true model. I grew up with a stay-at-home mom and breadwinning-and-actively-involved-in-our-lives dad who are still married to each other (now for over 50 years), in a community of families that looked like ours. Our home life was traditional, conservative, upper-middle class, and our extended family mirrored "The Thanksgiving Painting" by Norman Rockwell. We were privileged and happy, so naturally, it was assumed my siblings, Carrie and Kevin, and I would follow our parents' example. My friends, primarily Gen Xers and tail-end Baby Boomers, shared my expectations of a life designed around family. "I always figured that children would be in the picture somehow," my friend Liz told me, "but I never really had a specific game plan of when that would happen." Like me, she assumed she'd be lucky and it would eventually come together, which it did when she met a great guy and they welcomed their first child. As far as she, I, and our circle of girlfriends were concerned, this was the path to happiness and the mark of success.

But could I really make a satisfying version of this as a single parent? Only I could answer this dilemma. No mommy friend, celebrity, or online quiz could resolve it for me. Did I want this enough to gamble and sacrifice for it?

My pal Lori was an unexpected voice in this discussion. "I hate it," she confided to me over a rare catching-up lunch. She had married in her mid-40s and she and her husband rushed into parenthood, producing two children in three years. Once a go-getting career gal, she was now an exhausted stay-at-home mom to toddlers. The blood left my face and ran cold in my veins as I considered what she'd just said. "No, no," she hurried to explain, "I don't hate *my children*, I love my children. But if I'd known what I was getting into, I wouldn't have done it."

We'd talk more about her reasons for feeling this way later, but what it taught me in the moment was that, before I took my leap of faith, I needed more in-depth information from solid sources to be able to fully consider all my options and make the right decisions for myself in the short and very long term. And, okay, so...I also needed to embrace that in this situation I was not really a "leap of faith" kind of gal, but more of a "walk in someone else's shoes while weighing *all* my options" kind of gal. There would be no leaping with regard to this most precious and important decision. Instead of seeking answers from the marketing fluff found in books, magazines, and movies, I felt I needed to go about this wisely, taking in information from my heart, my head, my experiences, and those around me. I needed to try out being a single mommy. I needed, and wanted, a reality check. I needed...well...an internship.

And for once, my prayers were answered with exactly what I'd requested. My sister, Carrie, called with an extraordinary opportunity.

4

PERFECT VACATION PLANS

A phone call interrupted my dinner with the cast of Entertainment Tonight. It was a weekday night in the spring, a couple of months before my 41st birthday. Carrie was calling to ask a favor. A big favor.

"What would you think...?"

I set the TV on mute and gave her my full attention.

"We're planning a two-week trip to Europe this summer," Carrie explained. "First we're going to visit friends in Germany, then we're going to hike Cinque Terre in Italy. We were going to take Jake with us, but now that we've really thought about it, it would be crazy to take a 15-month-old on a trip like this, with messed-up sleep schedules and weird food and all."

"No kidding."

"So...and say no if you don't want to, there's really no pressure...but would you consider..."

"Yes."

"I haven't asked you yet."

"You were going to ask me to babysit Jake while you're gone, and my answer is yes."

"Really?"

"Yes," I repeated, my mind racing as I shooed Beau away from the coffee table and my oh-so-tempting beef-and-broccoli stir-fry.

"Do you want to do it just part of the time and he could stay with someone else the rest of the time?"

"No. I'll do it all."

"All two weeks?"

"The whole tamale."

Details would be worked out in subsequent phone calls and emails, but the basic plan was in place. I couldn't get over the timing of this. It was perfect. It was exactly what I needed, what I'd asked for, and I was elated. For two weeks, I would be my nephew's primary provider of food, comfort, fresh diapers, bedtime stories, entertainment, and discipline. For two weeks, I would play house in their home, run the household, and serve as caregiver of their precious kid.

For two weeks, he would be *my* kid.

So as not to disrupt his normal routine, Jake would go to day care Monday through Friday. This meant I'd also get to experience what it was like being a single *working* mother. Having him out from underfoot for six hours each day, I thought, would give me ample time to run errands, take care of household chores, and turn around projects for clients. Then, in the afternoons after I picked him up from day care, we'd schedule play dates, go to the park, play at home just the two of us, or visit my brother and his family. I'd manage it all beautifully, thus proving to myself that I was ready to do it full-time for real.

This was quite a leap forward from my previous childcare experience with Jake, and with Chloe, Ellie, and Quinn (Kevin and Molly's daughters). I'd never done anything beyond a few hours of daytime babysitting or sleepovers in the guest room with their parents in another room down the hall, yet I was confident I could handle this big undertaking while proving that my dream—and now big hairy audacious goal—of being a single mommy could become my reality.

Certainly, it would be more instructive than the high school health class assignment of carrying around an egg for a week. It was more like the working vacations I'd read about—and mocked. I mean, what kind of idiot *pays* to spend her vacation time working? I have to confess, I'd secretly snickered at people who took "vocation vacations," in which they tried out other jobs during a few precious days off from their existing jobs. My expectations were different from those people who hoped to escape grueling, demeaning, and boring jobs by test-driving fantasy jobs like horse breeding, landscape designing, running a bed and breakfast, chocolate-making, and sword-making. I wasn't interested in glamming up my life. I simply hoped to discover whether it was possible to bring home the bacon, fry it up in a pan, and never let my little guy forget he's The Man. I sought on-the-job experience with all of the highs, the dulls, and the doses of reality. Here was my chance to try out the one job I'd dreamed about since I was a child: I was going to be someone's mommy.

Like the vacationers whose testimonies I'd read, I believed my experience would inspire me, lead me out of my comfort zone, encourage me to look beyond my self-imposed boundaries, and motivate me to make life-altering changes. Everything was finally falling into place for me, and I was confident I would come home from my trial run with beautiful mommy memories and enough experience to make informed decisions about my future. This was perfect. This opportunity was better than anything I could have dreamed up for myself. It was going to be awesome, and I was going to be the best vacation mommy ever!

"Do one or the other. If you try to do both, both will suffer, and it's always your career that suffers most."

—advice given to Beth, a young woman trying to figure out how to have kids and a career, from her mentor (who chose her career)

"I'm not a big believer in 'doing it all.' You do have to sacrifice some things, and hard choices have to be made. I've missed opportunities. I've probably given up a 20-year cycle of focusing exclusively on my career."

—Liz, Dylan's mom, on if she has any regrets

5

BIG GIRLS DON'T CRY, THEY MELT DOWN

*P*acking, tidying up the house, typing notes for the house-/dog-sitter, scrambling to wrap up client jobs. In the last 24 hours before my departure, I engaged in a flurry of busyness that barely stifled my anxieties. It was as if frantic miners (Panicky, Clueless, and Vexful—*Heigh Ho!*) were chipping away at my subconscious and shoveling worries into overflowing piles. But instead of dealing with my fears about how poorly equipped I was to succeed in my coming venture as a single mommy intern, I bulldozed those piles of emotions aside. I'd dig into them, I told myself, another day.

Throughout the afternoon, I thought about how I should have acknowledged, from the beginning, that I was a living-alone-working-at-home gal whose typical day was full, yet structured and calm: gym, post office, walk the dog, work at my desk until lunch outside at my bistro table; several more hours of work, a few loads of laundry, dinner at the coffee table; settling onto the couch with a movie or book for company for a couple of hours, then to bed; repeat. Yet here I was, preparing to take on the needs of a toddler in addition to my work plus home-care plus self-care plus any crisis that might pop up.

I can do this, I can. Bulldoze, bulldoze.

I looked forward to finally experiencing the joy and laughter of mommydom, meals shared across a family-sized dining table, and sweet moments spent cuddling before bedtime. Meanwhile I rationally expected bites of reality that would make me better relate to friends with kids who wistfully commented on my freedom to come and go as I pleased, watch TV shows without annoyingly catchy jingles, read books without pop-up pictures, and wear white T-shirts more than once. I was in for who-knows-what kind of chaos, the kind that might involve spending designated working hours scrubbing barf out of the carpet, running to the grocery store to restock child-friendly menu items and prescription refills for the childhood disease du jour, or juggling a kid with a cold, demanding clients, and my own crankiness brought on by sleep deprivation. Would I be an overprotective hover-mother, or the one who was otherwise distracted while her toddler practiced his couch-diving skills? Would I recognize or miss the signs that he was starving, exhausted, and suffering from acute rash formations brought on by toxic diaper overflow? Would I exhaust myself by being on hyperalert for every little murmur, or would I snore through the three-alarm fire?!

Enough. Shhhh... Bulldoze. You have lots to do, and there aren't enough hours in the day to get it all done.

There weren't enough hours in the day to get it all done.

Oh, sweet God, what had I gotten myself into?!

It was late in the day when I felt myself being buried under a growing heap of anticipatory remorse, certain I was going to screw up my sister's vacation and a crucial period of my nephew's emotional development all because I was cocky enough to believe I—all alone—could handle it. The enormity of the responsibilities I faced, with minimal real-world planning and certainly no real training, were only the short-term fears. Long term was my life, the life plan I'd nurtured for decades. Now my future swung in the balance, on the cusp of before internship and after internship, and I felt like a patient who anticipates a life-altering diagnosis and the potentially harsh new reality after. Everything—*everything*—was about to change in ways I couldn't possibly imagine, and I was terrified of the prospect of the truly blank slate I would face if the answers I sought about how to achieve the mommy chapter of my life were not the answers I wanted.

Clutching T-shirts still warm from the dryer, I began pacing between the laundry area at the far end of my kitchen and the open suitcase in the middle of the living room. *Breathe, Kath.* Beau looked up at me from his spot on the rug, wondering if this was a signal we were going out for a walk, but he gave up as he saw that my figure eights around the couch and through the kitchen were not ending at the coatrack where his leash was stashed. With each turn, my breath came in shorter, more stifled gasps, as I fought the urge to kick something, hit something, scream. I threw the shirts onto the desk chair and compulsively opened and closed my fingers into fists, hoping to safely expel the dizzying energy. Yet it all came crashing down as one of my favorite pieces of music, a jazz arrangement for acoustic guitar called "Classical Gas," came on the stereo.

Those sweet, magical tones crept through my nerves like a stealth electric current and tingled as it exited my fingers and toes. As the guitarist plucked at the first slow, melancholy notes, the doors to my heart burst open, exposing and releasing all the passions and fears, hopes and longings I held deep inside. A cry tickled the back of my throat, and tears welled in my eyes, although I fought back. Spinning in a dance of flying notes and chords, I felt myself racing toward my dreams, grasping, reaching out to catch them before they slipped by me as brief memories or passing fancies. Suspended notes were the hopes I still clung to, the prayers for all my dreams to come true just as I had envisioned them. All I ever wanted, all I'd ever hoped to become, rushed past me like a movie playing on fast-forward. "Hurry!" the music said to me, "You are running out of time! Go, go, go!" I held my breath, felt panic rising in me as I reached for a chair, fell to my knees, then crumpled onto the cool hardwood floor. As the soaring music washed over me, I gave in to the sobs that flooded from my core. Curled in a ball, my chest heaving, my body shaking, I slowly rocked myself back and forth while inviting each of my fears to introduce itself.

I felt the enormity of the responsibility I had accepted and shuddered at the possibility of hurting precious Jake, inflicting serious physical or deep emotional injury. My heart ached at the possibility of his not taking to me, not trusting me, rejecting me. I dreaded the possibility that I could turn out not only to be a bad temporary mother but a bad aunt. If all went horribly awry, said my now despairing imagination, this could be my last experience of closeness with a child. My failings could mark me as an outcast in the only family I had, as the aunt who couldn't be trusted, the aunt who couldn't handle responsibility, the aunt who would never be deemed worthy of a seat at the big kids' table.

Lying broken on the floor, I pictured myself lonely and depressed, isolated from my child-rearing friends, relegated to spinsterworld. Hopeless, friendless, tragic, I'd live out my future days in a dull and meaningless routine until death ultimately claimed me. Hell, I'd be so forgotten, I wouldn't even rate a published obituary. For what would it say? *Single, childless woman dies alone. She had no one in her life to care.*

Well, that would have been my fate had I not chosen to take this risk, said my reasoning mind, which I was grateful was reasserting its voice. But I needed to face the possibility that the answers I found on my vacation mommyship would negate my fantasies, that when I gathered all the information and took a good look at the deepest question in my soul, the answer would be "No." *No, I'm not cut out to be a mother. The sacrifices are too much. No, I don't want to do this.*

There was a terrifying possibility that I'd spent most of my life waiting, hoping, wasting, and pretending. What brought out the most gut-wrenching sobs was the possibility that all my dreams would be unfulfilled and I would have to create new dreams, from scratch. I couldn't imagine how to begin to replace something as significant as motherhood in my life's plans. I was grieving the loss of something I might never have.

It was too late to back out. It was too late to change my mommy internship plans and my sister's vacation plans and reject this opportunity, this experiment, this gift that the Universe had given me. And so, as the song's final crescendo eased into gentle resolution—*pianissimo,* "very gentle"— promising strength and peace, I looked heavenward and made one last desperate prayer. "Dear God, watch over me and Jake. Guide me, help me. Show me my purpose. Please, please let me be a good mother."

Not quite spent, I sprawled on the floor and wallowed in a quieter expulsion of grief. Cry, clutch, wipe nose and eyes, repeat. Sensing that I was no longer a violent risk, Beau came over and nudged my back with his cold, damp nose, then curled up in the arc of my legs. I reached down and caressed the top of his head, seeking the solace only a dog can provide. I felt my body give in and give up as my breathing slowed and a balm of acceptance began to spread over me. *Sometimes that has to happen,* rational mind said to me. *Sometimes you have to be broken, driven to your knees, and have the path completely cleared before you can see the Light.*

I was still shaky, but I could put one foot in front of the other until I got on the airplane bound for Northern California, and then I would keep taking steps forward, doing the best I could with whatever I was given. One way or another, my life would shift, starting the very next day. My visions of what parenthood, specifically single parenthood, looked like, would be challenged in the next two weeks. By the end of my vacation, I *would* be a different person. I was going to lose a part of myself, perhaps my dreams, or perhaps the expectations, mine and others', that had hindered me from answering my true calling, whatever that might be. There was no going back.

I can do this, I told myself. *Enough thinking, enough imagining the worst. It's time for doing. I will* do *this.*

Finally, slightly embarrassed yet relieved that no one other than Beau had witnessed my overindulgence in self-pity and drama queen-ness, I rolled over to my side, pushed up to all fours, and planted one foot firmly onto the floor to launch myself up. Acting more courageous than I felt, I stood up straight, squared my shoulders, took one big cleansing breath, and went back to work.

My big-girl meltdown had served a purpose. I'd allowed my demons to spew their poison, and I felt semi-confident that would chill out for a bit and give me a break so I could begin the next stage of my journey. I was scared, and I was hopeful. I felt determined to return home from my vacation mommy internship either content at last to be the world's greatest aunt, or ready to google sperm banks.

With one last look at my packing list, I snapped shut my suitcase and set it next to the front door. An apple and a few slices of good cheddar served as dinner, and allowed for minimal cleanup. I flossed my teeth and brushed my hair, cleansed and moisturized my swollen face, slipped into cozy flannel PJs, and tucked my comforter around me. Beau curled into his spot at my feet.

"I love you, Beau," I whispered. "Dream of slow-moving cats."

He rolled over to rest his head on my leg. Before I drifted into a deep and restorative sleep, my last thought was how nice it would be to have my own little someone say "Love you" back.

6

MEET JAKE

The star of my vacation mommy story is a 15-month-old boy we call Jake, Jakey, and occasionally Jakester. If Jake had been born five centuries ago, he could have modeled for Botticelli's cherub. His skin was creamy, not yet dotted by freckles, religiously protected by generous dowsings of SPF 50 sunscreen for babies. His soft, round features radiated warmth, health, and joy, with rosy, apple-shaped cheeks you wanted to nuzzle. His pudgy limbs, still clumsy as he learned to master his muscles and reflexes, brought to mind the Michelin character, the Pillsbury Dough Boy, or a laughing Buddha. Sometimes, though, when I watched him sitting in all his roly-poly-ness, I could envision his potential future as a couch potato, reclining lazily in a Barcalounger, TV remote in one hand, a Budweiser in the other. It was an endearing image.

He laughed a lot, a laugh that started in his belly, opened his mouth, lit up his eyes, shook his whole little body, and infected everyone around him. At his first Christmas Eve dinner, he got a case of the giggles over who knows what, and 10 adults forgot more weighty conversations about recent headlines from around the world to laugh with him and at him. He had the power to lift up whatever mood I brought into the room.

At birth, Jake was long and lean and graced with dark, almost black, curly hair. Within a few months, this fell out, and fine, pale-lemony wisps grew in its place. Both shades complimented his clear blue eyes, the kind that looked into the deepest part of my soul but were filled with such love and delight that I felt safe under his scrutiny.

He shared those baby blue eyes with his grandfather, Kathy's father. The blond hair mimicked photos of his mommy as a toddler, though we suspect, as he gets older, the black curls will return, he'll sprout up tall, and come to resemble his donor daddy.

Wait...what? His mother Kathy? His "donor daddy"? Let me explain.

Jake is the son of my sister, Carrie (aka Mama), and her partner, Kathy (Mommy). Carrie and Kathy were legally registered and fully committed domestic partners, what California at that time deemed the separate but equal version of marriage for gay and lesbian couples. Together, Jake and his mommies comprise a gay family. I know there are people who will be quick to judge, and judge harshly, when I state that my sister's version is one of the best models I've experienced for a *loving* family. And I am well aware of the blessings of living in a time and an area of our country, our world, where a two-mommy unit doesn't raise an eyebrow. Carrie, Kathy, and Jake are a family. Period. No need for discriminating labels.

From the beginning of their relationship, Carrie and Kathy knew they wanted children, and since Kathy is two years older than my sister, they decided she would be the first to get pregnant. A close friend donated his sperm (donor daddy) and relinquished all parental rights while remaining a part of the extended family, kind of like a really, really special uncle. Kathy conceived Jake at home via a low-tech, child-sized medicine dropper. ("We got it from Walgreens pharmacy for free!" my sister told me.) Six months after his birth, Carrie legally adopted him. Jake's birth certificate lists Kathy and Carrie as his "parents"; there are no gender distinctions. A few years after Jake's arrival, Carrie planned to get pregnant with and carry their second child, also using their friend's donated sperm so that their children would be biologically related; Kathy would then go through the adoption process.

When they explained their family planning to me, I was impressed with how much thought went into it. After researching and exploring their legal options, they met with counselors and attorneys to make sure each mommy and the donor daddy was comfortable with her/his participation and future roles. They timed their pregnancies to allow each partner to be there to support the pregnant and new mother. In every way possible, they prepared themselves financially, physically, and emotionally—similar to what I was now trying to do for myself.

With plans in place, they got ready for Jake's arrival. Having already welcomed three nieces, I was familiar with the awesome heart-expanding sensation that occurred with each new addition to the Guthrie brood. I'd come home to messages on my answering machine with my brother coaching someone to say, "Hi, Aunt Kath"...

"Ha wah kah."

"How are you?"

"Ha wa wa?"

...and I'd fight the urge to go outside and hug the nearest stranger.

I was prepared, I thought, when Carrie and Kathy invited me to join the grandparents-to-be in the hospital waiting room.

But nothing prepared me for the awe, the rush of desire to love and protect, the acknowledgement of our divine presence, as I soaked up this miracle of a new person. Jake and I were briefly introduced for the first time about 30 minutes after he was born. He was getting his first sponge bath, and he was not enjoying it. Red, squirming, squawking in bursts of frustration —it was cold out in the world! I couldn't yet touch him, could only admire and coo, but it was love at first sight. He was the only person I had known since the day of his birth (I didn't get to meet my nieces till a month or two after their arrivals), so that also gave him a special place in my heart.

We became better acquainted when I held him for the first time several hours later. A photo from that day shows me in my favorite orange crewneck sweater, cuddling a bundle that looks like a flannel burrito with Jake's head. You could already discern his features.

"Hello, Jake. I am your Aunt Kath. I am so very glad to meet you. We are going to have a lot of fun. In fact, you and I are going to have many wild rumpusses together," I said, referring to the line from *Where the Wild Things Are*, my most recent contribution to the family library.

I slowly walked around the hospital room, humming nursery rhymes to him. I sat and admired his crinkly face, watched him yawn and stretch, and inhaled his newborn scent, part baby soap, part pixie dust. I hoarded every moment until I begrudgingly gave him up so his grandparents could all get their fair share of Jakey time.

My connection with Jake grew quickly as we became more familiar with each other. He was comfortable in my arms at family gatherings, he babbled on the phone with my sister's encouragement, and he was just darn cute.

Jake grew to love listening to stories, he loved to mimic what he heard, and he also loved to talk. Talking could mean two things: that fabulous gobbledygook babies speak as they experiment with their voices, and communicating through baby sign language. When Jake was six months old, Kathy started teaching him a vocabulary of signs, a simplified version of what is used for children and adults with hearing challenges. This technique was designed to help a toddler, who couldn't yet coordinate his voice with his thoughts, express his needs and desires through hand signals.

Standing quietly in the background, I'd watch with amazement while Kathy and Jake practiced. Frequently they did this during meal time, since many of the signs were for food, and Jake, strapped into his high chair, would have fewer distractions. With lots of patience and repetition, and help from an illustrated guidebook, Kathy got Jake to repeat her actions and then do them without prompting. Snuggled in a cocoon of their own making, eyes locked, their voices and movements were gentle, calm. Then, when something clicked for Jakey, they seemed to experience almost an electrical jolt. I could almost hear his brain working through the puzzle, then lock it into place. They'd both smile, laugh, and applaud his— their—achievements. His favorites: milk (squeezing his fist as if milking a cow), blueberries (tapping index finger to thumb, almost as if making the initial movement toward snapping), more (poking a thumb into the opposite palm), and all done (waving of both hands). My favorite was the one they'd created for "Aunt Kath": patting himself on the head. Carrie had told me about it in advance, but I still choked on tears the first time he looked up at me with those blue eyes, signed my name, and smiled in recognition, so proud of himself for getting it right.

At 15 months, he was well on his way to becoming a little boy. Big enough to pick himself up after a tumble, yet small enough that I could still scoop him up with one arm while lugging a sack of groceries in the other. He was walking, though still wobbly. He loved to sing to himself. He loved everything having to do with trucks.

I was head-over-heels in love with him. It didn't matter to me that we had no blood ties, no shared DNA, or that there was little chance people would one day say "he looks like you." My affection for Jake was as strong as what I felt for my nieces. He was family, and in my heart and mind, I was his always and forever, one and only Aunt Kath.

So, this special someone was to be my responsibility as well as my traveling companion on this great internship adventure. I would be the caregiver, he would be my dependent, yet I knew for certain he would be guiding and teaching me.

———

Carrie picked me up at baggage claim at the Oakland airport. We greeted each other with tight hugs, and I took her in: she shimmered with happiness and excitement. While waiting for my super-sized Samsonite to appear on the carousel (it felt like I'd packed that thing for a world tour), we chatted about her upcoming trip to Italy and Germany and my upcoming adventure with Jake. I was glad I'd made the decision to help out and allow them this long-overdue vacation.

My reunion with Jake came a bit later, since he was napping when we got to the house. Not wanting them to feel they needed to entertain me like a guest, I tucked into a corner of the living room couch, tried my best to be invisible, and pretended to read a book while I surreptitiously took in the activities of their household. Carrie and Kathy packed and prepped and bustled about. When Jake woke, he was a little shy around me at first. Didn't want to be held by me, buried his face in his mommy's shoulder. I didn't take it personally, didn't try to force my attentions on him. I knew from past visits that it took a little while for him to remember me, to feel at ease with me, and that soon enough he'd be crawling into my lap to listen to a story. I also wondered if he was more clingy than usual because he sensed his mommies were leaving. I'd seen Beau do this whenever I pulled a suitcase out of storage. He knew something was up, had kind of a sixth sense that he was headed for doggie day care. In Jake's case, he hadn't been apart from his moms before, and there had to be something in the air that signaled changes were coming.

With Jake's best friend, Jenni, with us, we headed out to an early dinner at a Mediterranean restaurant. Kathy met Jenni's mom through the mommies group that was coordinated by the hospital where the kids were both born, three weeks apart. They shared a nanny during the week at Jenni's home and traded babysitting duties to give each set of parents an occasional date night. Tonight was Jenni's parents' turn.

Jenni was a sweetie. She was blonde, like Jake, with big brown eyes and a pouty supermodel mouth. She was gorgeous as a toddler; she'll be gorgeous as an adult. She was mellow and observant, in stark contrast to the fidgety guy in the high chair next to her.

Kathy and Carrie had packed an insulated lunch bag with food for both little kids to eat while we enjoyed our hummus, baba ghanoush, and kebobs. But Jake had little interest in the delish food or in our attempts to engage him. To help him burn off his restless energy, we big kids took turns taking him outside for walks. When it was my turn, I watched in awe as he turned on his natural charm.

"Well, hello, little man," one woman said as he wandered along the sidewalk with me in tow. "Where are you off to?" asked another, laughing as he bobbed and wobbled from curb to doorway, intrigued by a strange plant or a colorful item in a shop window.

He looked up, flashed a smile, giggled, and got a smile in return before turning his attention to the next new person or distraction. Passersby looked at me with a sparkle in their eyes and said, "He's adorable!"

"Thank you," I'd say, not feeling I owed an explanation, but inwardly pleased that they assumed he was my adorable child.

After dinner, I squished my big-kid butt in between the kids in their car seats for the 15-minute ride home. Carrie, a natural comedienne with a range of silly faces and a gift for creating witty songs on the spot, was quick to provide entertainment.

"Sssssssss," she said, exaggerating the sound of a leaking hose. Jake and Jenni looked up with surprise, then gave their best imitations.

"Ssssssstthttthtthhhtttwwwttt!" they said, spitting out the last syllables and dissolving into giggles.

"Brrrrrrrlllllleeeeeeeee!" Carrie trilled, like the ringing of an old-time phone.

"BRRRRRRRLLLLLLLDDDDDDDDDD!" repeated the babies, and we all laughed hysterically.

"Thhhhttt!" Jenni stuck out her tongue and blew a fabulous raspberry, Jake copied, and then the grownups joined the chorus. We took turns creating and imitating new sounds, followed by more laughter till I was holding my stomach. In no time, it seemed, we were home.

Though it was past their bedtime, we still made time for a bath. It was sweetly intimate. Both kids were tired, but rallied to play in the tub, sitting in special seats with suction cups that held them upright and kept them from trying to stand or climb around on their own. This allowed the bath-giver to have both hands free, versus having to constantly hold a wet and soapy child to keep him/her from slipping and falling (and cracking a skull).

With Carrie busy shampooing Jenni, I moved to the side of the tub to help, and unwittingly sat on the end of the plastic shower curtain. In one of those horrifying split-seconds, with a foreboding jab to my stomach, I realized I'd made a wrong move that could not be stopped once it was in motion. Startled out of the quiet scene, I looked up and saw I had pulled the metal tension rod from the walls above us. The rod fell in a sickening slow motion yet still managed to slip through my grasping hands. *BANG-clang-ng-ng-ng-ng!* Though it didn't touch the kids, thank God, the loud clanging as it bounced against the ceramic tub scared them—and me!—and set them both off wailing. *Oh geez, oh geez!* I bumbled to my feet, frantically gathering wet plastic sheeting into my arms, while I panicked about what I'd done, what horrible calamity could have happened, and what I needed to do to make sure everyone was okay. "I'm sorry! I'm sorry! I'm so, so sorry!" The babies were already tired from being up later than usual, having their routines messed up by a visiting relative. Now the amateur mommy-wannabe had made it worse by scaring the bejeezus out of them and nearly injuring them. I looked to my sister to see if she was changing her mind about having me stick around as the vacation mommy, but she wasn't the least rattled.

"Shhhh, babies, it's okay," cooed the pro. "It's just a silly loud pole." She dipped the soft washcloth in the warm water and gently squeezed water around the shoulders of each child. I swear Jenni shot me a look of accusation, backed by all the disdain a toddler could muster. "So sorry," I whispered again, and turned down the sides of my mouth to express my contrition. Carrie continued talking in a mellow, soft voice, and with each slow caress on their backs, Jake and Jenni's cries became quieter whimpers till their lips stopped quivering and the trauma was forgotten.

I wanted my mommy. I wanted someone to tell me it was all going to be okay. I looked to my sister, who was still focused on calming and bathing the kids, and knew I couldn't rightfully expect her to calm me down too. I was a grownup, and any soothing I wanted was going to have to be administered by myself. I inhaled the lightly scented steam from the bath and willed my rattled nerves to calm down. *No one was hurt, everyone is fine. Breathe, Kath, breathe.*

We lifted each calm and clean kid out of the tub, dried them off with baby-soft towels, diapered and dressed them in PJs, finally getting them into bed around 8:30—the latest Jake had gone to bed ever. Both were sound asleep within minutes of hitting the mattresses.

They weren't the only ones who were wiped out: Carrie, Kathy, and I each had a small cup of ice cream and settled in the living room to watch the movie *Shrek 2*. In previous childfree days, we might have stayed up late talking about politics, religion, and the last great books we'd read, comparing notes and offering suggestions. We might have played Pictionary or pulled out a deck of cards for a round of Queens. I loved spending time with both of them, always learning something new from our conversations. Under other circumstances, I would have been sad to miss catching up with them, but this time, I was too exhausted to care. Within 20 minutes of starting the movie, I was asleep on the floor.

Carrie woke me for a few minutes to help pull out and flatten the futon, my guest bed on many previous visits. I didn't even have time to review the events of the day, tally up my moments good (learning from Carrie how to make a car ride fly by) and not-so-good (the disgraceful shower rod incident), or wonder if Carrie and Kathy had any doubts about leaving me on my own with their baby. If I'd had an ounce of extra energy, certainly *I* would have marveled at their trust in me.

Instead, I quickly fell into a deep sleep except for one brief interruption: At one point in the middle of the night, I woke up and for a few moments thought I was at home in my own bedroom. Although I was familiar with their home, having visited before, this night I was disoriented. As the windows, bed covering, and light patterns from the tall windows became clear in my consciousness, I reminded myself that the long-awaited adventure had begun. I'd prepped, packed, arrived, made my first gaffe and recovered from it. More surprises were ahead, more unfamiliar territory. My last thought before I drifted back to sleep was of hope that I could ease into my new role with some grace.

Breathe, Kath, breathe.

7

A CRASH COURSE IN RESPONSIBLE PARENTING

*T*eething is a painful experience for toddlers and their parents. Jake had a new tooth coming in, and was up intermittently throughout the night, with Carrie and Kathy taking turns getting up with him. Or so I later heard. I was blissfully unaware, because I slept like an old corpse. I was aware—and somewhat chagrined—that my ability to snooze through all the hubbub did not bode well for my new role as 24-hour caregiver. I hoped I would rise to the occasion in the very near future, and I felt only slightly guilty about getting a full night's sleep while everyone else started the morning capital-C cranky.

Jake did not want me to hold him; he didn't want to eat, he cried and was frustrated. He was also very clingy with both of his mommies, who were exhausted and stressed enough without the added burden of a weepy 25-pound child. I wanted to be more than the extra in-the-way body in the house, but also sensed that trying to pry him away wouldn't make things easier. I hovered around them all, quiet and observant, in case an opportunity presented itself for me to be helpful. It didn't, I wasn't, but we muddled through.

When morning nap time came, they finally got him down, which allowed Kathy to concentrate on packing and Carrie to give me my orientation and a crash course in responsible parenting. We set off in her car to run errands and explore my new town.

They lived on Alameda, a six-mile-long island just off the coast of Oakland, California. It sits in the San Francisco Bay with a view (on clear days) of the beautiful Bay Bridge to the north and the dramatic San Francisco skyline to the west. The Oakland Airport is about a 10-minute drive to the south, and crossing one of the three bridges or traveling through an underwater tunnel would give access to major freeways and the greater Bay Area.

Alameda residents take pride in being self-sufficient, with all the basic needs available on the island: schools, grocery stores, fabulous old-school hardware stores packed to the rafters, well-tended parks with climbable trees, city-exclusive utilities, boutique shops, and a mix of independent and chain coffee houses and restaurants. It is family- and pet-friendly, with a strictly enforced island-wide speed limit of 25 MPH. Almost completely flat, it is a great place to ride a bike to work, the twice-weekly farmers' market, and the local shops, or to push a stroller carrying one or more kids. It also has a healthy cross-section of races, ages, and genders, including a large contingency of gay families. Perhaps this would be an ideal place to raise my own nontraditional family, I thought. Certainly it is more communal than widespread and impersonal Los Angeles.

Alameda came of age around the turn of the 20th century, and brick and stone churches and civic buildings remain with cornerstone plaques that proudly announce dates of construction and historical markers. Alameda boasts the highest per-capita of Victorian homes in the country, many of which have been lovingly restored in recent years. Carrie, Kathy, and Jake lived on the top floor of one of those, a single-family home that had been converted into two still-spacious apartments that sported elegant period details, such as crown moldings, tall windows, and light fixtures hung on long stems from the high ceilings.

On our way to the main shopping center, Carrie pointed out Jake's doctor's office, kid-friendly cafés, Jenni's house (where Jake would go for day care), favorite parks, gas stations, any place she thought might be important during my stay. I followed along by referring to a rough map she had drawn for me, making notes of landmarks and easy-to-miss turns. We then completed a major grocery shop at Trader Joe's and Safeway, conveniently located next door to each other, and I noted for future reference the Walgreens pharmacy situated in the shared parking lot. The plan was to have me well stocked so that I would only need to go out to replace a few things, such as milk and fresh produce. We loaded everything in the car, drove one mile home, then lugged it upstairs to their second-story apartment and consolidated it into the refrigerator and cupboards.

Jake, post-nap, greeted us in a good mood, a playful mood, and he was eager to play with me (finally) while Kathy and Carrie worked around the house. I pulled out his blocks in the living room and together we built colorful towers that he would then demolish as I made appropriate sound effects. "Incoming! Bombs away! Ppoooschhh! Crwaaaaaaaaahhh! We can rebuild it!"

As I fed him lunch, with just the two of us in the room, I looked into his eyes for confirmation that we were bonding, that he was starting to remember me from previous visits, that he felt safe with me. Maybe now that he'd seen his mommies were okay with me around, he sensed he could trust me.

"We're cool, right?" I asked in a conspiratorial whisper.

He picked up a blueberry from his tray with his gooey fingers and offered it to me. I took that as an encouraging sign and wasn't at all discouraged when he changed his mind and shoved it into his own slobbery mouth.

During Jake's afternoon nap, Carrie and I had our lunch and went through all the paperwork that she had organized into categories and labeled "Jakey Instructions." Her comprehensive notes included outlines for typical morning and bedtime routines, emergency information and phone numbers, lists of favorite foods (tofu, frozen blueberries, pumpkin scones at Peet's), suggestions for places to go and things to do (story time at the library, free kids' music performance at a café), and "Things That Are Soothing" (milk, pacifier aka "binky," you, your cell phone). She gave me an overview of the "King Jake" ritual, which I would experience first-hand later that night, and demonstrated how to properly open and close the child-proof safety gate at the top of the staircase that connected the front entry way to their living quarters.

"Always, *always* make sure it clicks into place," Carrie commanded. "Don't just close it. Adjust it until it clicks. Don't take any chances that he could get past the barrier and fall," for the consequences could be crippling, if not life-threatening.

Open, click, open, click. She had me practice under her supervision until she was convinced I had the procedure down pat, then we moved on to other tasks and responsibilities.

I should have been drinking espressos to keep up with the volume of information I was trying to absorb, and I fought back tinglings of overwhelm. Of course I wanted to get everything right and hoped I could live up to the expectations implied in my sister's four pages of typed instructions. On the other hand, I was grateful to Carrie for giving so much thought to the duties they took for granted, the things I would need to master, and writing it all down for me. Having her operating manual, her lists and maps, took off some of the stress of having to remember all the details on my own or winging it. The experience was also sobering, as I started to take in all the tasks performed by two high-functioning adults, that I would now being taking on solo.

I was calm-ish, which made me nervous-ish. I mean, I felt I'd done the best that I could to prepare myself for my internship, but this was different from taking on a big job at work. This was huge! I felt the need to have all senses firing so that I would be prepared to anticipate and/or handle any missteps. In general, I liked to plan as best I could for any project so that when any unexpected challenges arose, I could better address them. At work, if I bit off more than I could chew, I could always ask for an extension on a deadline (not that I ever did this) or call on people for help. And that was part of what I needed to learn and embrace in this experience: There were other people who could help. My brother and sister-in-law were nearby. I had phone numbers for Jake's doctors and for neighbors and friends from the mommies group. If I completely lost it, I could call one of my super-mommy girlfriends, certain she would talk me off any ledge. I might struggle, but I was not going to bomb.

I thought about how I would handle this on my own, with my own child. In everyday life, I could outsource some of the to dos, such as arranging a grocery delivery service or budgeting for weekly housekeeping help. Since I would need to work full-time, day care would be a necessity, and that would take care of some of the childcare tasks. But I couldn't imagine asking any of my friends to step in and take care of my child while I took a mid-week business trip. I couldn't imagine asking my sister to take two weeks off to fly to Los Angeles and babysit while I went on vacation, although knowing that they owed me a favor, perhaps I could first fly to Alameda to drop off my child at their house for "camp" with the cousins. I made a note to myself in my journal to revisit this, to brainstorm how I might expand my village. I also wanted to later think about how I might be a better support to my friends back home who were parents.

But these were musings for another time, a quieter time. First, I had work to do.

"Motherhood, to me, seems more than just giving birth, or signing the adoption papers, or even having a well-organized diaper bag. It is more of an identity that might take time to get used to. You have to fit it in with who you think you are, at that moment in your life."

—*Liz, who became a mother after establishing herself in her career*

8

GETTING INTO OUR GROOVE THANG

*A*fter Jake's nap, to allow Carrie and Kathy time to finish packing in peace, I loaded him into the car and we drove for 20 minutes into the valley to visit his cousins. As we pulled up to their house, we were greeted by cute, screaming, excited girls waiting in the front yard. "Aunt Kath is here! Aunt Kath! Aunt Kath!" I felt my cheeks blush as a smile stretched across my face and my heart expanded with joy at their greeting. It had been far too long since my last dose of niece-love, and I felt lucky to have even a small amount of bonus time with them on this visit.

I unbuckled Jake from his car seat, carried him to the sidewalk, then pulled each of the girls in for hugs and kisses. "You've grown so tall!" I said, as I eased out of our embraces to get a full picture. Chloe was six and a half, Ellie would be five at the end of August, and Quinn would turn two on the Fourth of July.

"Aunt Kaaaa-aath," Chloe complained, rolling her eyes.

I shouldn't have been surprised. We're tall people, and I was always among the taller kids in my classes, so of course they would grow like weeds. Still, it was shocking—and bittersweet

—to see how much they'd changed between my infrequent visits.

"Come play dress-up with us." Ellie pulled me by the hand with all her strength, but I held my ground.

"I can't, loves," I said. "I need to keep an eye on Jake."

"But Aunt Kaaa-aath," Chloe protested, "can't you come play with *us* for just a little while? Jakey can watch a movie or something."

"I want to do your hair," Ellie added with a pout.

"You know I love love love doing all those things with you, but I can't just go into another room and leave Jakey all alone," I tried to explain, inwardly loving that I was in such demand. "It's my job to take care of him right now. But maybe we can find something fun we can all do together."

"Ohhhhhh," Chloe groaned, and Ellie looked up at me with her face scrunched into a scowl.

I sensed I was on the verge of losing my "Fun Aunt" title and scrambled to come up with a plan. "How about...we all go for a walk on the trail?"

"Yaaay!" the girls shouted, with more enthusiasm than I thought exercise, really, warranted, but I rolled with it.

With Molly's thumbs-up (I appreciated her vote of confidence), Jake, the girls, and I ventured out along the paved pathway that ran behind their home. At one time or another I carried each child. Chloe and Ellie whined, claiming, "My tongue is burning!" or "We've walked for *miles!* Puh-lease, can't we go home now?" when we'd barely turned the first curve.

Games. We needed to play games. I channeled my Uncle Tom, my mom's youngest brother, who was 17 years old when I was born and remained one of the "kids" through my early years (until he married and had a kid of his own). What would Uncle Tom do? We sang. We played Follow the Leader. We made up funny walks. We stopped to check out interesting bugs and rocks.

It was exhausting—for me and for them. We couldn't have been on the path more than 20 minutes, but the kids panted, groaned, and behaved as if we'd just scaled Mt. Everest. I was tuckered, too. It took a lot of work to pay attention to, corral, lift, carry, and entertain four little people.

Molly, in fully competent mommy mode, greeted us as we dragged ourselves through the back gate. Although she was six years my junior, she had filled those years with mommying experience. I had observed her on the sly on previous visits, and I knew I would be learning from her during my internship and into my future parenting. She impressed me with her calm and competency, and I hoped she'd be a patient mentor. I also had to admit that I was in awe of her, by how she seemed to take everything in stride.

I was definitely in awe—if not chagrined—when Molly immediately picked up that Jake was looking for food. How had I missed the signals? Was he chewing his lip, sucking on his fingers, gnawing his shirt? Aack! I'd have to watch for and learn how to better read his moods.

I gave him half a stick of string cheese to tide him over, then we all sat down to share dinner on the back patio. Scents from the barbecue reminded me of many summer nights my family and I had enjoyed at a beach where I grew up. I was flooded with memories of fruit salad, hot dogs and burgers, corn on the cob roasted in husks on the coals of a fire, marshmallows toasted for s'mores, all accompanied by silly songs we made up with Dad on the ukulele. These were cherished memories I longed to recreate as an adult with my own circle of loved ones.

I was trying to hold Jake in my lap while we ate, but Molly said I could put Jake down and we'd all watch him.

"Just keep an eye on the back stairs," she warned, pointing out the three paved steps that led from their sliding glass doors to the slate patio below.

"The first time we watched Jake…," my brother began.

"...I think it was the first time Kathy and Carrie had let anyone ever babysit Jake...," Molly interjected.

"...Jake did a somersault down those steps and landed on his head," Kevin confided.

"He was fine," Molly quickly added, "although we never told Carrie and Kathy about it."

I swore myself to secrecy and inwardly felt relieved. I considered Molly and Kevin, who were now expecting their fourth child, to be parenting experts, so if they were capable of letting a kid in their charge fall on his head—actually somersault down steps before falling on his head—and he came out of it okay, I had good odds for doing an acceptable job.

As the big kids lingered around the table, Ellie took it upon herself to keep Jake entertained. But as I periodically checked on him, I could see that his eyes were falling to half-mast. He finally wandered over to my chair, looked at me with anticipation, and when I asked if he wanted up, he responded by barely lifting his arms, as if they were each weighted with a wet blanket. Once in my lap, he proceeded to drape himself over my left arm, and it was impossible to misinterpret the signals. It was time to take us home and him to bed. I gathered our few belongings, said a hasty goodbye and thank you, and buckled a limp Jake into his seat. By the time I got to the freeway, five minutes from Kevin and Molly's house, he was out. It was 6:45.

I noticed that I drove the posted speed limit while I was going home. That was new! Usually I'm a lead-footed driver, going as fast as the flow of traffic will allow, and always hoping to shave a few or more minutes off my travel time. It seemed I was already, even subconsciously, taking my parental responsibilities to heart, better protecting his safety and well-being as well as my own.

The quiet time allowed me to mull over the afternoon's

adventures and wonder how I might create a kind of family interaction among my circle of friends in LA. I thought about who might step in to fill the role of cool aunt or uncle or who might have children, close to my child's age, who could grow up as honorary cousins. A few candidates came to mind, including James and Teri, a childfree couple, work colleagues, who had told me their teenaged nieces and nephews still thought of them as the last standing fun adults in the family. They would be perfect.

Back at the house, I stayed out of the way to allow Carrie, Kathy, and Jake a few last minutes of family bonding time over Jake's bath and bedtime routine. They had an early morning departure scheduled, so we agreed I would take over Jakey duties starting that night. My shift had started, I was on call, although I still had Carrie and Kathy as backup, should I need them.

At 10:33 PM, I heard Jake crying. I waited two minutes to see if he would settle himself back down, then decided I couldn't take it and got up to check on him. I entered his room through the dining room just as Carrie came through the adjoining door from their bedroom. *Ah, crap!* Had I blown it? Had I waited too long to go in? Carrie didn't scold me, and I certainly didn't bring it up. Besides, we had Jake to attend to, and he was crying hard. I picked him up and considered the possible causes for his discomfort. Ah ha! A very full, very wet diaper. Carrie supervised while I changed him, then, when he asked for milk, using his sign language, I heated a bottle and gave it to him. He promptly spit it out and all over himself.

"He's all yours!" Carrie said with a grin as she headed back to bed. I changed his PJs then carried Jake to the rocking chair. We rocked for a few minutes and I soaked in the loveliness of holding him close. He felt hot, but not feverish. I felt like I was holding a beating, squirming hot water bottle; his soft breath on my neck was soothing. It took a few moments to get him back to sleep and several minutes for me to feel ready to give him up and place him gently back in his crib. I touched his forehead and wished him sweet dreams, then tip-toed out of the room.

————

Carrie and Kathy's shuttle arrived at 5:45 AM, so I saw them off, then took advantage of the extra time to shower, quickly review the morning activities on the Jakey Instructions, and pull myself together. I popped down to the entryway to make sure the stroller was ready for duty, then, with one hand on the railing, I counted the number of steps up the steep staircase to the living areas: 21. I wanted to have this number in my head for times when I might have my hands full and couldn't see ahead; I could at least count to make sure I wasn't skipping one and risking a tumble. Obsessive, I know, but I didn't want to take any chances. I locked and double-checked the child-safety gate, took a deep breath, and started our day.

When I heard Jake stirring, I got him up, diapered, and dressed while he was still a bit groggy. He wandered through the entire house, probably looking for his moms, but he didn't get upset when he didn't find them. I let out a big sigh of relief, having not realized I'd been holding my breath in anticipation of a meltdown.

We had breakfast together at the small table wedged next to the washing machine in the kitchen. For me: a protein shake out of a can, a simple no-prep routine I would come to greatly appreciate in the days ahead. For Jake: a toasted waffle, cubes of tofu, and frozen blueberries. When I poured out the blueberries, they came out of the bag onto his tray in a big gush, and he laughed and laughed, then dug into his meal, picking up and eating each individual bite with his fingers. I liked having company at breakfast. I liked his company and appreciated his apparent interest in my company, although I wondered if the attention he was giving me wasn't something akin to how dogs love the human who feeds them.

I was okay with that.

Following breakfast, we played together on the floor for a short while with a mid-size ball—throwing, kicking, bouncing, laughing. Then Jake entertained himself in the living room while I cleaned up from breakfast and packed his lunch sack. One of his CDs was playing on the stereo, and when I peeked around the corner from the kitchen, curious to see what he was up to, I found him dancing. He was in his own element, moving to his own beat. Random. Spontaneous. No obvious rhythm or flow. The best way I could think to describe it was that this must be where Julia Louis-Dreyfus came up with the inspiration for her character Elaine's herky-jerky dance moves on the sitcom *Seinfeld*. Jake was having a great time and was totally adorable.

My body hummed with delight as I watched him. I turned up all my senses to imprint the memory, recognizing that I was getting a glimpse into one of the rare joys of motherhood. Maybe this kind of everyday entertainment would be something I'd take for granted over time once I became a full-time parent. But in that moment, I acknowledged what a precious, fleeting gift it was, and I stored it deep inside me. Spontaneous moments of joyful entertainment was definitely going onto my pros column.

The spell broke when I looked at the time and realized we needed to hustle to stay on schedule. As I gathered up his gear, he wobbled along behind me, sticking close as I went from room to room to pick things up or put them away. I loved having a shadow, and frequently looked behind me to see if he was still there. I did a quick diaper check, loaded the kid, his lunch, and his stuff into the stroller, and we headed down the street to his friend Jenni's house for day care.

The 40-minute walk took us past the high school, across the main street (Park Street), past the fire station, over a small park with a Victorian-style gazebo, and through a neighborhood of charming homes. At times, we'd chat, as in: "Look at the big red fire trucks, Jake!" I'd lean over and direct his gaze across the street. He responded by bouncing up and down and spewing out excited gobbledygook. We—well, I—sang, "Do your ears hang low/Do they wobble to and fro?/Can you tie 'em in a knot/Can you tie 'em in a bow?" He took in the scenery while working a binky, quite contented for several moments at a stretch, and I got into my own rhythm of breathing, walking, singing, and pushing.

Jenni and their nanny greeted us enthusiastically, but Jake suddenly became clingy. He started crying, tried to follow me out, grabbed at my legs and then at my feet. I have to admit, I liked it. It felt good that he was attached to me and didn't want me to leave. But being a clingy mommy is not being a good mommy, so I got him engaged in a stack of plastic blocks with Jenni and, moments later when I observed him laughing, I quietly slipped away.

As I walked home, I was shocked to discover that my heart ached. I missed him already.

———

Back at the house, I dashed around multitasking. Started the dishwasher, ran a load of laundry, and vacuumed traffic areas—but that came only after getting on hands and knees and prying the safety plug outlet cover out of the electrical socket. Designed to keep wee ones from poking forks or their fingers into outlets and possibly electrocuting themselves, installing these rubbery things is included on every to-do list when you're babyproofing a home. While simple to insert, they require untold levels of strength, dexterity, and patience to remove.

Cuss words were used as I struggled to gain access to the outlet, and I wondered, safe from whom?

Ultimately, I achieved removal of the damned safety plug, vacuumed as planned, and charged up my laptop. When I finally sat down to do some work, I realized how bushed I was —and it was still morning. I persevered, got a few items checked off the to-do list—motivated in part by my limited time —and made a mental note of how important quiet was for me. I wondered how, during long periods at this pace, I could sustain the necessary levels of creativity and productivity to meet the requirements of my work. I'd have to figure out how I'd balance my mommy responsibilities with my work responsibilities, and devise a schedule and pace that was most effective and efficient for me. These next couple of internship weeks, I knew, were my opportunity to experiment and perhaps establish my revised daily to-do list.

After lunch, I gave up the fight and indulged in a 40-minute nap, but I woke several times thinking I heard him. Maternal hallucinations? Weird.

I was eager to see Jake again by the late-afternoon pickup time, but by then, he was antsy, and he struggled with me as I tried to get him into the stroller. Remembering how Kathy and Carrie had encouraged him to burn off extra energy when we all were out to dinner that first night, I stopped at the park near Jenni's house and let him run around the grassy areas. A few minutes of turning in circles, chasing after birds, and watching squirrels scramble up trees, and he was winded and pliant. No fuss this time as I eased him back into his seat. Genius.

At busy intersections, while standing at the corner waiting for the signal to change, I "gunned" the "engine" of the stroller by making sound effects ("rumm-mm-mm") while pushing it back and forth. When the light changed, I burned a little rubber ("eeeeeeeee!") as we sprinted into the intersection, switched gears ("eeeee-Eoooooooo") as we flew along the sidewalk, and screeched to a halt at the next corner ("errk!"). Jake laughed and squealed and gasped with delight. "More! More!" he signaled. I took a deep breath and fired up my engine.

I could see where this was leading, and in that a moment, I fully understood my friends who expressed their frustrations at having to sing the same songs—and read the same books and watch the same TV shows and play the same games—over and over again. But for me it was still new, and it was definitely still fun.

———

During the hour or so before dinner, we initiated a routine that we would basically follow for the rest of my stay. I joined Jake in the living room for play time, engaging in whichever activity was attracting his interest at any given moment. We stacked and demolished towers of blocks, took breaks to dance, each in our own style, and sang along with the CD on the stereo. We leaned over the back of the couch, pushed the drapes aside, and watched guys across the street build a picket fence. We made noises in concert with a menagerie of music-making toys. We fired up a crazy apparatus that ran lightweight plastic balls through a clear maze, then POOF!, shot each one into the air for us to try to catch and then feed back into the maze, all to the soundtrack of frenzied, mechanized, kid-friendly classical music. It was so simple and yet so entertaining, for both of us. The breezes through the tall windows gradually cooled, and the sun shifted, turning the walls from a soft to a deeper mauve, a warm color that embraced me, made me feel pleasantly drowsy, and signaled the shift to dinner time.

Dinner for Jake was a delish dish of a veggie dog sliced into Jake-size bites, steamed peas and carrots, and the ever-popular Trader Joe's Os and Puffins cereal. To encourage him to eat, I made noises like at a NASCAR racetrack ("rmmmmmmmm") while moving Jake's spoon around in an oval. I made the sounds quieter when the spoon was at the far end of the oval ("rmmmmmmmm"), then louder as I drew closer to Jake's mouth ("RMMMMMMMmmmmmmmmmmmmmmmm"), and closer and closer to his lips each time I came around. On about the third time around, he had his mouth open and I popped in the food. "Mmmmm," he quietly murmured, a sound of contentment that resonated inside me.

I was quite pleased with myself, for my ability to entertain, feed, and nurture. At the same time, a small nagging voice questioned how I'd have the time and energy to keep this up day after day after day. Would I be the mom who gave in to exhaustion and boredom and wished away her child's childhood, eager for the moment when he could feed and fend for himself? Possibly. Not too soon, I hoped.

"More," he signed, and I quietly made my own sounds of contentment.

After he finished eating, I left him to his own devices in the living room while I prepped his lunch for the next day and got started on kitchen clean-up. While I was doing the dishes at the sink, he came up behind me, threw his arms around my right leg, and kissed me on my calf, then headed back to the living room to play.

My world stopped.

I put my hand to my heart, closed my eyes, resumed breathing, and called out in a cracking voice, "Thanks, Jake!"

It had been...what...months? I couldn't recall, but months at least since anyone had kissed me anywhere. A surge of energy coursed through me, tingling my limbs and igniting a fire, whetting a hunger for more. More affection, more physical contact, more random acts of kindness. More hugs, more caresses, more sweet acts that washed away all my anxieties in the moment.

I knew I was tired from the long day and stressed about coming days, but the flood of emotions that were released with my body's physical response to Jake's kiss overwhelmed me. I'd never before experienced such genuine sweetness. What shocked and scared me was realizing how long I had gone without physical contact and affection. Depravation had been my "normal" back home in LA, and I hadn't even noticed.

I hadn't even noticed.

What was it I longed for, really? Sure, I wanted that still-elusive romantic connection, and frustration bubbled up from my core because I felt I had no control over finding it. However, I could take charge in creating my own little kissing human. I could create a family and nurture it with cuddles and caresses, with healthy meals and silly games, with all the love that I had been saving up for someday. I made a vow to myself to create more moments like these by making my single mommy goals come to fruition.

"You can do this," I said to myself, as I rubbed tears off my cheeks with the back of my rubber-gloved hand. "I *will* do this."

———

Bath time was very fun, very playful. When simple splashing in the water wasn't enough entertainment, I balanced a plastic cup on the edge of the tub, then nudged it slightly and repeatedly until it slipped over the side of the tub and crash-landed into the water. Jake threw his head back and *howled* with laughter. When that act got too familiar, I upgraded it and managed to increase the volume and intensity of his laughs by balancing the cup on top of my head and leaning forward until it fell. He laughed, which made me laugh. It felt so good to laugh with so little effort.

After lifting his slick, slippery clean body from the tub and onto the floor mat (*Bend your knees, Kath. Use your legs.*), I draped his special blue towel over him and gave a cursory drying-off. We looked at each other and a small signal passed between us: It was time for the nightly ritual. His towel had a built-in hood, which I placed onto his head. Still on my knees, I raised my head and announced to the imaginary crowd: "King Jake!" We exited the bathroom and commenced with the parade.

With the towel flowing behind him like a regal cape, otherwise-naked Jake marched around the house, periodically looking back to check for me, as I chanted, "King Jake, King Jake, King JAAAAAAAAAAAAAAKE, King Jake, King Jake...!" He beamed the whole time as he passed through the bedrooms to the hallway to the dining room and then retraced his route. I bowed dramatically to him as he strode past me, which he found hilarious.

As he rounded the final curve back into the dining room, I gave one last bow. "Your majesty," I said, "shall we proceed to Bedfordshire?" He giggled as I scooped him up and kissed his bare tummy.

After I got him into a fresh diaper and PJs, he joined me for a snuggle in the rocking chair. That lasted 20 seconds before he squirmed out of my arms, still running on a tiny reserve of energy.

Guided by the Jakey Instructions, I read a few books aloud while he wandered around his bedroom. His attention span for actually looking at the pictures and giving full focus to the story was about half a book. When his eyes started to droop and his breathing deepened, I coaxed him back to the rocking chair with me. When I was fairly certain he wouldn't get a second wind, I carried him to the crib, lifted him over the side (*Use your legs, Kath. Save your back.*), and carefully deposited him on the mattress. After arranging a few toys, books, and binkies within easy reach, I stroked his forehead and whispered, "I love you...sweet dreams." I didn't mind that he didn't say anything back. I had enough love and sweet dream wishes for both of us.

With the baby monitor close at hand, I settled onto the couch for a movie on cable and some semblance of grownup food for dinner—tortilla chips, salsa, and ice cream.

It had been a full day, a novel day, fun in its newness as we discovered and created our routines. I was pleased with myself for getting through it with some grace.

But I was also exhausted because I felt like I had to be "on" all the time I was with him, either alert and keeping an eye out for his safety and comfort, or entertaining and engaging. I even felt the need to be "on" when he wasn't with me, still thinking about and anticipating his needs. Maybe I would feel less obligated as time went on, as I grew more comfortable with the fact that he would be okay and could be more independent. Maybe I'd ease up a bit if he were my own child, although it was hard to imagine being less diligent. Maybe, like so many mothers I knew, I'd figure out my own imperfect path, my own groove, and find the balance that worked best for me and my family, one that allowed me to keep up with my work and my kid while managing all the other important things like paying bills, running laundry, feeding dogs, lining up jobs for the week, and reaching out to friends.

I mean, because, really, women have been "working mothers" since time began. I could almost hear one of my ancestors telling me to "Suck it up!"

"I tended the farm, raised livestock, and hunted for food...while bearing and raising children."

"I cooked and cleaned and nursed and kept the community running while our menfolk went off to explore and 'conquer' new territories."

"I housed and fed our neighbors and extended family, caring for young and old without complaint, during times of warfare."

"I traveled over miles of uncharted terrain *in a f-ing wagon* to carve out new homes and towns in wilderness."

"And I did it all while wearing petticoats and a corset."

It was time to follow my foremothers' examples and grow up, because I knew what I wanted, and I knew I could draw on their courage, strength, and persistence to go after it: I wanted more tiny helpings of shared meals and more little kisses on the backs of my legs. What kind of wimp would I be if I couldn't figure it out with all the conveniences and support of the 21st century?

When I could no longer kid myself about keeping my eyes open, I dragged myself through my own bedtime ritual (floss, brush, wash off mascara) and collapsed into bed. I needed some solid rest so I could repeat everything the next day—and the next—so I could begin consciously laying the foundation for my future.

9

LESSONS & SIGNS

*M*olly credits me with teaching her girls how to pull the sides of their mouths open with their fingers, stick out their tongues, and say "laulahahuh lahluh." It's not pretty, it's kind of obnoxious, but it cracks me up and I have photos hanging in my home of them doing this. I don't recall initiating this boorish behavior, but also can't deny it with complete certainty.

Now that I was a mommy, I reminded myself that part of my job was to be a role model—a positive role model—and teacher to Jake, and I took this seriously. There would be no learning how to show off "see" food (i.e., opening our mouths to reveal chewed food), no demonstrations of arm farts, no burping contests (in which, for the record, my sister is a champ). Instead, we had lots of fun with Jake's ability to communicate with baby sign language.

I did some online research and learned that a typical 15-month-old can speak five to seven words: Mama, Dada, three familiar nouns (cookie, ball, dog), plus frequently used words such as "no" and "more." They understand additional words and phrases, but do most of their communicating by pointing and grunting. Jake was still testing out his vocal cords and spoke very little beyond his gobbledygook, yet he was able to communicate effectively because of the baby sign language.

We talked a lot when he ate. With Jake strapped in his high chair, I sat facing him and, while I encouraged him to eat and occasionally picked food up off his tray and popped it into his mouth, we practiced.

"What would you like, Jakey?"

He pinched his fingertips together.

"B-lue-be-rrie-s." I pronounced the word slowly, emphasizing each sound.

He poked his thumb into his opposite palm.

"More?" Emphatic poking. "More?" I poured berries onto his tray until he waved his hands. "All done. Good job, Jakey!"

One morning after I'd wiped mashed food off his face and hands, I signed and said out loud, "Aunt Kath (patting myself on the head)...loves (I giving myself a hug)...YOU (pointing to him)!" He watched me closely, then grinned and responded by giving himself a hug and simultaneously pointing back at me in imitation of my movements. I repeated my actions, he repeated, and I told myself surely on some level he understood what it all meant.

I introduced a few new signs, using Kathy's sign language book as a guide. I tucked "airplane" and "helicopter" into my mind for the right opportunities, knowing we'd see both since the Oakland airport was nearby and planes flew overhead several times a day. We were playing with a ball in the front yard when the first sighting occurred. Jake stopped still. His eyes grew wide, then he tilted his head back to search the sky overhead. He'd detected the roar of the jet engines before I could hear them. "AIRPLANE!" I shouted, as I stretched out my arm and pointed my index finger straight to the sky. He looked at me, startled. "Airplane!" I reached over, lifted his arm up, and gently positioned his finger into a point. "Airplane! You got it!" I clapped, he clapped, then I hugged him till he giggled.

The next time he heard one coming, he looked to me, watched as I enthusiastically thrust my arm toward the sky, then quickly followed suit. Awesome. The sign for "helicopter" was similar, except instead of pointing just an index finger at the sky, I pointed all fingers up and turned my hand like I was opening a doorknob. Helicopter flyovers were less frequent, so we got very excited whenever we saw one and did the sign together.

My cousin Karen, who came to visit one afternoon, is a teacher and student of sign language in addition to being the mother of four teenagers. Jake was enthralled with her. I was entranced as I watched her teach him new signs that he took to immediately.

Sitting on the couch, with Jake standing at her knees, she spoke in a tone of voice of a beloved elementary school teacher: "Dog." She stuck out her tongue and panted. Jake mimicked her, panted, grinned. "Dog," she said again, continuing to pant. He would later try this out with a neighbor's dog, leaving me in awe that he'd made the correct association, and then added an "ARF!" We were both disappointed when the dog didn't talk back.

"Cat." Using her fingers, she stroked imaginary whiskers on her face, then reached over and stroked imaginary whiskers on Jake's cheek. He giggled and squirmed, delighted with her tickling, then focused again on her face as she repeated the action. "Cat." With his eyes glued on her, he slowly tried the motion for himself. While watching them both, I became mesmerized by Karen's hands, hands I recognized. She had inherited them from our grandmother, and I felt my heart expand at the realization that they were loving a new generation.

Karen had lessons for me too. While I fed Jake his dinner,

Karen sat beside me. Jake was playing with and throwing his food. "Don't throw your food on the floor, Jakey!" I said, a little perturbed, and Karen burst out laughing.

"That is so funny coming from *you* of all people," she said.

"Really? What do you mean?"

"When you were about Jake's age," Karen explained, "when I was about eight, we came to visit you and your mom and dad. Your mom had you set up in a high chair in the middle of the kitchen on top of a huge sheet of plastic. I couldn't understand this...until I saw you eat. You were a mess! You threw your food *everywhere!*"

Karen laughed out loud at the memory, then shook her head. "Your poor mother," she said. "You must have made her nuts."

I was my parents' first and only child for three years before Carrie arrived, and all I'd ever heard about was how my mom loved sewing us matching outfits, how she loved brushing and braiding my hair, how much my parents loved hearing me sing (hours and hours of reel-to-reel recordings, circa 1968). I didn't have older siblings to tell me stories about me as a little kid, to tell me the truth about how I'd brought total chaos into my mother's neat and orderly world. But I did have an inkling that Karen's tale was true because I have a copy of a poem our grandmother wrote after she babysat me one afternoon:

"That's enough of that!" I said sternly
And her blue eyes gazed at me firmly.
Then
"Wuv oo," she said sweetly
Patting my head
As I knelt, cleaning the floor
Of the food she had spread.[1]

I imagined how annoyed I'd feel having to clean gunk off the recently restored hardwood floors at home. Not the ideal picture I had of mommyhood. But, hey, I could pick up a big sheet of plastic at the hardware store. Add that to my to-do list. No problem.

"Listen," Karen said, and got down to business. "Try teaching Jake using positive terms." I paid attention. "Instead of 'Don't throw your food on the floor!' say 'Food goes in your mouth, please.'"

"Food goes in your mouth, please," I said to Jake, who crammed a handful of cantaloupe cubes into his mouth, half of which landed in his lap, and gave me a look that said, "Huh?" I would need to practice.

"And when he gets older," Karen continued, "give him choices that lead to the same result. For example, instead of announcing 'Bed time! NOW!' say to him 'Would you like to walk to your bedroom yourself or would you like me to carry you?' Both options will get him into his room for bedtime while at the same time empowering him with being able to make the choice himself."

Have I mentioned my cousin is brilliant? I tucked her tips into my mind for future reference, as well as a reminder to call on her for parenting advice in the future.

Like Jake, I was an eager student and quick learner. There's so much I didn't know about parenting simply because I hadn't needed to know it. Some knowledge would be instinctual, some would come from books, and some would come from drawing on the experiences of all the experts in my circle of family and friends. I felt grateful that there were loving and patient teachers like Karen around to encourage and guide me.

———

My vacation wasn't all about observing, evaluating, and trying to make major decisions about the Rest of My Life. I gave myself the tremendous gift of being present, of simply being with another human. That meant that tiny interactions, ones that might bore or repeatedly annoy a full-time parent, were fresh sources of entertainment for me, and I relished them. Take telephones, for example.

Phones are fascinating, even to a 15-month-old kid who couldn't yet carry on a real conversation. Pretty much everything Jake could hold in his hand stood in for a telephone.

During playtime, any one of the painted blocks or plastic stackable rings or one of my shoes, pulled from my suitcase specifically for this function, could serve as a phone. On my first day, Jake picked up one of my sandals and carried it over to where I was sitting on the futon.

"For me?" I asked, feigning surprise and delight that I was getting a call. I took the shoe and held it up to my ear while Jake looked on attentively.

"Helloooooooo," I said in a sing-songy voice. "Oh!" I opened my eyes wide and smiled at Jake. "I'm so glad you called!"

Jake smiled back and looked as though he was holding his breath.

"Really? Really! Oh, my," I said, glancing at Jake, who was taking in every bit. "Well. That *is* very exciting news. I'm soooo happy to hear it."

Jake edged a bit closer to my legs and leaned in, as if he were hoping to pick up snippets of the caller's end of our conversation.

"You know," I continued, "Jake is right here with me and I think he'd like to talk to you too."

Jake reached up to take the "phone."

"Here he is now," I said, then handed it to Jake. "It's for you."

Jake took the shoe and listened, looked at me, listened. Then he handed it back.

"For me again? Thank you."

I chatted a little longer, with Jake looking on. We handed it back and forth, with me carrying on lively one-sided conversations, until he grew tired of the game and toddled off to a new distraction.

When my shoe was otherwise engaged, Jake might hold his fist up to his cheek. "Hi? Yes, yes...yes," he'd say, then he'd listen for a few moments, then reply with an animated string of baby talk as he paced the room. He also had a toy phone, a Jake-size cell phone that beeped and chirped on command. It beeped and chirped spontaneously from various hiding places, which could be really annoying. Really, really annoying. Especially late at night when I fought for every possible minute of sleep.

Actual phones, including the house cordless model and my own cell phone, worked well for him, too, though I kept a sharp eye on those to make sure he wasn't calling Singapore.

My old cell phone died a few days before I left home, so I was still getting accustomed to the ring tones on my new model. On more than one occasion I missed actual calls because I thought the ring I heard was from Jake's toy. I explained my late response to one long-time client, who, I'm relieved to say, found it hilarious.

Carrie and Kathy called to check in with us when they reached Sienna. I held the house phone in my hand as Jake rested his face against it and listened. He said "Hi" very softly a couple of times, but otherwise didn't contribute to the conversation. Ironic, since he could be quite chatty with imaginary callers.

At home, I'd started to notice that my phone rang less and less as girlfriends married and started families. I got it: They were busy, they had a ton of new responsibilities. But I hoped this was just a phase, and I hoped once I had a child and mothering experience of my own, those connections would be rekindled.

As I watched Jake on his phone, and as I participated in his playacting, I got a taste of what I had been missing: social interaction with real humans. On my list of pros and cons for being a mommy, I added "Having someone to play make-believe with" to the left column.

[1]"My Granddaughter" by Mima E. Guthrie.

10

TOUGH LOVING

*O*ne morning, as I walked home after dropping Jake off at day care, two good-looking guys on bicycles checked me out. *That's right, I'm hot!* Feeling cute in the running shorts that showed off my long, fit legs, and the bright orange baseball cap that accented my long, blonde ponytail, I responded with my best open and encouraging smile. *Shall we meet for a quick get-acquainted coffee?,* I tried to signal with a coquettish tilt of my head, *or perhaps you'd like to join me for a stroll along the coastline?*

It didn't happen. Once they caught a glimpse of the empty sippy cup in my right hand, their let's-get-together smiles morphed into have-a-nice-day-ma'am nods, and they went on their way.

I swear a wedding band would have marked me as more available.

Which makes sense, if you think about it. As a single mom, I was ruled by nap and feeding schedules, new teeth and ear infections. If I were merely married, I would be able to sneak out while my fella was at work or traveling. I could even go out to dinner past 5.

Would being a single mom be the end of my dating life?
Did I care?

I got another taste of reality bites as I tried to coordinate get-togethers with the handful of friends I wanted to see while I was in Northern California. "I'll be there for TWO WHOLE WEEKS!" I crowed in the emails I sent out shortly after I booked the flights. I assumed there would be plenty of time to socialize between caring for Jake and working. In my mind I had idyllic visions of gathering Jake from day care and trekking off with him for thoughtful explorations in the park or mellow play dates with friends or contentedly sipping cups of java in hip coffee houses around town.... Riiight.

Here's how things worked in my real world: On a Wednesday, I picked Jake up from day care at 3:30. As part of my plan to include exercise in my daily routine, I had left the stroller there in the morning, with Jake, with the intention of walking the round trip in the afternoon.

Unfortunately, my arrival woke Jake prematurely from his afternoon nap, so he was predisposed to crankiness before the front door closed behind us. Within the first couple of blocks, all hell broke loose. He wanted to be carried, refused to walk, threw a fit when I tried to get him into the stroller. The latter was really the only option, since his 25 pounds were too cumbersome for me to lug more than a block or two.

He cried. He screamed. He kicked off his shoes. He *spit!* All in the first three minutes of what was, under the best conditions, a 40-minute walk. *Jesus, Mary, and Joseph,* this was not good!

I sang. I made soothing sounds. I pleaded. At about the halfway point, I tried another tactic. I stopped at a café my sister had recommended, a place where they knew Jake and he would feel comfortable. I ordered a cup of whole milk for him and a lemon-verbena iced tea for me. The nice young man (yes, I also became an old fart in that first week) behind the counter took pity on me and carried our beverages while I juggled Jake in one arm and the stroller with the other through a narrow passageway to the café's charming, fern-rimmed, back patio.

Jake calmed down. He chugged some milk and stretched his back. He wandered around our wooden picnic table and, when he squatted down to check out a bug, rewarded me with a peek of his adorable plumber's butt crack. He was intrigued by two preteen girls who were playing Scrabble at a nearby table and toddled over to make friends. One of the girls had a Tamagotchi toy, a handheld digital "pet" that could be set up so that its young owner could feed, play with, and raise it. Jake was fascinated, and the girl kindly let him play with it (after I made sure he couldn't accidentally reprogram it).

My shoulders relaxed and my blood pressure dropped as I sipped my iced tea and enjoyed watching my sweet darling interact nicely with the other kids.

Too soon, it was time to give the toy back, and Mr. Hyde reemerged from Dr. Jekyll's façade. I then carried my kicking, screaming monster past the couples chatting on the patio and the individuals quietly clicking away on their laptops at the bistro tables inside, and once out front, wrestled him back into his stroller straps. Not even milk or a binky would appease him at this point.

As we trudged the rest of the way home, I imagined what other people thought of me when they saw us. *What a horrible mother. There's a woman waaay in over her head. Why can't she control her little brat?* Or maybe, I hoped, they took pity on me.

I hauled the kid and all our gear up the stairs and into the house. We headed into his room where he proceeded to roll around on the floor, kicking at the furniture and roughly in my direction. He was not happy with me at all, and we were going into our second hour of theatrics. Screaming, energy-sucking meltdowns were totally going into the cons column of my list.

I called my sister-in-law Molly. "Help me, pleeeeeeeease!"

"Stick in a video," Molly recommended, "any video. It will distract him."

I found a copy of *Holiday Celebration with Mickey and His Pals* on DVD. It didn't matter to Jake that it was the middle of summer and we were watching Mickey and Pluto play in the snow. It did soothe him, though not completely, but enough so that I could shortly thereafter get him into his high chair for dinner.

Dinner is what brought him—the real him, the baby I loved and adored—back to me. He even let out a big "aaah" of contentment after finishing his meal and chugging several gulps of water. Maybe he hadn't had enough to eat at lunch and had simply been hungry. Maybe handing over a bag of Os as we left day care would have calmed the beast.

I tried to think of other ideas for how I could have better handled the meltdown, but my body was too tired from all the effort. The events of the afternoon left me physically and emotionally wiped out, with no energy for taking care of myself. Extending my day's experience into my future possible life, I acknowledged I definitely didn't have the reserves for dolling up my hair and makeup and reenergizing myself to be "on" for a date. I couldn't imagine taking what little steam was left in me to listen to a partner's issues or work on a relationship or be, well, steamy.

This made me uneasy as I was planning a date with my friend Braden. We had met three months earlier and had just started to get to know each other via emails, phone conversations, and the occasional in-person dinner date. He lived in San Francisco, not far from my siblings, and I lived in South Pasadena, a suburb of Los Angeles where he had grown up and still had family. Since we each traveled frequently to each other's neighborhoods, we were encouraged to get acquainted. So far, I liked what I saw: smart, successful, handsome. A great guy. He was my age and had been married once before, but was widowed. I didn't yet know the details, but I sensed getting back into the dating scene was challenging, and I was happy to move slowly. I looked forward to getting to know him better.

It seemed conceivable that we could meet up at least once during my two-week visit, and when I suggested it, he was enthusiastic. He even offered to come to us one weeknight, to meet Jake, to work around our schedule. I knew he didn't have kids of his own, and I wondered if he had any idea what he was in for. It wouldn't be a quiet evening. It would be an early evening, in light of Jake's bedtime routine, which began at 5:30. It couldn't involve anything too fancy; even if I managed to keep my clothes relatively clean, everything I'd packed was very casual. And there certainly wouldn't be much in the way of romance. With what little energy I had, I was focused on my responsibilities in caring for Jake. He was the priority.

As I thought this through, I realized if I decided to pursue mommyhood on my own after this, I could pretty much rule out dating and mating for myself. In my current day-to-day, it was hard enough to make time for a boyfriend/spouse with a full-time job, a household to run, and a life, let alone working around a kid's needs too. I supposed a single dad might be more open to it, would be more understanding, but only if the kids' schedules were in sync. Maybe that was what I should pursue: I'd look for a dating service that skipped chemistry and went right to matching nap times. "10–12 and 2–4 seeks same."

Or maybe someday some wonderful guy would surprise me. A "Sensitive New Age Guy" who would share diaper duties and midnight feedings, who thought a Sunday afternoon spent watching kinder-soccer was the height of great entertainment. One who valued family and recognized that the sacrifices were minimal compared to the rewards.

Maybe my priorities were changing. Maybe having a child in my life was enough and I didn't need the adult companionship of a spouse. My dating relationships thus far had been disappointing, so maybe trading romantic love for maternal love was my way to happiness.

But then, it didn't seem fair to have a child to fulfill my needs for affection. I caught myself thinking like an immature woman who gets pregnant because she wants someone to love her. I had always been quick to judge, but now, kinda in her shoes, I kinda, like, understood.

I was back in limbo. Even after a meltdown or a tantrum or a rough patch, as soon as I left my little buddy behind at day care, I missed him. I also enjoyed the attention from the cycling hotties as well as the anticipation of another great date with Braden. I hadn't forgotten the wonderful all-aflutter feeling that comes from connecting with someone special. I also carried with me the heart-flipping feeling of being at the receiving end of one of Jake's big, drooly, baby-toothy smiles.

My pros-cons list was running about even. I still wanted it all.

———

A nightmare? A wet diaper? Is he hurt or sick or scared?

When Jake woke crying in the middle of the night, I flew to the rescue. "It's okay, you're okay, I'm here," I said in my most comforting voice as I lifted him out of his crib. I dried his tears with kisses, took audibly deep breaths and gently rubbed his chest until his breathing calmed, then changed his diaper. I wrapped him in a favorite blankie, popped the binky back in, and held his warm sweet body close, rocking us both slowly in the rocking chair, until I felt certain his droopy eyelids would stay closed.

Four times or more of this in any given night and sleep would become a long-lost luxury. I knew I couldn't keep up this pace. Beyond some suggestions for calming and easing Jake to sleep before bedtime, the topic of how to get him to sleep through the night on his own was not addressed in detail in the Jakey Instructions, and certainly I had given no thought to fully discussing it when she'd prepped me. Fortunately, during one rough wee-hours-of-the-morning crying session, I found the remedy in a guidebook tucked among old issues of *Time* and *Parents* magazines in the living room: *Helping Your Child Sleep Through the Night: A Guide for Parents with Children from Infancy to Age Five.*

"Let him cry," the book advised.

"Are you f-ing kidding me?!" I said out loud to the Universe, quietly, of course, so as not to further upset my weeping baby. That seemed counter-intuitive. While patting Jake's back to bring up what I'd hoped was only a bubble of gas, I skimmed ahead to the midway pages. There had to be other—better, more humane—options.

By 15 months—yup, that's us—a child should be sleeping through the night, I learned. Basically, indulging him by jumping into action at the first cry is "training" him that this is the way to get a response, to get attention from me.

Well, crap. It made sense, but it was going to be hard putting it into action. With another deep breath and a gentle shake to strengthen my resolve, I committed myself to toughing it out for at least two nights. Perhaps getting him into a sleeping routine would be another gift I could give his mommies.

I had a mission.

On the second night of my mission, I had an unfair advantage. Carrie had warned me that they thought Jake might be getting a new tooth and gave me the okay to administer Baby Tylenol to bring down any slight fever. His temperature was slightly elevated, so—after triple-checking the Jakey Instructions—I gave him the minimal amount, which appeared to ease his discomfort and work as a sleep inducer. He slept through the night. I slept in short bursts, checking every 30 minutes or so to make sure he was still breathing.

The real test came a few nights later.

I followed the book's instructions to ignore him initially, to let him "self-soothe" back to sleep. If he continued crying for a prolonged period (by my definition, about 2.6 minutes, although it felt like an agonizing 10), then I could go into the room and *verbally* reassure him that he was okay.

I called Molly the expert for confirmation that the book's method was effective and humane. She gave it the thumbs-up.

"Ellie once cried for two hours straight," she explained, "then got herself back to sleep."

Two hours straight. Yikes.

"You can rub his back, give him milk, and even lie down beside him—not in his crib, obviously, but on the floor," Molly continued, "but what you can NOT do is pick him up and hold him until he stops crying." I gave myself a little asterisk that said if he was hot, I'd take his temperature and break all the rules.

Okay. I can do this.

We went through the bath and bedtime routine, he went to sleep without much fuss, and pretty much slept through the night. He woke once. I went in, rubbed his back, and he was fine. He softly cried himself back to sleep within a few minutes.

The next night, I heard sounds over the baby monitor that sounded like he was choking. I panicked, dashed through the house, and burst into his room, which, of course, woke him up. He was fine. He observed me groggily then drifted back to sleep. I think he must have been rubbing up against the rubber pads that go around the sides of his crib. I never did figure out the source of the "choking" noise.

That was it. He was out till 6 am.

Me? I was awake most of the night, anticipating a disaster that never occurred.

The book said there are two exceptions to the tough love rule: separation anxiety and illness. I'd need to be sensitive to the missing his mommies part, but now that his fever had subsided, I sensed I could forge ahead.

The following night he was awake at 2:05. I went in, rubbed his back, and handed him his binky. He cried hard, but went back down. *Oh please, oh please...I think it worked...Hallelujah!* He woke two more times, and I put the monitor to my ear and listened for signs of distress, but he got himself back to sleep without my having to even get out of my bed. *Wahoo!*

The next night, I got up only once, crept into his room, held my breath, and listened intently, but he was making soft murmuring sounds, probably just talking through a dream. I finally went to get him at 6:45 the next morning, and he was quietly playing in his crib. Mellow, happy. His diaper was the fullest diaper I had ever seen. No poop; all pee. It looked like he had leaked on his PJ bottoms a bit, but his bed was dry. This debunks the myth that a wet diaper would wake a sleeping baby and that I needed to get him up for a change.

Three nights in a row he slept through the night with only minor interruptions. *I am SUPER (substitute) MOMMY!*

I was proud of my success, except for one small thing: *I* still wasn't sleeping through the night. I'd hear a small whimper, and would sit straight up in bed, shocked out of any stage of sleep. Holding my breath, trying to still my racing heart, I'd listen. *Another cry?* Nope. *A louder cry?* Not yet. *Wait for it....* Okay. Deep exhalation. I'd lie down and try to get back to sleep.

It was taking a toll on me during the days, but I felt I'd achieved my goal overall. I had made a plan, exercised self-discipline, and followed through with the tough love. We were in a routine, and he was thriving.

His mommies were so going to love me!

11

ALL IN A (VACATION MOMMY'S) DAY'S WORK

I was scrambling to get myself out the door when Dad called to check in.

"What are you doing today?" he asked.

"I just dropped Jake off at day care. Now I'm on my way to meet a former colleague and potential future client for lunch, then I'm seeing the girls, then I'll do something with Jake."

"Sounds like it's become a real vacation."

"Huh?"

"I mean because you're being so social," he explained. "It's not like you're working."

Ouch.

I'd been up since 5. I loaded the dishwasher, double-checked the grocery list, prepped items for laundry, took a quick shower, made a call to another writer about a job opportunity, cleaned up the mess from Jake's breakfast, dressed myself, dressed Jake, and delivered him to day care. Hardly my definition of *vacation*.

Even though I'd notified clients that I was technically on a vacation, I had agreed to be available to work, in part because I thought this would be a great opportunity to test out my single working mommy plans. It's a good thing I hadn't promised any rush turnarounds, because I quickly learned that wasn't feasible in my new reality.

One morning, after I'd dropped Jake at day care, I sat down for what I thought would be a block of several open hours of productivity. It didn't take long before I caught myself re-reading the same paragraph of a marketing report without any comprehension. My intent was real, but my focus was blurry. Sleepless nights, inadequate nutrition, and a lack of quiet thinking time had taken a toll.

With determination and handfuls of Puffins, I managed to write, edit, and submit a front-of-book piece to a magazine, send out an email announcing that a short story was being featured on an online site, and cobbled together the first draft of a client's product description barely ahead of the deadline. Not my typical level of productivity, but it was better than taking an all-consuming nap and calling it a "mental health day".

Although my industry is known for its wonderfully addictive creative chaos, I'd excelled by imposing some order on it, by acknowledging and employing the discipline that makes a freelancer's life tolerable and profitable. Framed by deadline pressures and my own high standards, my work required management of short, manic bursts of creativity, periods of solid rest and mental replenishment, and designated hours of butt-in-chair research, analysis, and problem-solving. I'd built my business on being reliable, clear-headed, efficient, and effective. That wouldn't change, I told myself. It was my sense of order and scheduling that needed to be flexible.

I'd made adjustments before, such as when I switched from working regular days in an employer's office to working from an office in my home. Switching to working from home with a kid would just be another tweak. I'd find my new rhythm eventually, and somehow I'd find and make the time to meet regular deadlines, churn out the volumes of copy needed for client jobs and my own writing, cover the occasional rush job— a welcome, and often necessary, component of any freelancer's budget—send out regular invoices, balance the books, keep up with emails and social media, promote and market my services, pursue my passions, make a viable living, and take care of the kid and myself. Sure, it would be a struggle at times, but I was determined, and game, to tackle the challenges. As long as I planned and prepped and stayed my course, I thought, this would be a piece o' chocolate cake!

My good intentions and careful planning all came crashing down, as reality bit once again, the first time I tried to work while Jake was at home with me. I set Jake up with his basket of toys in the living room, then set myself up with a workstation at the dining room table, a vantage point from where I could keep an eye on him. I felt distracted by the tugs of my conflicting responsibilities, and I hoped I wouldn't be interrupted by a shin-bruising accident or a spillage of blueberry yogurt. The tug-of-war continued between the copy on my screen and the little dude who found my long computer cables more fascinating and attractive than his myriad of brightly colored, jingly-jangly toys. When the situation became dangerous— both for him and for my laptop—I cried uncle.

I shut down work and played with him, hoping I'd remember my train of thought a bit later when he went down for his nap. Assuming I wouldn't also give in to the siren call of napping, I felt mostly confident I could complete my tasks in the windows of time available to me.

I later thought about some of my favorite authors, women who were/are professional writers and also mothers, and from my quite-distant perspective, they had excelled at both. Anna

Quindlen and Anita Shreve topped my list. But part of what differentiated them from me is that neither of them had to be the family's sole breadwinner when their children were young. Quindlen's husband was an attorney, and Shreve's husband worked in insurance. Now I don't know what their financial situations were early in their writing careers, and maybe these women had to work beyond fulfilling their creative endeavors.

I also wondered about what they sacrificed to make time for their pursuits. Perhaps they felt guilty about "neglecting" their children and delegating child-rearing to hired help. Maybe the house was declared a hazard zone, overflowing with unwashed laundry and half-empty boxes of rotting takeout. Maybe the neighbors complained about weed-infested yards, or friends drifted away after months of unreturned calls and emails. I'd feel a little bit better about myself if they all had let their gym memberships lapse and, well, could they at least have gotten slovenly?

I thought back to the week before I left home, when I sat in a chair in a salon for the better part of four hours getting highlights, base color, a trim, and a blowout. No way could I fit that into my life now. And if I did have a spare four hours, I'd rather be sleeping.

I got it. Something would have to be sacrificed: my career, my lifestyle, my freedom. It was a matter of priorities, and I remained convinced it would be a worthy exchange.

———

I stood in the middle of the master bedroom, not really thinking, not doing, just standing, not knowing if I was coming or going. I was wiped.

It was a Saturday. In my single girl life, it might have been a day to catch up with friends and family, a day to catch myself up on rest and rejuvenation. Or it could be the day when I caught up on filing and billing, and cleared the decks in preparation for another busy work week.

This was not one of those Saturdays.

I longed for sleep the way an addict craves the warm rush and sweet peacefulness of her next hit. Or so I imagined. *I'll just close my eyes for a moment*, I thought. *I can wake up any time I want*, my inner sleep-aholic whispered. But I had things to do and a baby to mother.

The previous night had been especially rough with multiple crying jags and overall fussiness. Jake's, not mine, although I was on the brink of my own weepy, delirious, shoe-throwing meltdown. Whoever coined the phrase "I slept like a baby," which I've always understood to mean "I slept deeply and through the night," clearly had never been around a real-live small child. I'm guessing this genius was a man.

I tried to remember if I had actually taken a shower that morning, but I must have, because it appeared my legs had been recently shaved. I was fully and appropriately dressed, which seemed like a promising sign.

I had a vague recollection of putting on some makeup, not because of any visual clues, but because I remembered Jake had joined me in the bathroom, still fussy, so in an effort to calm him, I had lightly brushed his cheeks, forehead, nose, down the bridge of his nose, and in circles around his tummy with my blush brush, a sensation he clearly relished. He then reached and grunted, insisted on taking the brush from me so he could do it for himself. When his coordination failed him, he turned to sucking and chewing on the handle and drooling on the bristles. "That's alright, you keep it," I said when he offered it back.

Back in the present, my gaze refocused on the mirror and I stared at a woman who looked familiar but seriously needed to reconnect with her hairbrush. "Pull yourself together, woman!" I said to her. Because this was it; these were the lessons I had asked the Universe to teach me. I was learning exactly what Real Life with a job and a baby and an endless to-do list of responsibilities and no one else to share them with would be like. This would be my life, and I was going to have to figure out how to manage it all.

I shook myself a little more awake, squared my shoulders, and got back to work.

———

Jake worked off the sugar rush from a midmorning pumpkin scone by dancing around the living room as I went to work with household chores: folding and putting away laundry, running a new load, cleaning out the fridge, arranging the groceries I'd picked up the day before, chopping and steaming veggies, putting small servings of Jake's favorite foods in containers to be added to lunches in the week ahead. I can't believe I'm committing this to ink and paper, but I experienced a Zen-like state while I did all this. I found it almost meditational as I got into a rhythm. It was peaceful and serene and beautiful.

Yep. I was that zonked.

Mercifully, Jake's battery finally ran down. By the time I tucked him in for his morning nap, I was in a zombie-like state. I ran the vacuum around the living room and family room to pick up the Os he had dropped. Earlier I had given him a small bowl so he could feed himself, and at least half of the snack had ended up on the floor. A few times, much to my amusement, he did a Downward-Facing Dog, his little bum up in the air, and picked up the O's with his lips. Others he ground into the carpet as he danced.

I now understand why parents sometimes run the vacuum when they are trying to get their babies to fall asleep. It is a very soothing sound. It worked on me. I think there should be a warning label on it: MAY CAUSE DROWSINESS. DO NOT OPERATE WHILE SLEEP-DEPRIVED.

I returned the vacuum to the linen closet without incident or accident and dragged my worn body to bed for as much of a nap as I could fit in while Jake slept.

Not much, apparently.

Nap time is sacred. Homes with small children should be equipped with those lights outside film studios that go on to indicate filming has started inside. "Quiet on the set!" Incoming phone calls should automatically be redirected to voicemail. All traffic should be diverted. Neighbors who feel the need to build fences during this time should be heavily fined. (I'm not naming names, but the family across the street with the cute new white picket fence, I'm talking about you.)

Shortly after my head hit the pillow and my brain entered a blissful state of REM, Mom called to check in. A friend returned my call about the possibility of meeting for lunch later in the week. And then the doorbell rang.

I stumbled and grumbled down the 19...20...21 stairs, relieved that there was no reaction from Jake's room to the doorbell. I opened the door in my bedraggled state and was greeted by two Jehovah's Witnesses, a man and a woman, professionally dressed and nonthreatening in appearance.

"Good mor...," one began, annoyingly cheerful.

"This is not a good time," I croaked, my eyes squinting in the bright late-morning sun. "My baby and I are in the middle of a nap."

To my amazement, the woman had the balls to stick her foot in the doorway, encroaching on my personal space. *Seriously?! You want to mess with a woman whose baby you've just woken? Does this method really work? Do you really win converts this way? Well, bring it, bitch!*

I did not say any of this out loud, but I hoped I communicated it telepathically through my bloodshot eyes.

She extended her hand with a booklet, which I made no move to accept.

The man chuckled and said, "Yeah, you sort of look like you're in the middle of a nap."

Ya think?

I gave him a small, tired smile of appreciation. If he could be gracious, I could be courteous. I mean, aside from the foot-in-the-door move, they weren't completely obnoxious.

They departed without leaving anything behind, and I was pleased I hadn't been rude.

As I trudged back up the stairs...*19...20...21*...and tumbled back into bed, I thought, "I am soooo using the 'my baby is taking a nap' line for unwanted solicitors back home." It's a mommy's trump card.

———

Later that day, refreshed from our naps and a half-decent late lunch, Jake and I went to the Oakland Zoo for a few hours with family friends. Jake was adorable, charming, more fun to watch than the playful chimpanzees. He spoke to the sheep in the petting zoo ("baaaaaaaaaaa") and petted and brushed a goat. He waved to the giraffes; he did the baby sign language sign for the elephants (waving his arm up and down to mimic the movement of an elephant's trunk). He discovered a love for ice cream sandwiches, and turned what had been offered as a "taste" into devouring half my treat. He also stayed awake for the whole time, well into the period for his usual afternoon nap.

Back at home, Jake was still on a high from the day's adventures. The energy reserves of a toddler are astonishing, and I'm sure the sugar rush from the ice cream added fuel to his fun. While he danced and played around me, I dozed on the living room floor. I had closed off access to the kitchen and stairs, and knew he'd be safe in the living room if I let my guard down for a few minutes. Having been "on" for hours, all the adrenaline had drained out of me and I was so friggin' tired.

I felt a little nudge and cracked open my eyes to discover that Jake had brought me his teddy bear, tucking it next to my arm. He returned a few moments later with a binky. *Oh, how sweet,* I thought, my heart swelling. *He's comforting me and helping me to fall asleep*

He toddled off again toward his room and soon returned with a book; Jake liked to go to sleep surrounded by his books. How precious that he loved his books so much he treated them like his favorite toys.

"Thank you, sweet pea," I said.

Then he raised his arms up to me. And grunted.

He wanted me to lift him into my lap. *Ah-hah.* His gifts were not for me; he was furnishing his nest so that he'd be comfortable while I read to him.

He popped his binky into his mouth, scooped the bear into his arms, and grunted again, my signal to begin reading.

———

Even though we skipped an official afternoon nap that day, dinner and bath and bed times ran smoothly. After settling him in his crib and watching him drift off to a peaceful sleep, I retreated to the living room for a five-star gourmet dinner of my own. Not really. I ate a tragic combination of half an apple left over from Jake's dinner; tortilla chips and guacamole; slices of deli roast turkey, which I rolled up and ate with my fingers; and a bowl of chocolate chip ice cream, which I ate with a spoon. Fruit, meat, dairy, grains, dessert...I think I covered all the necessary food groups.

It was painfully apparent to me that if I was going to keep up with this overextended lifestyle, I would need to work out a sustainable routine for shopping for, prepping, and actually eating healthy meals. Right after I laughed out loud at the concept, I mentally added "Develop new routine" to my to-do list.

I cleaned up from our dinners, surveyed the house, and felt a mild sense of panic rising in my throat. A stack of work folders and a hastily scribbled schedule with pressing deadlines lay neglected next to my unopened laptop. I noticed crumbs from my dinner had fallen on the floor, the floor I had vacuumed clean just a few hours earlier, and I almost wept. Almost, because I really didn't have time to cry or in any way suffer a breakdown. *Must focus. Must stay on top of things. Must be strong. Must sleep. Dear God, please let me sleep tonight.*

I stood there, having lost all sense of feeling in my exhausted body, and then I got distracted by my parched and sore hands, with embarrassingly ragged cuticles. *A manicure would be nice. A full-time live-in housekeeper would be nice. A million dollars would be very nice. I'm going to need a vacation from my vacation.*

If I had been less tired, I might have been more rational. I would have told my inner perfectionist to "Shut it!" I would have told myself it was silly to cry over a few crumbs. I would have chosen a quick nap over a quick vacuuming.

I thought about Martha Stewart and *Good Housekeeping* and all the role models from my youth that set me up for failure. It was impossible to do it all, to have it all. It wasn't about being perfect, contrary to the message I'd been hearing most of my life; it was about being good enough. I could do many of the tasks in my sleep, which was essentially what I had done all day, wandering around in half a trance while muddling through what most needed to be done. Jake was eating, he was sort of sleeping, the top-of-the-list client work was getting done on time, the house was not a health hazard, we were having some fun, and I wasn't yet dead, broken, or completely unrecognizable. Things were good enough, and that would have to be enough.

This must be a perpetual state of being for moms with young children, I thought. I couldn't imagine how anyone could keep this up full-time, year-round, year after year. I couldn't imagine how a single mother could keep up this pace and successfully hold down a full-time job, something that I would need to do to keep us both housed and fed. I had to laugh at my naïveté in choosing my profession, having thought working for myself as a freelancer would make it easier for me to be flexible, to better manage and balance home life and work.

And—oh, right. If/when I embarked on my real-life single mommy adventures, I wouldn't be a feisty twenty-something who could pull off repetitive late- or all-nighters; I'd be a pre-menopausal forty-something with seriously limited stores of energy.

I was surprised to discover that the weekends were hardest of all when child and home care was 24/7. Aside from brief nap times, breaks when I also would have loved to catch up on sleep, I felt like I couldn't get anything done. So many to-dos were calling for my attention, and my sleep deprivation had me feeling more scatterbrained than usual. I realized I'd made lunch plans for three days in the coming week, and now I was regretting it. I wanted to get stuff done, both work stuff and household stuff. I needed to get out and socialize and network, yet I also felt the need to "catch up." Does anyone get caught up? Ever?

I had two revealing ah-hahs from all this. One: I realized it had been days since I'd looked at my personal emails. I should have been checking daily. I owed replies. But I couldn't find the time or the focus to even consider it. I would, I knew, be much more understanding of my friends and work colleagues who are moms when they didn't return my calls or messages right away.

Two: I did not *want* to do this by myself. It was no fun. Being a single parent was hard work. Really hard work. Even the small things, such as the few minutes I spent every night—every night—picking up Jake's toys, added up. Even after-work and spare weekend hours would be devoted to catching up on work, answering messages, paying bills, and other necessary tasks. There was no one else to pass the buck to, to hand the child off to, to share the chores and responsibilities and give me a breather. My time was not my own. There was no down time. There was no time or energy to take care of myself, to read a story with an adult protagonist or write a letter to a friend or dream up a novel. Hell, I didn't even have the energy to think straight.

I'd been tired before, from pushing myself in a physical workout or pulling all-nighters or traveling across time zones. But I always had a reprieve. There was no time-out for parents, especially single parents.

Yet...there had to be a way, I thought. Assuming I didn't have a partner to co-parent, I was sure I could create my village of caregivers and care-sharers. I'd meet other parents through Mommy 'n' Me class or preschool, and like my sister's and Jenni's families, we'd devise a way to share day care. Like my mom, I'd build my network so that I'd be one-fifth of a carpool team, thus giving me four days off of kid delivery service each week. I recalled how aunts and uncles and friends' parents would host sleepovers to allow my parents date nights, how Sunday school and summer camp and Girl Scouts and basketball practices gave my mom those few extra hours to catch up on to dos.

I could do that too.

———

A Short List of Pros for Being a Single Mommy

- I get to be the sole disciplinarian. No compromising on what are good manners and acceptable behaviors. And no good cop/bad cop games, as in I won't have to hold my ground when I'm up against "But Dad said I could!"
- I won't have to deal with a spouse who is jealous that our child gets a bigger share of my time, energy, and affection than he does.
- I am the sole recipient of the child's affection.
- No meddling in-laws (as in, I won't have to bite my tongue while hearing a running commentary on how I *should* be raising my child).
- Only one set of grandparents to accommodate on vacations and holidays.
- I get to be a mommy. Period.

———

Late one afternoon, Jake followed me into the bathroom while I unloaded the dryer. I hadn't noticed that he'd followed me, until out of the corner of my eye I saw the stack of neatly folded clean laundry topple over to the floor. *What the...?!* I looked down at him, he looked up at me, all innocence. I sighed and scooped up towels and clothing to refold and restack. When I turned back around, Jake had taken a bright yellow thong of mine and wrapped it around his neck like a scarf. Classic. I threw back my head and laughed. Welcome to my life!

The work would get done, deadlines would be met. Maybe the laundry would pile up and eventually be stuffed into drawers unfolded. It wasn't pretty, it wasn't perfect, but it was occasionally fun, and at least I still had my sense of humor.

12

ROLE MODELS

I am pumped with nervous energy, standing in a client's lobby as our creative team gathers for an important production meeting, a meeting I, as senior copywriter, am going to lead. I am in my element, confident in my agenda, confident in my skills. Still nervous, though, because I want the meeting to go well. I want the client to be pleased, if not impressed. Hoping no one notices, I wipe my sweaty palm on my skirt, switch my heavy briefcase from my right to left shoulder, and shift my weight in my kick-ass "I'm a successful businesswoman" heels.

One of the designers walks in. We've worked together on several projects in the past, although most of our interactions have been via email. I haven't seen her in months, and I express my delight and congratulations for her hugely pregnant belly.

"How far along are you?" Seven months and counting.

"How long are you planning to take for maternity leave?" At least six months, but she's a little worried she'll be bored making the switch from full-time designer on a busy team to full-time mommy of a non-communicating infant.

"Are you and your husband all ready for your baby's arrival?" Is anyone ever ready?

We both laugh. I'm happy for her, and my blood pressure calms as we engage in this easy conversation.

Then another woman, someone from the client's marketing department, arrives for the meeting. She, too, is expecting, and she joins our chat.

Cloth diapers versus Pampers?

Day care at church or an au pair?

Cheap but stylish maternity clothes from Target or deals on designer duds from the consignment shop?

I've paid attention to friends and family members when they went through this stage, so I know a bit about each of these topics. I open my mouth to contribute to the conversation. But each time I start to speak, I'm drowned out by one of the mommies-to-be. Slowly, subtly—and, I hope, subconsciously—as they connect over their common bond, they angle toward each other until I am literally looking at their backs. I feel as though I'm standing on a sinkhole or a patch of quicksand, and no one notices as I become invisible.

This was not a nightmare that came about after eating too much ice cream before bed. This wasn't one of those anxiety dreams you have about walking into your calculus final and realizing you haven't studied (and then waking yourself up by remembering you graduated from college years ago). No. This was real life.

This exchange happened with two women I liked, who I believe liked and respected me. This wasn't a grown-up version of mean girls, with me being intentionally rejected and excluded, nor was this a manifestation of my envy for what they had and I was still being denied. But in that dagger-to-the-heart moment, as I stared at their backs, I finally recognized that there had been previous social slights, and their frequency and intensity were increasing as I closed in on and moved past 40, still single, still childless. This feeling of being shut out for not living up to the "norm" was real. This phenomenon of becoming invisible was real, and I'm sure I wasn't the only woman to experience it. It starts in your own small sphere and expands into society at large, where suddenly you discover advertisers and TV executives and women's magazine editors don't just diminish your worth because you're not a member of the mommy club, they ignore you. Because you are invisible.

I reappeared when I became Jake's vacation mommy.

———

At Peet's Coffee, two men leaned across the aisle to interact with Jake in his stroller and to chat with me about their grandkids. On our walks around the neighborhood, Jake and I were stopped by strangers who complimented Jake on his cuteness and initiated cordial conversations with me about our family's plans for upcoming Fourth of July celebrations. At La Piñata, a casual Mexican restaurant, a woman one table over, with a daughter who looked to be about two, asked me, "How old is he?"

"Fifteen months," I answered, as I expertly crushed tortilla chips into Jake-size nibbles.

"Isn't this a fun age?" she said, with a knowing smile.

"I'm loving every minute of it," I replied with my own smile.

At the park, I briefly registered the sign informing me adults were not allowed in the play area unless they had a child with them. A necessary precaution, I supposed, though it still felt cruel. I shook off the implied accusation (*Childless people are up to no good!*) and focused instead on how I instantly felt part of the community when I realized everyone there was keeping an eye on everyone else's kids. There was a silent expectation that I would join the ranks. "Your son is adorable," one woman said to me. I chose not to correct her and just said "Thank you" while I kept my eyes on the one-man show being performed for an audience of one. Jake dashed from the slide to the swing set to the monkey bars, showing off his skills, and glanced back frequently to make sure I was paying attention, admiring his stunts, and applauding his enthusiastic performance. My heart swelled to bursting with love and pride. "Well done, Jakey! You're awesome!"

I felt like I was playing a role in a play and it was the best acting gig I'd ever had. I was all Method: I was someone's mommy, I was Jake's mommy. I'd studied this demographic in my friends and family, so I knew the language, I knew the emotions and the expressions. I'd rehearsed during get-togethers with girlfriends who connected over their shared wife and mommying experiences. They weren't ignoring me on purpose, I know, but even when I could chime in with the occasional pithy story about a niece, I was left feeling like an invisible (i.e., worthless) wanna-be (i.e., loser). While I felt painfully ashamed that I was still struggling to fit in, I listened and learned. So now I had my character down, and I was so confident in my skills that I found myself engaging other people in parenting conversations, aka "mommy talk."

I gave an award-worthy performance when I visited a friend for lunch midway through my stint as Jake's mommy. Instead of introducing standard topics like work, politics, or pop culture, I dove into discussions about self-soothing, encouraging kids to sleep through the night, picky eaters, healthy food choices, play time—topics I knew she, a mother of two young boys, could relate to. And, for the first time since we'd been teenaged coeds, I felt legitimately like her peer. I felt interesting and useful, glowing and beautiful. I felt proud of my child and my job performance. I was an accepted participant who spoke age-appropriate language. I looked and acted the part, so other people assumed I knew what I was doing. I was finally a member of the club, and I didn't feel like a fraud.

And I found myself wondering what percentage of my longing for kids was really about a longing to belong.

I was most grateful for my newfound confidence when I

spent time with my sister-in-law. Molly amazed me. She was a full-time stay-at-home mom to three young daughters and was pregnant with number four. She made mothering and running a home look easy, although I knew she worked hard, was very disciplined with herself and her kids, and ran her household with efficiency. I also admired how she kept balance in her own life. She worked out daily, went on weekly date nights with my brother, and had a full social life with friends and nearby family. And she was gorgeous. Six years my junior, she was everything I wanted to be when I grew up.

Now that I was a mom, too, I could commiserate with her about my concern with Jake's fever during my first nights of mommying and how stressful it was to use the Baby Tylenol. (It had worked like a charm, his fever went down to normal the next morning, but I was still scared about giving him the correct dosage—not so little that it was ineffective and not so much that it induced a coma.) I appreciated her expert advice, such as when she recommended popping in a video to calm Jake's fussiness after a long day. I loved being able to talk with her as an almost-equal.

"You're doing a great job taking care of him," she said to me one day, and I basked in the glow of her praise. It was like having Julia Child tell me she loved my beef bourguignon.

Less than a year earlier, I'd felt invisible at the family Thanksgiving gathering. While Molly, Carrie, and Kathy bonded over a discussion about childcare hits and misses, I'd silently wondered if I should throw in the towel and join the discussion about Elmo at the kids' table. Now, another holiday was coming, and I'd hoped this time I'd be encouraged to join in the adult-appropriate chatter and laughter I'd previously observed as a sideliner. I didn't want to be a contender; I wanted to be a contributor. I wanted to demonstrate and prove my worthiness by having *my* life experiences and wisdom heard and appreciated.

I wanted to emulate my mommy role models and become one myself.

―――――

It wasn't just the mommies I wanted to emulate. I also had some role models for the cute, clever, and precious kids I longed to mother.

Meet The Guthrie Girls. Chloe is focused, dramatic, independent, and inquisitive ("Do frogs sneeze?" she asked me when she was three). Ellie is a natural comedienne, social, compassionate, loving, and whip-smart ("That Ellie Guthrie is going to *Harvard!*" her preschool teacher had once proclaimed). Quinn, the baby sister at the time, is funny, feisty, a bit of a show-off, and has the most infectious giggle I've ever heard.

Early in my trip, I couldn't be quite as playful as usual with them because I was responsible for Jake. But auntie time was special to me, so I arranged to cram a couple of visits—with just the girls—between mothering and work duties.

One afternoon, while Jake was in day care, I attended Chloe and Ellie's swim lessons, then took everyone—including Molly and Quinn—out to lunch. I caught Molly up on my get-Jake-to-sleep-through-the-night program, during which Chloe piped in with, "Thank goodness for Baby Tylenol!"

"Wow," I said as I turned and stared at her. "You were listening carefully to what I said, weren't you?"

She just looked back at me and beamed.

There's that saying "Little pitchers have big ears," a caution to parents that children listen in on your conversations when you're not paying attention to them and they understand more than you realize, and then they repeat inappropriate things at inopportune moments. I'd forgotten about this, even though it had been less than a year since I'd been called out by my nieces over my use of a naughty word. Chloe, Ellie, and I had gone for a long walk together. We'd looked for fairies, played Follow the Leader, sang songs. But instead of telling their mom about our grand adventures when we returned home through the back gate, they ran to the house yelling, "AUNT KATH SAID A BAD WORD!"

Oh, crap! I thought to myself, completely mortified. *What did I say?*

Poopie. The offending word was *poopie*. We had seen a woman let her dog poop on the trail, and I called the woman "a poopie lady" when she didn't pick up the poop. I can't remember how Molly responded because I was preoccupied thinking *I am capable of so much worse!*

At home, surrounded by other consenting adults, I never censor my language. I don't think I have a potty mouth...oops, that word is also a no-no...I mean, I don't think I have a *dirty* mouth, but I was learning that I needed to be more aware of how I behaved around my little tattletales...um, imitators.

Toward the middle of my mommy vacation, with Jake at day care and during Quinn's nap time, I loaded Chloe and Ellie's booster seats into the back seat of Carrie's car, made sure the girls were properly buckled in, then headed out for what I called a Special Date. We started at Cold Stone Creamery for ice cream. They each had a scoop of chocolate ice cream with white chocolate chips and gummy bears. *Gr-ross.* I had a scoop of chocolate ice cream with chocolate chips, and felt only slightly envious of their gastronomic adventurousness.

From there we went to a nail salon for manicures. The girls carefully considered all the choices of colors before Ellie selected red for her toes and white for her fingers and Chloe selected all red, in the spirit of Independence Day. Chloe also picked out my color: a metallic yellowish-goldish-orange, what I would later describe as "Metallic Bile." It was completely hideous, but she said she liked it because it looked like fireworks. Okay then.

It was supposed to be a date for just manicures, or technically, $7 polish changes. But I got worked by a masterful pair of manipulators.

"But Aunt Kaa-aaath! What do you mean we can't get pedicures?"

"We only made appointments for manicures."

"Mommy said we could get pedicures too," Chloe said, putting on her best mopey, sad-puppy-dog face to cover an obvious fib.

"Since I'm paying for it, we're only getting manicures."

"But that's not fair!" Chloe continued. "And the only reason I wore flip-flops was so I could get a pedicure."

"That is so not true. You wore flip-flops so your feet would be cool and comfortable in this heat."

"But Aunt Ka-ath!"

My best argument was that we didn't have time to do both because I needed to be back home in time to pick up Jake.

"But they do it at the same time!" Ellie countered.

They didn't, but at this point I folded.

One very patient lady painted Ellie's toes then fingers, then Chloe's toes and fingers, then my fingernails. The girls did their best to sit still at the dryers, but were quickly distracted.

"Aunt Kath, I'm bored...," Ellie whined.

Jesus, Mary, and Joseph...

"THEY HAVE STICKERS!!! Aunt Kath..."

"NO!"

I faked an itchy nose and rubbed my face on my sleeve to conceal my laughter.

God, how I loved being their aunt. I had to wonder if I would still be as amused by the attempted fleecing—if I would retain my patience and sense of humor—if I were the parental figure in this scenario. Honestly, I think it would have rubbed my last nerve after a while, and I didn't relish the possibility of becoming just another cranky grownup in their lives. I couldn't image their wanting to spend time with me, either, if that was the case.

But, oh, it would be worth it, I thought, if my own kids were this adorable.

———

As we crossed the parking lot back to my car, I wiggled my hips, threw out a few Disco Kid punches, and struck my own version of a Vogue pose.

"Oh, Aunt Kath," Ellie said, as she giggled and climbed into her seat. "Sometimes you're funny."

It reminded me of a recent conversation I had had with my friend James. He and his wife, Teri, have been married for several years and were discussing whether or not it was time to start a family of their own.

"The thing is," he confided in me, "I really don't want children."

"Seriously? Why not?"

"Well...I like our life. I like our marriage, and I really like that I am still the 'fun uncle' to all of our nieces and nephews."

"Can't you still be fun when you have kids of your own?" I asked.

"Not really," he said. "Think about it. You have to be responsible, a disciplinarian. My brothers and their wives are always too tired to play, too stressed out."

I'd never really thought about this before. I'd assumed I'd always be fun, but I could see how parenting could take a toll. I thought about my aunts and uncles—all had their own kids to raise—and saw the reality of what they had chosen. We had close relationships when I was young, but they had always been an extension of my parents. Giving up the "fun" title would be a painful sacrifice for me.

"Teri and I get to be silly and funny," James said. "We get to be outside and play games with the kids while the other adults sit around and gripe about how burned out they are. They were once fun, too, but then they had kids. I want to be the fun uncle as long as possible, maybe forever."

I thought a lot about our conversation as I now weighed the pros and cons of joining the mommy club. I loved being the one who made silly faces, danced like a lunatic, got down on the floor to play "surfboard" (as in I was the surfboard, and the girls stood on my back to ride the waves), and allowed my hair to be teased into a mess of tangles by budding stylists. Maybe I could still do that with my own kids to some extent, but I didn't see how it was possible. My parents were pretty cool, but they were still my parents. Even now I can't imagine my mom being okay with having her hair mussed.

It's not that I wanted to be a Peter Pan, someone who never grows up, never takes on responsibilities. This also wasn't about giving into the kids' every whim, then handing them back to their parents when they had sugar meltdowns. Like James, I loved my relationship with each little human in my family, and I wanted to nourish those relationships. With them, I wanted to hang on to my kid-like sense of play, I wanted to be the good guy (versus the disciplinarian), and I wanted to (occasionally) be the troublemaker who helped impressionable youths master critical life skills, like arm farts. I wanted to be the grownup they adored. I wanted to always be The World's Greatest Aunt.

At the time, I was making six or more trips each year to see them for birthdays, holidays, and other special—or not especially special—events. While there were no guarantees they'd want me around in their teenage and busy young adult lives, I hoped to over time expand my role to friend and trusted confidante. I didn't think I was an exceptional aunt, but I could see that I had something special with my nieces that my mom friends couldn't create or sustain with their nieces and nephews: I could give them the time, energy, and attention my friends were spending on their own kids.

If I achieved my goal of becoming a mom, everything would change. Everything.

"Limited interaction with nieces and nephew" went to the top of my cons list.

13

CORRECTION: #1 ON MY CONS LIST

*D*uring the day, Jake liked to turn all his noisemaker toys on at one time for a jangling, jingling, beeping cacophony of sounds. I could deal with most of them. The piano-kind-of-thingy that played familiar jazz tunes when you pressed color-coded blocks was actually kind of cool.

However. I hope the person who created the duck-faced, pusher-toy-thingy with the fish handle, currently has a teenager...who is a limitedly talented drummer...in a heavy metal band.

At the slightest nudge, or from a miniscule shake from the reverberations of a passing truck, this evil gadget broke out into loud techno nursery rhymes. It was especially annoying when I was exhausted, was stumbling around in the dark, and was trying not to make the teensiest noise that might wake a slumbering baby. Like a highly sensitive car alarm, it announced its presence to the world at all hours of the day and night. More than once it had jarred me from a few precious moments of deep sleep into a toy-icidal rage.

I fantasized about smashing it into a thousand quiet plastic pieces.

Noisy toys, Legos that maim bare feet, and similar instruments of torture were not things I looked forward to in my future parenting adventures.

"Aunt Kath, why didn't you ever want to get married?"

"It wasn't that I didn't want to get married, I just haven't met the right guy."

"Here's what you've gotta do: Go to college, meet a boy, get his phone number, call him up, and tell him you want to get married."

"That's a great idea, except I've already been to college and I didn't meet a boy I really liked. And I don't think I want to go back to college."

"Hmm."

"What do you think I should do to meet a boy?"

"I don't know."

"Maybe I should just go to the store and buy one."

"Oh, Aunt Kath! That's the funniest thing you've ever said!"

—with Ellie, age 5

"Can't you get one of the boys at work to marry you?"

—Chloe, age 6

14

DATING...WITH KID

For the first time in my life, my body was being used for something other than getting me around or getting me attention. There was more to hot vacation mama than met the eye. You see, it turned out I had hips. Not swaying, sexy, child-bearing hips, but the kind that developed aches and pains and debilitating cramps. I also discovered new nerve endings and muscles in my back, legs, shoulders, and arms.

After just a few days of toting around a squiggly 25-pound kid, leaning in odd angles to deposit him into the stroller or pick him up from the bathtub, or reaching behind and under furniture to retrieve wooden blocks, my body was crying uncle. I was shocked the first time I swung my legs over the side of the bed to jumpstart a day only to have sharp pains shoot through my hips and lower back.

"HOLY MOTHER!" I silently screamed, not wanting to wake and scare the kid in the next room.

I popped Advil with my vitamins and briefly considered bumping grocery shopping off the schedule to allow for a 90-minute massage.

By the end of each day, my lower back was threatening to go

on strike, along with my hips and knees. For hours my body had twisted at weird angles as I lifted Jake from seats, over railings, out of the crib, into the crib, from his car seat and out the car door, from his high chair, from the living room floor and onto the couch. "Use your legs, Kath," my inner personal trainer told me, but I ignored the advice as I continued to focus on taking care of the kid first. As a result, I felt stiff and achy and stooped and older by years rather than hours.

This got me thinking about the realities of being an older mother. An online search for information yielded the expected articles about the sharp decline in fertility after the age of 35, the decrease in the number and quality of my eggs, the increased risk of chromosomal abnormalities for the child. The strain of pregnancy on an older body, I learned, also included higher risks for gestational diabetes, complications from a C-section (more likely because an older uterus doesn't stretch as well as a younger one), and heart damage. The stress of pregnancy on the heart was likened to the stress of running a marathon, which would be compounded on an older, weakened heart muscle.

Lordy.

I was disappointed, although not entirely surprised, that the articles that offered solutions focused on IVF treatments. I didn't want to go there. I wondered how many of those clinics were candid with their potential clients about *all* the physical risks.

Meanwhile, I still wanted to know about the realities of raising a child after 40. Scientific articles reported cardiac complications, a higher risk of developing breast cancer, and the compounding of normal aging conditions such as high blood pressure and cholesterol.

The anecdotal information I found in discussions and mommy blog posts supported what I'd heard friends complain about. Commenters wrote about being less able to keep up with active children, about sleep deprivation in the first year and lack of physical energy as the children grew. They shared their fears of dying while the children were still young, about not living long enough to see their children become adults. A number of grandparents who we were raising grandchildren weighed in too, and one woman lamented her biggest challenge: juggling her grandchild's active schedule to accommodate her water aerobics classes for adults with arthritis. That was so going to be me, and I grimaced at the image of my future crone-like self, shuffling through the day while my tween-ager Rollerbladed circles around me.

While the outlook for my physical decline was not bright, there was some encouragement. Older parents reported feeling more emotionally prepared, self-aware, and stable. "I'm mellower than I would have been in my 20s," and "I don't sweat the small stuff" were among the more encouraging comments. Life experience counted for something. Another plus was that several people wrote that they were able to cope with the challenges because their young children kept them feeling young.

I suppose I could look at the physical toll as a tradeoff for the kisses and cuddles. One of the harsh realities of being single and living alone is how little physical contact you receive. As a single adult, if you want regular touching, you have to pay for it, via a massage or a pedicure. Or you engage in a soulless fling, accepting brief embraces in lieu of true affection. Or you find substitutes for your soothing in such things as wine and chocolate. Eighty-two percent dark chocolate was my big-girl version of a binky.

Pros and cons, cons and pros. From my (bad) dating days, I'd learned I deserved more than relationships that were "good enough," that provided fleeting moments of tenderness but required I squelch my loving nature. Now here I was, sacrificing the needs of my own body to meet the needs of another in hopes of getting a tiny bit of affection in return. I could hear my inner critics battling it out in my head:

"Don't be so selfish! Give up everything to take care of the kid!"

"Didn't you want the kid for selfish reasons, to see a mini-you, to create someone who would love you? We all have needs—stop being such a martyr!"

"You knew there would be sacrifices going into this. Take your Advil, eat your chocolate, and get over yourself!"

It felt less and less like I could have it all. It was "either-or," not "and," but I wasn't ready to convince myself that it was good enough for me.

————

I wasn't ready to give up on having it all.

Conveniently, Braden, the guy I'd been getting to know over emails and a couple of casual dates during his visits to family in Southern California, followed up on his promise to take me— plus Jake—out for dinner. He suggested meeting at family-friendly La Piñata, a half-mile from home. Thursday night, 5:30. What a trouper.

We'd met through an online dating site, something I'd signed up for in an effort to "put myself out there." Honestly, I didn't have very high expectations for finding The One, but I wasn't finding Any One on my own or through my friends, and I figured it couldn't hurt to expand my circle. Among the creeps and cheaters who popped into my inbox (Me: "You've seen my photo, I'd like to see yours." Cheater: "Why?" Me: "Are you married?" Cheater: "Why would you ask that?!" Me: *Buh-bye.*), he was a lovely exception. Better than that, he was funny, intelligent, handsome, and genuinely kind. I looked forward to spending more time with him.

I had a slight tan from all the walking and strollering and playing in the park. In ivory linen shorts, a form-fitting white T-shirt, with my hair in a sleek ponytail, I felt fit and sexy. I was a hot mama and I was going on a date!

Following a mellow walk through the neighborhood, I rolled Jake and his stroller to a table in a corner of the busy restaurant, where I could corral him. Braden arrived a few minutes after we had gotten settled. Through the big picture window, I watched him pull up in a light-blue, convertible BMW (nice). He had come straight from work in the City, so was dressed in a tan suit and stylish tie (hubba hubba!). After a quick hug hello (did my heart just flutter?), I insisted he take off his tie and relax.

We caught up a bit on work, family, and plans for the summer, all interspersed with Jakey interruptions. I had brought food from home for Jake, and he had some of my chicken quesadilla, which I cut into Jake-size pieces and doled out in small amounts to keep him occupied. He also loved the tortilla chips, which I crushed and deposited in piles onto the tray of his high chair. I kept him entertained with a few toys I'd brought along—I was learning!

What impressed me about Braden this particular evening was how great he was with Jake. Not just that he made the effort to interact with a 15-month-old, but that he didn't get frustrated or impatient. It was clear that having an in-depth, continuous, adult conversation was impossible, especially when Jake finished eating and I released him from his chair so he could explore the area around the table. But Braden didn't make an issue out if it. Other single, kid-less guys might feel offended that I wasn't giving them my full attention, or frustrated that they couldn't finish making their point, or embarrassed because the kid was getting antsy in a public place.

Braden flowed with the flow.

"Dinner's on us," I said, when the waiter came to ask if we wanted churros or flan. "It's the least I can do, since I essentially got you out on a work night to come help me babysit."

Braden exchanged a grin with our waiter, who then told me, "It's taken care of." Braden had slipped his credit card to him before joining us at our table. He wouldn't even let me pay the tip. I wasn't sure what pleased me more: that he'd paid for dinner for all three of us, or that he'd pulled off such a smooth surprise. "Nicely done," I said, blushing with delight at his kind gesture. "Thank you."

Under different circumstances we would have lingered over dessert and coffee, or perhaps a glass of wine, getting better acquainted and sussing out the potential for future dates. Instead, he helped me—without the slightest complaint— gather up our gear so I could get Jake home, bathed, and asleep within range of his normal bedtime hour. Like I said: trouper. I made a mental IOU to devote my full attention to Braden the next time we were together, and to stay out until long after sunset.

We walked to the end of the block together, then Braden held the stroller steady while I wrestled a now-cranky kid into it. Jake was doing a fake cry and struggling with me. I held his binky in my mouth to free up both hands, grappled with flailing arms and legs, and strapped him in. I gave Braden a quick hug goodbye, thanked him for meeting us and treating us to dinner, and turned the stroller homeward.

He has nice eyes, I thought to myself as Jake settled into the rhythm of the stroller. *He has a great hug.*

I resisted the urge to start imagining how our children would look (his big grin, my high cheekbones, athletic builds— oops, maybe I thought about it a little bit). I wondered if he really had daddy potential or if he was just making nice, because this was not *my* kid he needed to charm to get to me. He wasn't interviewing to be my future partner and my kid's future stepdad. We weren't even to the point of discussing how we might facilitate our dogs' cohabitation. He seemed to have had a nice time that evening, but I didn't know what kind of impression I had given him. Cool aunt, sexy single lady, or loudly ticking biological time bomb? I hoped I hadn't come across as Bachelorette #3, but there was a part of her in me too.

I really liked this guy. And while I knew it was waaay too early in the dating game to put all my eggs in one basket with one guy and address family planning issues, I was over 40. Sometime soon, I needed to know if family/children was something he wanted for himself, something he'd be willing to do with me. It was equally scary to think that one day I might have to ask him if he was okay with my going ahead and having a baby on my own—without the expectation that he would commit to co-parenting—because my precious eggs had expiration dates. I wanted to allow us all the time we needed to get to know each other better and decide if we had a future together, yet time, clearly, was not my friend. What a quagmire.

These worries paused briefly as I gave Jake his bath and gently wrapped him in his towel. I melted inside as he gave me a sleepy, sloppy kiss on my chin after I helped him into his PJs. I held my sweet boy in my arms as I rocked him into slow, deep breaths, then carefully lifted him into his crib. I watched as he settled in, among his books and binkies, and committed every precious moment to memory. Was this a harbinger of my future, or...?

"Fools rush in," says the wise adage, and if there was one thing I knew, it was that I didn't want to rush this relationship with Braden. I wanted it to unfold naturally, comfortably, respectfully. I looked forward to seeing him again and hoped that our date night with kid hadn't scared him off.

———

Oh, f***! The fish! Carrie and Kathy had also entrusted me with the well-being of a small school of fish and teeny, tiny, skinny-legged frogs, inhabitants of an aquarium stationed in the hallway. By some miracle I managed to feed them during my morning stupor, though most days I had no memory of doing so. A daily pinch of flaky fish food sprinkled along the surface of the water plus another pinch of seed-like frog food released just underneath the surface was all it took. It seemed simple, but on my to-do list, it could easily have been overlooked.

Much to my relief, all the creatures were still alive. No floaters.

Remembering to feed myself was another story. My healthy, planned-menus, five-small-meals-a-day routine was shot. It was entirely possible that my body was running on ice cream.

I thought about my sweet dog, Beau, and how guilt nearly leveled me whenever I cut walks short due to my busy schedule. I imagined adding him to my current scenario and wondered how I'd remember to feed and nurture him, wondered what all this neglect would do to my health, wondered how long I could survive on poor self-care before I collapsed and couldn't take care of any of us. The fish could be flushed, no problem, and though it would break my heart to give up my sweet Beau, I suppose I could do it from a place of wanting what was best for him. But this tapped into one of my deepest fears about becoming a single parent: that something would happen to me, that I might get sick or be seriously injured or otherwise become incapacitated. Or worse, that I simply wouldn't be able to hack parenting on my own and would have to give up my child.

Oh, for Pete's sake, snap out of it, Kath!

I shook myself out of my overly dramatic nightmare and tried to tap into the fishes' Zen. *Breathe in, breathe out.* As I stood there in the hallway, watching the fish swim in lazy, full-bellied circles, I found myself thinking how much easier (ha) it would have been if I'd been one of those women who never wanted children.

My first encounter with a childfree-by-choice peer came shortly after college. Annie had gotten married over the summer and we met for lunch to catch up that fall. "I have big news!" she told me on the phone when we confirmed our plans. Naturally, I came prepared to plan a baby shower.

"Oh, good god, no!" she said, laughing at my assumption that she was pregnant. "I don't have the mommy gene. I've never wanted children."

I couldn't understand how that could be. Weren't all women born with an instinctual desire for children?

"It's not that I don't like children," she explained, "I adore my niece. I just never wanted any of my own."

I would meet more women like Annie over time. Rather, I'd discover this about more of my friends as we became closer and the topic came up. They weren't child-haters, they didn't have "bitter wombs," they weren't married to their careers—although many of them had thriving careers that never would have been possible between flu season and PTA meetings. They were...what was it about them? They were content with their lots in life. They were comfortable in their skin. They had no problem with people who questioned them about their lack of offspring. They laughed off meddlesome strangers who suggested they were selfish or said unhelpful things like "You still have time."

Contrary to what I assumed was public opinion, the childfree women among my friends had solid self-identities and self-esteem. And as I stood in Carrie and Kathy's hallway getting hypnotized by the fish, I wondered if I could be content among their numbers.

Hmmm...nope. As much as I wished life were simpler for me, more black and white, I couldn't fathom ending up in No Kids Land. Or rather, I couldn't imagine being happy there.

So back to work on the plan.

Meanwhile, in the moment, I was fine. The fish were fine, Jake was fine, I trusted Beau was fine. I'd almost dropped the ball on something tiny in the great scheme of things. Big whoop! Whatever path I chose, I'd get the hang of it. I'd find my rhythm.

"Breathe, Kath, breathe," I said to myself as I pulled away from the aquarium and back to my to-do list.

Somehow I'd figure it out. Somehow, I'd get it all done.

15

INTERDEPENDENCE

I had big plans for the Fourth of July. In anticipation, I'd packed my red linen dress and red, white, and blue sandals. For Jake, I'd laid out a coordinating red, white, and blue striped T-shirt and navy shorts. I could pretend for the day that we were our own little family, as we joined extended family for holiday fun, and I imagined how cute the matchy-matchy photos of us would look on my shelf at home.

Together, we'd head out early, to beat the closing of the island's streets for the local parade, and travel over the bridge to join my brother, Kevin, Molly, and the girls for a traditional Independence Day celebration. We'd go to their town's parade, return to their backyard for a BBQ with homemade ice cream for dessert, play some games, then hang out with them or return home to watch fireworks light up the skies. It was going to be crammed with family activities. It was going to be perfect.

Growing up, the Fourth of July was a major holiday for my family. Typically we'd celebrate in one of two ways: We'd either gather together with neighbors and friends for barbecued burgers, corn-on-the-cob, watermelon, ice cream cranked in the garage, and sparklers waved around in the cul-de-sac. Or, we'd go to our grandmother's, about an hour's drive from our home, and walk from her house to the high school, spread a picnic blanket in the middle of the football field, and eat cold fried chicken, olives off the tips of our fingers, bread-and-butter pickles, potato salad, and Gram's chocolate cream pie. Then we'd lie back on the grass or climb into the stands to watch a spectacular fireworks display, whooping or applauding or laughing with delight at each thrilling bang.

One year, just to mix things up, we spent the day at the beach, playing in the surf and sand all day, grilling dinner over the open fire pit, toasting marshmallows for s'mores, and singing along to the accompaniment of my dad on the ukulele. But by the time it was dark enough for fireworks, the fog had rolled in, thick enough so that the much-anticipated presentation being shot off the nearby pier appeared to us as muffled colorful glows in a smoky sky. It was cool in its own way, and it wasn't lost on me that family being together was the common thread through every variation of the holiday.

All of these experiences stood out in my memories as idyllic, and it stood to reason, then, that I expected to someday host my own star-spangled celebrations with extended family and friends, complete with tri-color decorations and a spread of food worthy of a Martha Stewart–styled magazine photo shoot.

But that was still an elaborate fantasy because I was, as you know, single.

As a young adult, with family scattered and doing their own things, I occasionally hoped for an invitation to a friend's party. If a family gathering was coordinated, it made more sense for me to travel to a sibling's home, since I didn't have to travel with children. For the same reason, I'd never been the host. Families were hosts; single women were lucky to be invited. Most years, however, I spent the day alone. Maybe I'd read a book or take a nap or watch some weepy chick-flicks. If the holiday fell in the middle of the week, there was a good chance I'd just work through it. Memories of those lonely years fueled my determination to make my holiday with Jake live up to—if not exceed—my expectations.

Despite all my advance planning (and coordinated outfits) for this year's festivities, I hadn't given a whole lot of thought to how a 15-month-old child would react to the excitement of the Fourth. My cousin Karen brought it up during her visit and suggested using white noise to help Jake remain calm through the startling and potentially frightening sounds of revelry. She pointed me toward the radio Jake had in his room, which I sometimes set to a low volume at night to help him fall asleep. Per her instructions, for a couple of days leading up to the Fourth, each time he went into his room for a nap or bedtime, I turned the radio on to a mellow music station and gradually increased the volume each time. He didn't seem to notice the difference. After tucking him into bed on the night of the 3rd, I congratulated myself on being proactive.

It wasn't enough. The music on the radio initially helped him fall asleep, and stay asleep during what sounded like an official presentation over loudspeakers somewhere in the neighborhood. But as the night progressed, we both were awakened in near panic by random explosions and the booming, snapping, and crackling of nearby fireworks (or gunfire—it was hard to differentiate, and I really didn't want to know if it was the latter). At 3:27 AM on the Fourth, I finally accepted that neither of us was going to achieve the REM stage of sleep.

By that point, his cries upon waking were more tortured than usual, plus I'd been having nightmares about him. Each time he'd cry out, my dreams would go into a scenario in which he was in a dangerous predicament. In the last one, he was standing atop the fireplace mantle in the master bedroom, about to take a header. I shot up in bed, heart pounding, breath coming in frantic bursts. I rolled out of bed, stumbled to his room, lifted him out of his crib, put him in a dry diaper, inserted a binky, and rocked him back to sleep. We both needed soothing. Knowing that both he and I were going to be extremely tired in the coming day was not encouraging. I worried that we would be cranky guests for Kevin and Molly, but there was nothing I could do to change the course of events. I marched on.

———

At 6:30 I gave up and dragged myself into the day. I got myself dressed and spiffed in my holiday-themed attire, then rallied Jake. As I propped him against me to get him dressed, his eyes were still at half-mast and he was wobbly on his legs, but we managed to get the right shoe on the right foot, left shoe on left foot, and our breakfast routine went smoothly. After cleaning hands and faces, we called Quinn and sang "Happy Birthday" to her, then headed out.

Barely ahead of schedule, we drove through the neighborhood and got a preview of Alameda's festivities. It was fun to drive down Park Street and see all the spectators lined up along the curbs, waiting for the parade to begin. People in beach chairs, children on shoulders, banners and balloons decorating the storefronts, an air of excitement and anticipation throughout. I smiled to myself, envisioning my future alongside them.

When we arrived at the Guthries' house, we were greeted by the three girls, still in their PJs and very excited to see us. Chloe and Ellie pulled us into Quinn's room to show us how they'd TP'd it, a family tradition in which other family members sneak in while the birthday girl is sleeping and "decorate" her room. The mood was playful, inviting, and celebratory. But Jake was a wreck already, fussy, cranky, and agitated. I put him down in Quinn's bed soon after we arrived, in hopes he would nap and make up for some of the night's sleep deprivation. Sweet Quinn tried to help by bringing him her binkies, blankets, and stuffed animals, but he was inconsolable. I did the best that I could, holding and caressing him, carrying him around, talking to him in soothing tones, and encouraging him to play with his cousins. This worked for short periods and he would display moments of Jake-ness during the day—cute, playful, happy—but he never quite made a full recovery from the stress of the previous night.

We did manage to wedge in some family fun. We watched some of Quinn's videotape of her life so far—her first birthday celebration, her first steps, Christmases—and I allowed myself to imagine creating records of my own child's milestones. I joined Chloe and Ellie to play with their dolls for a while, trying to give them a little of the attention they craved, then we all gathered together in the living room to participate in a relatively new family tradition: watching Nathan's Famous Fourth of July Hot Dog Eating Contest. Live from Coney Island, professional eaters raced to see who could down the most hot dogs in 12 minutes. ESPN hosted the broadcast, complete with commentary and instant replays, and we watched with horror, awe, disgust, and disbelief as the competitors crammed hot dogs and buns into their mouths and washed them down with soda or water. Or didn't. We writhed on the couches and tried not to watch the "reversals," in which the competitor gags and barfs back up what he—or she—has eaten. And then—"Oh, my gawd!"—s/he re-eats it so as not to lose the credit.

"This is *disgusting!*"

"I'm going to barf!"

"I can't watch this anymore!"

It was riveting, and hilarious, and the big winner—Joey Chestnut from nearby San José—won the title by keeping down a nauseating 66 dogs.

Although we were running late, we decided to try to attend some of the festivities in Molly's hometown, one town over. We loaded the kids into car seats and piled in their gear. Kevin drove a gigantic, gas-guzzling Ford Expedition that seated eight passengers, so we were all able to ride over together. The 15-minute drive provided a reprieve as we all pitched in to try to cheer up Jake—who was whimpering his way into a monumental meltdown—by singing along to a kid-friendly CD. Our off-keyed enthusiasm helped distract him.

Once I had wrestled him into his stroller at the fair, he became calm and stayed mellow, while the girls started to complain. This was all possibly due to the fact that it was 106 degrees. It wasn't just hot, it was fry-an-egg-on-the-hood-of-the-car hot. I longed to give in to the crankiness that lurked just below my limp linen-dressed mommy/auntie façade. I was as tired, uncomfortable, and irritable as the rest of them. Hell, no one got sweaty and sticky in my picture-perfect holiday fantasies. *Martha Stewart can bite me*, I thought to myself, but that attitude wasn't the example I wanted to set for my nieces. Sometimes being a grown-up sucks.

With rivers of sweat running down our bodies, Molly and I pushed the younger kids around in strollers, while coaxing the two older girls to keep up. We'd missed the parade, so we just dragged ourselves around the perimeter of the park, checking out the booths, bribing the kids with candies, hoping for a breeze that would bring cool relief. We lasted for one miserable rotation before we gave up and returned to the car.

Back inside their air-conditioned house, I fed Jake, then the rest of us celebrated Quinn's birthday with lunch, cake, and delicious homemade peach ice cream. I started to hope Jake had turned a corner.

Nope. Attempts at getting him down for his afternoon nap were a disaster. I put him in Quinn's crib, again with the girls offering comforting items such as toys and binkies, but he couldn't unwind enough to sleep. Their household was anything but quiet, so I'm sure he was distracted by the activities in surrounding rooms, probably longing to be part of the fun despite his fatigue. Kevin tried carrying him around and talking to him. Molly offered milk, snacks, and other mom-proven methods for soothing him, but nothing worked. Red in the face, shedding big tears, and hoarse from crying for so long, the poor little guy was just wiped out. It broke my heart to see him so distraught. Plus, I was disappointed in myself. I had thought that by now I would have had enough mommy experience to know what to do to calm him, make him happy, and work out his stress and frustration. But my own patience was worn out and my forced cheerful demeanor was fraying at the edges. When do mommies get to have their own meltdowns?

It was time to take him home. As much as I wanted to stay and play—and the girls wanted me to stay and play—I decided to be a good mommy and put him first. This wouldn't be the year I would stay up late with the nieces to watch fireworks or sit at the table for hours playing cards with my brother and sister-in-law. My first responsibility was to the soggy, overheated little guy in my care. And by this time, with my own discomfort and growing angst, giving up my Fourth of July dream was a relief.

With the sun still scorching down on me, I loaded up the car, got Jake strapped in and plugged up with a binky, cranked up the A/C, and waved goodbye. As soon as we hit the freeway,

Jake dropped his binky under his car seat (*just shoot me now*) and proceeded to *wail* all the way home. I was amazed he had that much energy left. At the first stop light after we exited the freeway, I was able to dig his sippy cup out of my purse, and that little bit of cool milk kept the peace until we got home.

Up the stairs and straight to bed, no fuss, no fight. With him down, I returned to the car to unload the stroller, locate the tossed binky, and gather all the gear. I was sticky and stinky and tired and grumpy and I soooo wanted this "holiday" to be over.

The thick, fluffy master bed called to me, and my aching body was craving a rejuvenating nap. But...as I balanced the stroller on my hip while I locked up the car, I noticed Kathy's car parked down the street. Or rather, it wasn't her car I noticed, but the glaringly bright orange warning sticker that had been pasted onto the front windshield. I lugged the stroller alongside me (because in my burned-out state I didn't think about opening it up and *rolling* it) and trudged down the block to investigate. The big black letters on the sticker shouted that this vehicle would be impounded because it had been parked in the same space for more than 72 hours. This, folks, is illegal in the city of Alameda, California. Other cities might be concerned with things like drive-by shootings and hate crime vandalism, but HERE, the big offense is parking your friggin' car in front of your friggin' home!

One of the neighbors must have reported the car, and now I had to find Kathy's keys, drive it around the block for appearances' sake, and pull it into a new spot. *Bastards!* What a pain in the ass. What if I had been home sick with the flu? What if I had been a new—single—mom, recovering from a C-section and unable to drive for two weeks? What if I had actually died, but my neighbors were more concerned with the car than their dead neighbor and her abandoned child?!

In my head I drafted a fiery letter to the editor of the local paper, cursing whomever felt the need to patrol this safe neighborhood for the dangerous criminal who would—gasp!—leave her car in the same place. My letter would lay it all out: the sleep deprivation, the temper tantrums, the stress of responsibility, and the agony of no air conditioning in this suffocating heat. (Like most homes and businesses in Alameda, Carrie and Kathy's old Victorian didn't have air-conditioning.) I imagined the pathetic little tattletale cringing as he (it couldn't have come from woman, she would be more understanding) recognized himself and his petty deed in my tale of woe.

But for now, I just...needed...that...nap. I filed my rant away for another day, moved the car over two spaces, peeled the sticker off the windshield, and made a mental note to move it again three days in the future.

After glaring at the houses in the vicinity, mentally spewing hateful curses upon the person who had felt the need to report our offending car, I climbed back up the stairs and headed for the shower, hoping it would help ease me into a more tranquil state. Although I had no quite spent all my patience dealing with Jake's hysterics, I desperately needed the two hours I estimated I could grab to nap or simply lie in front of the fan while he slept.

Twenty minutes later he was up. Over the monitor, I heard animated and nonsensical (to me) chatter. He was having quite the conversation with himself, an imaginary friend, or the books that he took to bed with him. No way to tell, but we were up once more.

We went through our usual nighttime routine, the only variation being that it was even hotter inside than on previous evenings. To keep Jake cool, I put him to bed in just a T-shirt and diaper. Then I turned on the fan and the radio for white noise and prayed for an uneventful evening as I stripped myself down to a T-shirt and undies and eased into bed.

The digital clock read 10:46 when I heard Jake cry out, just once. *Is he sick? Hot? Starting another meltdown?* I held my breath and listened closely to the baby monitor for other indications of the night ahead. Outside, fireworks were going off like crazy from different neighborhoods, but he didn't make another peep. I breathed a sigh of relief and felt grateful that I did not have to get up, then I felt guilty about putting my own comforts ahead of his. My hesitation to deal with an ongoing tantrum possibly made me a bad mommy, but I was just too tired to give a flying fig. Oh, sure, if he'd continued to cry, I would have gone in and taken care of him, but it wasn't like I was *eager* to jump up and repeat the exhausting drama from earlier in the day.

I managed a few hours of fitful sleep, but by the "dawn's early light," my mind was in overdrive. I thought back over the past 24-plus hours and gave myself credit for getting through it. We did the best we could under the circumstances, and when I recognized the signs that it wasn't working out, I made the right call to take us home. Good mommy-ing! He probably would have no memory of any drama, and I'd catch up on my sleep later. Someday. Over a future holiday weekend, perhaps.

Ah-hah. There was one of the benefits of being single and childfree. If I wanted, on any given national or religious holiday, I could stay home, read a book, watch a movie, or sleep all day. I'd gotten a taste of what a family-focused holiday was all about. I'd experienced the realities behind my Norman Rockwell–perfect illusions, and it was exhausting. A parent of a small child has to be constantly in care mode, constantly on alert for potential catastrophes, thus sacrificing their participation in the festivities. Multiply that by two or three kids, and another decade of being part of the fun flies by.

I knew in part that I was looking at one extreme, but it was painful having my dreams crushed. Coming off such a long, punishing day, it was hard to imagine how I, as a single parent, could produce traditional Christmas, Thanksgiving, Easter, Halloween, and birthday affairs, even with the help of family and friends. I'd already missed out on so many holiday festivities over the years because I was the odd single gal out, and now that I had had a glimpse of what the odd-single-gal-plus-toddler scenario looked like, I wasn't sure I was willing to "waste" any more.

Maybe I wanted to just hang out with my siblings and friends and the kids they already had. Maybe what I wanted more than the all-Americana, *Sunset* magazine–worthy imaginings I had held onto for so long was a sense of connectedness that comes from being part of a village, part of a tribe. I wasn't expecting to be catered to, to be a pampered guest; I would be happy to help with the preparations and cleanup, and even pitch in with childcare. Maybe I could look at holidays with a new perspective. I could appreciate the calm and quiet, or I could be more proactive about creating the kinds of gatherings I would enjoy and that would honor and entertain my circle of friends. It didn't have to be about the decorations or the fancy foods or any of the over-the-top hostessing hoopla, it could simply be about being together with whatever kind of "family" I wanted to be part of my "family holiday."

Acknowledging this, taking the pressure off myself, and committing myself to making it my reality, gave me a surprising glimmer of peace.

———

Early on July 5th, I remembered to recharge my phone and check for messages. Braden had left a message, and my heart skipped a beat when I heard his voice.

"Just wanted to tell you how much I enjoyed having dinner with you and Jake!"

What a sweetheart. How nice to be reminded that nice guys do exist in my world.

I pressed the key to save his message and allowed myself to

dream for a moment: *Can I start hoping about having a future with him? Is he making plans too? I wonder if he likes peach ice cream, big fireworks shows, and traditional holiday get-togethers? (Oops, there I go again with the food and traditions and hoopla.)*

I shook my head to clear my thoughts and turned off the phone. *Breathe, Kath, breathe. All will be revealed in good time.*

16

"NOT ON MY WATCH, KID"

*T*he way I saw it, my #1 task was to return Carrie and Kathy's child to them in perfect condition. No broken bones, concussion, bruises, burns, or cuts that required stitches. A living, breathing child would be best.

As the queen of klutz myself, in charge of an active toddler who had barely mastered the art of standing up and still walked like a drunk, the cards were stacked against me. But with a dose of diligence and an ounce or more of paranoia, I thought Jake and I could get to the end of our cohabitation pretty much intact.

There were some close calls, like the night Jake and I met Carrie's long-time friend Heidi for dinner at a local pizzeria. Jake was fussy, but still rallied to eat all the croutons out of my salad and half the mild sausage from my pizza. While Heidi and I attempted to catch up on life, love, and work, Jake entertained himself by rocking back and forth in his standing high chair. At the moment he tipped back a fraction too far, I shot out my left hand and firmly caught hold of his upper right arm. "Not on my watch, kid," I said to him as I set him back upright and placed my left foot on the frame of the chair to keep it firmly planted on the tiled floor.

On many afternoons, we went for walks in the neighborhood. As his enthusiasm bubbled over, he'd gleefully try to run, but his upper body motion moved him forward faster than his little legs could carry him. At just the right moment, almost by instinct, I would reach out and catch him by the back of his shirt or shorts, just before his nose skidded atop the pavement. "Not on my watch, kid," I whispered to him, as I scooped him up into my arms to plant a kiss on his belly.

As a parent-in-training, I prided myself on these great saves, but I also had to acknowledge that the accidents he *did* have on my watch were totally my fault.

A couple of days into my stay, as I puttered around doing household chores, Jake followed me into Carrie and Kathy's room. Instead of playfully—one might say "safely"—chasing him out of the room or picking him up and carrying him out when I finished sorting the laundry, I plopped him onto their three-feet-off-the-ground queen-size bed. Apparently I added a little English to my toss, for he promptly somersaulted backwards over the other side of the bed and landed flat on his back, the wind completely knocked out of him. In the horribly silent moment after he disappeared from view and made contact with the carpeted floor below, I scrambled over the top of the bed and looked down at his unmoving form. It could have been a tragedy. Thank God, it wasn't. I sensed he was okay, though his mouth was open, his eyes were huge, and no air was entering or leaving his little body.

"Breathe, Jakey, breathe," I whispered, as I caressed his chest.

He sucked in a big gulp of air and wailed.

I scooped him up and covered him with kisses and apologies and examined him for any injuries. Somehow he'd escaped with not even a bruise, nor did the experience scare him away from me. He would have been entitled to look at me with wariness whenever I approached him in the future, and I imagined him thinking, *Here comes the bad auntie who throws me off big beds!* But the near-disaster did not imprint on his developing mind, and the rest of our evening was uneventful.

Another morning, my sweet boy indicated he wanted to help clean the kitchen. As I swept, he grabbed hold of the broom and pushed it around the floor, trying to imitate my sweeping motions. I wet-mopped the back half of the room, then told him, "Please go into the living room while I finish up because the floor can get very slippery." He took one step...right onto the wet portion. His little feet flew out from under him and BAM! Tiny thick baby skull meets moderately unforgiving linoleum. I recognized the stunned expression on his face as he lay flat on his back.

"Breathe, Jake. Let it out," I coaxed as I crouched down on the wet floor beside him.

Big suckage of air, then WAIL!

Again I got lucky, since there was no bleeding, bruising, or apparent permanent damage. But I still had the grandmother of all near-catastrophic accidents ahead of me.

The site of my worst infraction was in the main entrance to their house. I had been cautioned about this passageway, and whenever I carried Jake up or down the long, steep staircase that led from the front door to their second-story living quarters, I moved slowly and deliberately, counting off each of the aforementioned 21 steps. I wanted to avoid stumbling, so I talked quietly to soothe Jake and to discourage any wiggling that could knock me off-balance.

Well.... One afternoon after picking Jake up from day care, I scrambled to get him, his gear, the stroller, my bulging purse, and the groceries out of the car and into the house. First I carried up the kid and settled him into the living room. Or so I thought. While I ran back down to the car, he followed me out to the top of the stairs. As I re-entered the front entryway, I looked up to see him push open the unsecured child-proof safety gate—the same gate Carrie had emphatically coached me through carefully closing. As Jake took a first, lethal step into the void, my heart stopped. The air froze. A scream bubbled in my belly, up through my throat, over my tongue:

"NOOOOOOOOOOOOOooooooooo!"

Before I could so much as drop the overstuffed grocery bags to the floor, he was in motion. *Oh dear God, no! Please!* If I'd had any more time, I would have sold my soul to the Devil to avoid this catastrophe, or at least sworn to God that I would never again waste my prayers asking for winning Lotto tickets if he would spare Jake. But there wasn't time. Though the motion seemed life-alteringly slow to me, it all happened in less than a second. He rolled down three steps, a blessed three versus the possible 21, then miraculously stopped and immediately burst into tears. I wasn't sure if he was crying because he was (a) scared, (b) hurt, or (c) freaked out by my yell and the look of utter terror on my face. I'd hoped (a) or (c), ran up the steps, scooped him into my arms, and clicked the damned gate into place.

"You're okay, Jakey. Aunt Kath has you."

He was okay, and within moments, he was squirming to be released from my hold so he could go play.

Aunt Kath, however, was a wreck. I wanted to bawl. I wanted to call on someone bigger and stronger who could rush to hold me tightly and tell me everything was going to be okay. I wanted to gulp down a sippy cup full of wine. But I couldn't do that, because I was still responsible for the kid and needed to have all my faculties on alert. I was still on duty.

That night, after he was tucked into bed, I replayed the scene over and over. Dread gripped my heart and stopped my breath as I considered how close I'd come to not just injuring Jake, but seriously injuring him. I went so far as to imagine the transatlantic phone call to his mommies, in which I would deliver news of a tragedy. Shivers ran through as I shoved aside chilling visions of their anguish and my self-loathing for having caused this imaginary catastrophe. It took all my energy to focus on the good news: Jake was fine.

And because Jake had come through all of these accidents relatively unscathed, I was spared having to tell his mommies the details. Had he been a couple of years older, I'm pretty sure he would have ratted me out. "Aunt Kath threw me off the bed!" I imagined him crowing to his parents as soon as they walked through the front door. I'd figured I'd play it by ear after they'd unpacked and settled in a bit. Really, did they need to hear a complete rundown of all my demerits? Probably not. I'd hoped not. I suddenly felt like a six-year-old who had gotten away with stealing a cookie but was riddled with guilt. This, however, was much more serious. And certainly, if he'd ended up with any severe or visible injuries, I would have made sure he received the very best care and treatment (and I would have fessed up).

I was surprised to discover how much and how often I worried about Jake. Obviously, I had a responsibility to take care of him when he was with me, but even when he was in day care I worried and obsessed about him.

In the past, I'd had nightmares about my nieces' safety and well-being after watching unimaginable stories about abductions, abuses, molestations, and crippling accidents on the nightly news. The concern factor must multiply tenfold for real parents. I don't know how they do it. I don't know how they send their precious child, the one they planned and prayed for, out to play in the big, bad world, and still sleep through the night. Every day there are terrifying possibilities for pain, suffering, and death, not only outside the safety of home, but also right inside its protective doors, with opportunities for broken bones and chicken pox scars and hurt feelings. And the worry never stops. Even when the child is grown and on his own, you still fret and hope he's okay, he's safe, he's happy.

Certainly there was the possibility I would grow with the experience, that in time I would find I was more able to let go and let him learn from his mistakes and pick himself up after tumbles. As he and I got older, it's likely we would both become more at ease with the everyday accidents that just happen. Perhaps that was the real lesson here, that parenting is also a form of growing up, and I, too, would have to release my expectations and fears to let him fully develop into his own self, for better or for worse, with all the physical and emotional bruises that come with the territory.

Parenting is a life-long commitment, even more binding than marriage, I realized. As I continued to weigh the pros and cons and contemplate my future, I had to ask myself if I was up to the challenge of single parenting. Did I even want to be? Or would I be content to sip my wine, keep all my croutons to myself, and go to sleep worry-free while being protected from the terrors that come hand-in-hand with the joys of being a mommy?

———

At the end of another full and exhausting day, I took one last peek at Jake on my way to my own bed. I leaned over his crib and gently placed my hand on his back, confirmed he was breathing, and let his sweet warmth travel up my arm and flood into my heart.

He was fine. I was fine. The next day we'd get another fresh start, with all the risks for owies and catastrophes, and all the opportunities for soul connections and precious memories. He'd grow a little taller, and my heart would grow a little bigger.

"Sweet dreams, Lovie," I whispered before I slipped out to the next room.

Was having a pure love like this in my life worth all the scares, hardships, challenges, and sacrifices?

Yes.

17

FOR THE LOVE OF SHOES

"*S*hooos," Jake cooed, one of the few words in his colorful, baby-babble vocabulary that I could understand. Actually, he made himself quite clear on this one.

"Shoooooss," he said, while pointing to his feet, for once not needing any fancy sign language to communicate what he wanted.

"Shooos!" he crowed upon pulling his choice for the day out of the lowest dresser drawer.

"Shoes," I said, pointing to the bright pink, flower-covered sandals I was wearing and carefully sounding out the word for him.

And "shoes," he repeated, ever so quietly, mimicking my pronunciation and rolling the new sounds around in his mouth.

During the two weeks I spent with Jake, shoes played a big part in our daily activities. In the mornings, I'd pull out a shirt and shorts for him to wear, setting aside a sweatshirt in case it was cool. As his head popped through the collar of his shirt, he'd look up at me with a big grin and we'd both burst out laughing. I guided his arms through sleeves and moved him in close to lean against me for balance as I pulled up, zipped, and snapped his shorts.

Once I had him dressed, Jake liked to carry his shoe selection over to me. He'd hand them to me, then sit down on the floor and scoot his little bottom over until he was leaning against me. I cradled his soft body in my arms while sliding his feet into place. "Left foot, left shoe," I'd say, while attaching the Velcro strap on his brown leather sandal. "Right foot, right shoe," I'd say, as he pushed his foot into my palm until every toe was in its proper place.

I'd hoist him back on his feet, and then he'd stomp on the carpet or dance around his bedroom to complete our getting-dressed ritual.

His fascination with shoes didn't end there. Jake loved getting into my suitcase and pulling out one or both members of a pair, trying them on, carrying them around the house, and, as I mentioned earlier, using one as a substitute for a cell phone ("Hiiii. Yes, yes, yes."). As the day progressed, I might discover one of my black sandals under the bed, in a cupboard in the kitchen, or tucked among his toys in the covered basket in the living room. Fortunately, it also became a game at the end of the day to gather up all of Aunt Kath's shoes and put them back into the suitcase, so I never lost anything for long.

In times of supreme crankiness, Jake's shoes also became instruments of his displeasure with me. In a final moment of defiance, at the tail end of a tantrum after binky, blankie, and Trader Joe's O's had been discarded over the side of the stroller, Jake kicked off his shoes and threw them onto the sidewalk. Of course, he immediately wanted them back, and "Shooooooos!" became a wailing cry of impatience.

Jake loved his shoes.

Then, one night, as I was cleaning up the peas and tofu Jake had squashed onto his high chair tray at dinner, he appeared around the corner of the kitchen entry to present me with my fuzzy black slippers. My heart leapt at his sweetness and with astonishment that such a young child could be so thoughtful. He beamed with pride as I stepped into my slippers, then squirmed away after I gave him a quick kiss of thanks, eager to get back into the living room and whatever next caught his attention.

I couldn't remember the last time anyone had brought me my slippers. And then it struck me: He was Eliza to my Professor Higgins! The analogy didn't end with Jake's bringing me my slippers at the end of a long day. I had, it's true, cast myself as his older and wiser mentor who would teach him his words and their correct pronunciations as well as important things like how to put on shoes. But my intention was never to make him subservient or dependent. Instead, someday soon he would be getting dressed all by himself, zipping his own pants, tying his own shoes.

I, on the other hand, was the one becoming more dependent. I loved the feeling of belonging, of being needed. I loved our morning ritual. I loved the smell and the feel of him as he rested his small body against me. I loved how he trusted me, how he came to me when he needed soothing. I loved when we talked about shoes or any other topic. My heart ached at the thought of having to give all that up.

I'd grown accustomed to his face, and I wasn't anywhere near ready to let go.

18

"I WON'T MIND"

*A*round the time my first niece was born, I decided we needed to have a song, our song, and the moment I heard Audra McDonald sing the tender lyrics of "I Won't Mind" on her *How Glory Goes* album, I knew that was it.

"Auntie Lizzie," the narrator of the song, had desperately wanted to be a mother. But after years of hoping and a devastating miscarriage, she had just been told that she would never be able to bear children of her own. Originally created for *The Other Franklin*, an unfinished musical[1], Lizzie sings to her infant godson, vowing to always be there for him and painting a picture of the unique and precious relationship they will share, one that will include hours and hours of singing, skating, building snowmen, and playing peek-a-boo. The song's title comes from Lizzie's promise that she won't mind playing a supporting role in her beloved boy's life, that not being his parent—just being his auntie—would be enough for her.

With a few changes of phrase, I was able to sing this to baby Chloe from her "Auntie Kathy." When Chloe was five weeks old and I was meeting her for the first time, I stepped away from the family circle for a few minutes to sing to her and make my own vows about the kind of auntie I hoped to be.

Six years later, she wasn't all that interested in hearing me sing a serious song and didn't have any recollections of whispered moments shared in her family's rocking chair. Instead, we talked more about Troy and Gabriella and the other cast members of *High School Musical*. But I don't mind. In her sweet lifetime, we've created our own special bond, one that may not be as idyllic as my original vision, but one that I am grateful for, one that I nurture by appreciating and encouraging her unique interests.

I chose and practiced songs for Jake before I left on my vacation mommy adventure, and sang to him frequently during our time together. Elton John's "Your Song" and Ella Fitzgerald's arrangement of "I've Got a Crush on You" were my personal favorites. Jake, however, was much more enamored with my falsetto imitation of Ron Moody as Fagan in the musical *Oliver!* "MORE!" he signaled emphatically, as I changed his poopy diaper. I sighed as I let go of my expectations for sentimental moments, took a dramatically deep breath, and began again.

But as the day approached for Jake's mommies' return, "I Won't Mind" played again and again in my mind, a semi-weepy soundtrack to my live performance as I made silly sounds to entertain him on our walks, while he splashed in the bathtub, when we marched through the house in our nightly King Jake parade.

I clung to a hope that being Jake's auntie would be enough, if that's where my life was headed. And there was truth in it, for, like Lizzie, I took pride in teaching Jake new things, such as the baby sign language signs for apple and airplane, and learning his left foot from his right foot. Like Lizzie, I promised to be there to catch Jake when he fell, and to kiss away his hurts. And my heart swelled when Jake ran directly to me when he slipped and tumbled or bumped into things or just needed someone to hold on to. Even my brother commented on how attached to me Jake had become, how safe he seemed to feel with me. What was becoming more apparent to me, however, was how much I was growing attached to him, and how much I was growing accustomed to being needed.

I shouldn't have been surprised to recognize jealousy in my heart two days before Carrie and Kathy were scheduled to return. The pros and cons swam in my subconscious, and my head and heart battled for the microphone:

"You'll never be a mom, so start work on your Plan C."

"You can do anything you want, as long as you want it bad enough."

"You loser, you waited too long!"

"Why, God, why have you denied me a Jakey of my own?"

"There's still time! You deserve every happiness. Don't give up!"

"All this love needs to go to someone!"

I fought to shut down the voices in my head, then had a few words with God about how I hoped he knew what he was doing and had something wonderful in mind for my future. Then, as much as I dreaded facing and making difficult choices once I returned home, I first had to deal with what I was experiencing in the present. I ached at the thought of Jake's running to Carrie or Kathy, when given the choice, instead of to me. The tearing of emotional tissue had already begun as I imagined losing the connection he and I had grown over the past days. I didn't want to share.

Yet he wasn't mine to begin with. Sharing wasn't an option. The natural state of order was for him to run to them in times of joy and sorrow, fear and fun. I briefly toyed with the idea of weaning him from me before the hand-over happened, but rationalized that (a) I couldn't drop the ball of taking care of him, (b) I didn't want to freak him out with any more abrupt changes, (c) he was a kid, he'd deal. Most of all, I knew *I* wasn't ready to let go, so I selfishly clung to what little I had.

On our second to last night together, I stayed awake as long as possible. I didn't want our time together to end. I didn't want to miss a moment. I was even tempted to wake him up (I know! The worst possible bad-mommy thing I could do!) to spend more time together, even if he was screaming in my ear.

I began gathering memories like a camel stores water for an excursion across the Sahara. I imprinted on my mind the image of him toddling around after me, shadowing me around the house. I thought about how I felt all warm and fuzzy when, on our walks, he'd peer through the clear plastic window on the top of his stroller and stretch up a hand; our fingers and our eyes would meet, and he'd grin, so tickled with our game. I smiled at the memory of seeing his pride in himself when he finally figured out how to tilt his head in the bath so rinse water would run down his back instead of into his eyes. And I swelled with some pride at the realization that I had mastered recognizing and addressing his moods, from cranky to gleeful to ready for nap time.

During the previous 24 hours, we'd had some play time in the living room that was so simple, such perfect pleasure. We played with the maze-like, vacuum-powered tube that pumps out brightly colored lightweight balls to the frenetic tune of "Flight of the Bumblebee." I tried to put them back in really fast, started screaming and scrambling. Jake laughed so hard, he got red in the face. Which made me laugh, which made him laugh even more, which made me want to cry.

We also played "Hop up!" I held his hands while he "hopped up" onto my right foot, then I walked around with him alternating between balancing on and slipping off me. It was a fun trick, and he loved it. *We now have* our *game,* I thought, *something for just the two of us.* Even then I knew I was being delusional because certainly this was something he would play with his mommies. The likelihood of his remembering that I was the one who made it up with him was nil, unless I became one of those annoying aunts who always reminded him of the fact.

I wasn't going to become one of those aunts.

Our last night together was uneventful. Dinner and story time went smoothly, and I resisted the desire to keep him up with me past his bedtime. My responsibility as worthy caregiver demanded that I deliver a happy, healthy kid at the end of my tour of duty, not one who was fussy and out of his routine.

Around 8:00 PM, Carrie and Kathy called to let me know their plane had landed in San Francisco. All of a sudden, just like that—it was over.

I greeted them from the top of the stairs as they came across the landing around 9:45. Carrie held the WELCOME HOME! sign I'd helped Jake decorate with colored markers and tape to the front door. They looked great. Not worn out, although they were both tired from their long journey. After quick hugs with me, they went into Jake's bedroom and gently woke him, not wanting to wait until morning to be reunited. (Yes, I know I resisted the same bad-mommy transgression two nights before, but under the circumstances, their transgression seemed permissible.) He whimpered a bit as they hugged and kissed him, and I noticed Carrie had tears in her eyes. I peeked around the corner to his room, then felt it was inappropriate to intrude on this family moment. So I retreated to the futon in the living room, my usual guest accommodations, and pretended to watch *Lethal Weapon* on TV.

An hour later, everyone was in bed. Carrie had told me I was "off the hook" if Jake cried because they wanted to get up with him. They even had me turn off the baby monitor so I wouldn't be disturbed. Like I could have slept.

I should have prepared myself better for this. But how?

That morning after dropping Jake at Jenni's, it had struck

me that this was like preparing for death. *If I had only X days to live, and I knew about it, what would I do?* Put my affairs in order, certainly, but mostly take in every moment by being present. I'd be with the ones I love. I'd enjoy the last breakfast, the last bath, the last dance, the last bedtime story, the last cuddle, even the last meltdown.

I'd done my best to enjoy and take in those final moments, but now that my vacation mommy time was over, my resolve to hold myself and my emotions in check crumbled.

Oh, my God, this was hard. I felt:

Not needed

Not wanted

Pushed aside

Invisible

Used

Used up

Like the hired help

Insignificant

Meaningless

Tragic

Pathetic

Worthless

I was not ready to "give up" *my* baby, yet it had already been done. I was back to playing a supporting...well, really, a character role. It was my place to step back so the leading players had him to themselves.

Really, I won't mind.

Except that I did.

The family was back together, as it should be, and my work here was done. The time had come for me, much like Mary Poppins, to pack up my magic carpetbag (the one filled with shoes), catch the south wind (via Southwest's Oakland to Burbank flight), and move to the next family who needed me (for now, my dog, Beau).

I didn't have regrets, exactly, but oh, how I wished I could have family and love in my life. I was grateful for my place in our extended family circle as aunt/sister/caregiver/role model, and, I hoped, friend. In the same heartbeat, I was fearful that it was too late for me to have my own immediate family, to pass along genes, traditions, games, songs, and memories to my own new generation. Would I forever after be, at best, on the sidelines? Was this wonderful two-week adventure as good as it was ever going to get for me? Possibly.

I wrapped my arms around myself and pulled my feet in close. I cocooned myself in the comforter, then pulled pillows around my body, imagining they were a warm body spooning me. Someone—someone who loved me—was holding me close, safe, and warm, and I waited for sleep to quiet my mind and obliterate my sadness.

Sleep was long in coming, for deep inside me, kept in a place where I could deny it, was a black hole that housed a secret. I loved playacting that Jake was my own. I loved feeling that I was needed and wanted. I loved every moment of physical connection, from the tiniest touches to the prolonged cuddles that warmed me to my core. I loved when strangers assumed I was Jake's mommy. I didn't want to give up any of it.

I knew I would grieve in silence. I would bury all my longings and play my part with a smile on my face. I imagined no one would ever notice how much I minded and how profoundly alone I was.

[1]Music by Jeff Blumenkranz, lyrics by Annie Kessler and Libby Saines.

19

PASSING THE BABY BATON

*L*eading up to my last day, I grocery shopped and prepped food so Kathy and Carrie could get back into their groove and enjoy their reunion with Jake instead of dealing with mundane tasks. I steamed veggies, put small servings in containers for quick Jakey lunch assemblies, caught up on the laundry, watered the plants, and vacuumed all the traffic areas. I also organized my stuff, packed what I wouldn't need for my last day and flight home, and moved it all from the bedroom out to the living room. Keeping busy was better than allowing myself to relax, which would open me up to the flow of emotions that threatened to bring on a new big-girl meltdown. At least I had good things to show for my efforts.

In addition to being pleased with myself for being such a thoughtful houseguest, I was quite proud of myself for handing over Jake in great shape upon Carrie and Kathy's return. By some miracle, there were no cuts, no scratches, no bruises, not so much as a runny nose. Gold star for Aunt Kath!

On their first full day home, before the day had even reached the halfway mark, Jake took several diggers and face plants, resulting in cuts, scratches, and bruises. None of which were my fault! I felt a wee bit better about the...ahem...tumbles he had taken on my watch.

In the early afternoon, we were all in the master bedroom while Carrie unpacked and Kathy downloaded photos to their computer. I sat on the floor while Jake ran around pulling things from suitcases and entertaining himself with my shoes.

He ran over to Kathy, apparently expecting her to catch him and pull him up into her lap, but she missed. Instead, he tripped over his and her feet, slipped down the front of the desk chair, and whacked his head on the base of the chair. Hard. There would be a bump and a bruise. He cried hard, and Kathy scooped him up to comfort him.

"That was totally my fault," she said by way of apology to Jake and to all of us in general. As an experienced mom, I could commiserate with her about how kids so easily get hurt at this age, and how they recover just fine.

Though I was sad Jake was hurt, I was surprised to sense that I was calm and that there was a bit of a sting in experiencing the shifting of responsibilities.

He's no longer on my watch, I thought to myself.

It was a bittersweet realization.

———

Part of me wished I could go into hiding. It was difficult to be an outsider, an observer of the family reunion. But having completed all my pre-travel tasks, and with little else to do, I had no choice but to put a smile on my face and choke down the lump in my throat.

Jake wanted little to do with me once he had his mommies back. He played with them while they unpacked and settled back into home life. He was much more affectionate with them than he was with me, I noticed, giving more kisses and throwing himself into their arms for more cuddles. (Is this how it was with babies and their actual mommies? Was this the next level of what I had to look forward to?) It was fun to watch them interact, to see their inside jokes and silly routines, goofy voices, wacky dances, and made-up rituals along the lines of "King Jake." He also was very clingy with them, barely napped, and ate little, as though he didn't want to miss a moment with them.

I heard details about Carrie and Kathy's trip throughout the day and got a preview of the 500+ photos they had taken. Gorgeous. *Cinque Terre: Must add that to my list of places to visit before I have kids.*

In the afternoon, we all walked to a new gelato shop I'd discovered while they were traveling. How perfect to come home from Italy and have a new taste of Italy right down the street. Jenni and her mom joined us, and we sat in the warm sun on the benches in front of the shop's picture windows while we enjoyed our creamy treats.

While the tone of the day would have appeared light and joyful to a casual observer, I was wrestling with painful demons. While my face smiled and laughed along with the fun around me, my insides were already adjusting to the realities of transitioning out of the family tableau: emptiness, quiet, isolation, and a lack of responsibilities. Despite all of the challenges, there were parts of being "on watch" that I really liked, such as having a sense of purpose, being needed.

I hadn't known the depth of my need for companionship, hadn't known I'd been missing it. Now I held close the small, everyday moments Jake and I had shared, such as mealtimes when we talked through signs or hummed or entertained each other with silly facial expressions and sounds. I relished the new sense I had developed of knowing that Jake was tagging along behind me, acting as my shadow, not because he needed anything, but simply to be close to me. I noted how I missed him, how I felt the absence of him on a deep, cellular level, as soon as I had dropped him off at day care.

In many ways, it was the physical sensations that were most deeply imprinted on me. The surprise kisses, tiny little pecks delivered to the underside of my chin while I was reading to him or drying him off from a bath. The sweetness of how he entwined his arm with mine and kissed my hand while I settled him on the changing table or tucked him in for a nap. The full-contact feeling of having him cling to me, with his tiny hands clamped onto my arms and his legs wrapped around my ribs. The weight and warmth of holding him close on my chest, my arms cradling his body, his head heavy on my shoulder, as he fell asleep.

I was aware of how each moment filled my heart and also made me acutely aware of the emptiness that had been there before and would return. During the two weeks with Jake, I had felt needed and wanted in a way that I'd never before experienced in my life. I felt like I was part of something that mattered, that I was, in my own small way, contributing to something bigger than my humble existence or our country's economy or world politics or any other contemporary social issue. For once, I was not just a hamster on a treadmill to nowhere or working my butt off to fill some CEO's bank account or feed my own ego. I was helping to raise and mold a good human.

My heart begged me to book an earlier flight and run away from the painfulness of sitting outside the family circle; my head told me to put off the inevitable face-the-music moments at home. Once I was completely removed from my internship, I knew I would have to face the questions about how I would incorporate my learnings into my life, into what my purpose in life was going to be.

I had to trust that the joy and the pain and the fun and the little stings were all part of the process of discovering who I was to become. I'd completed my mission. I'd done all the doing I could do, and now I needed to allow all the information I'd gathered to percolate and bubble up with some answers.

Floating above this soup of emotions was a strong sense of gratitude. By some chance of fate, I had been given the tremendous gift of living the mommy life for a short period of time. Certainly I had come full circle in that I had left home as a woman alone in the world and was returning as such, but with so much experience and wisdom. The memories I had created weren't just heartwarming, they were heart-expanding. I was starting to see and give value to the larger purpose of my life experience, for perhaps the whole point of my internship was to experience my own rebirth as a love-filled and love-giving human. It was who I had always been, who I was at the core. But in the midst of stressing about pursuing the lifestyle I thought I wanted to live, I'd simply forgotten who it was I wanted to be.

I looked forward to getting better reacquainted with myself.

"I'm glad you're a fighting part-Irish gal!"

—how my Gram signed her letters, always reminding me I could
achieve anything

20

(MAYBE) HOME IS WHERE YOUR DOG IS

*A*s I buckled into my seat and prepared myself for the early morning flight from Oakland to Burbank, I thought back on one of my last precious moments with my little guy. He was standing on the couch, with me nuzzled beside him to prop him up and keep him from tumbling backwards. Together, eyes glued to the clear summer sky through the picture window, we eagerly watched for airplanes to soar overhead. I discreetly inhaled his scent and flipped through my mind's dictionary to find the one term that best described it: *warm.*

When, if ever, would I get to experience this again? I wondered as I hoarded the memory. Sardined between two strangers on a crowded flight, I shook off the chill that threatened to melt into tears, swallowed my loneliness, and bit my stiff upper lip as I bravely looked toward home.

Fifty-five minutes later I was back on the ground, and in no time I was with my other little guy. As soon as I arrived at my back gate, I called out to Beau, and he bounded over the porch steps and across the small yard to greet me.

"Hello, Love!" I dropped my purse and crouched down to

dip into his squirrely greeting. I buried my nose in his head and inhaled grass, dirt, and a bit of muskiness I really didn't care to identify but altogether smelled like Home.

My sweet Beau. No one greets you better than a dog. No one else is this full of glee to see you every time you return home, whether it be from an absence of hours or weeks. He jumped, whimpered, danced in circles, sniffed, nuzzled, jumped some more, and bounced along beside me as I heaved my luggage up the back steps and into the house. With my darling furry companion happily shadowing me, I opened the windows to allow a fresh breeze through the house, started laundry, and sorted mail. Whenever I sat down, he curled all 50 pounds of himself on top of my feet.

Feeling an itch to be outside, in the late afternoon I loaded Beau—who I called "Jake" twice during that first day—a book, and a beach chair into the car and headed toward my favorite park. I needed a playground fix, and although I didn't have the requisite child for entry, I could observe and listen to the joyfulness of other people's children from a short distance away.

I walked with Beau around the park's perimeter, then settled into my chair in a shady spot and watched children and their minders at play from behind my book. The sights and sounds tugged at my heart and threatened to release tears, but they also soothed the ache in my soul a bit; a masochistic pleasure, to be sure.

I wished I knew how to create a healthy, step-by-step transition process for myself. The shift from Jakeworld to Kathworld was shocking. I felt off-balance, like being on a seesaw but with ever-changing partners so that you never quite get your rhythm down. It felt weird to not be operating on Jake's eating schedule, weird to not have a schedule. I missed companionship, I missed having a clear purpose. I missed smiles and kisses and even dramatic tantrums (to a point).

Despite all the stress and uncertainty and chaos I had just gotten through, I wasn't ready to go back to my normal world of relative calm. Normal now looked boring in comparison, while at the same time I was faced with an open future that felt scary, but not in the thrilling way you feel when you're anticipating the next stomach-in-your-throat drop of a rollercoaster.

I wasn't clear what these feelings wanted from me. Were they telling me to go back, to embrace the life with child, to accept that chaos and uncertainty? What was my gut telling me? Was it saying that the life I had created at home was not the right fit? Or was it simply another form of jet lag, in which I simply needed a day or two to regroup, catch up on sleep, get back on schedule? What was I ignoring? What was I denying? What couldn't I bear to face?

No clear answers rose from my subconscious.

After the park and a dinner of takeout burger and fries, I took Beau out for a walk around our neighborhood. It was one of those perfect summer evenings: warm with a light breeze, so you could comfortably sit outside and enjoy a glass of chilled Sauvignon Blanc after the sun went down, eventually cool enough so you could sleep.

I went to bed tired, not so much from the lingering sleep deprivation or the physical exertion of traveling, but more from the emotional after-effects of my adventures. My home was quiet. Too quiet. Jarringly quiet. And in that quiet, my body, heart, and mind churned into overdrive. I pictured Jake and replayed our bedtime routine, hoping to imprint it in my memory, hoping to distract myself with denial, but it was no good.

My body felt hug-deprived. My heart felt...hungry. I still wasn't sure how I was going to feed the longings and emptiness I was experiencing. I wondered if I was indeed back "home," or if this was to be another brief, temporary stop on my journey toward...something. Was I on the cusp of jumping into a new life path as single mommy, or was I facing a new life path that was open to suggestion, one that was a clean slate, one that I was going to have to figure out from scratch? The thought of that was overwhelming. Where would I start? I mean this wasn't like choosing between Italian or Mexican for dinner. This was trying to make the right choices to choose which path would lead to my life. My Whole Life.

No pressure.

It was too soon to invite the demons back in to play, to face all my fears and doubts, to do a thorough examination of the information I'd brought home with me as well as all the exhaustion, confusion, and fretfulness I carried inside of me. I was aware enough to acknowledge that there was too much noise happening internally for me to be able to explore my options and accurately interpret any signs or directions about what I was supposed to do. And frankly, part of me still hoped that my new direction would soon be revealed, effortlessly, magically. It could happen, but I suspected that it was more likely my process would take some hard and painful work on my part to evaluate, sort, and review my experiences.

That first night home, I forced myself to focus on gratitude. I was grateful to be back in my own bed, with my own dog in his proper place at my feet. As the warmth of my little cocoon embraced me, fatigue finally triumphed, and I found escape in a sweet, deep sleep.

———

Over my first several days back home, I pictured Jake frequently: his smiling face as we talked over dinner, his endearing quirky-jerky dancing, his sleeping form dominated by his huge diaper-padded bum sticking up like Mt. Rainer rising over the Seattle landscape. I'd smile at the memories, then feel the crush as my emotions claimed their toll and I all but doubled over as the pain of emptiness coursed through my arms and chest. I missed him, and I missed who I got to be when I was with him. I missed being needed, and I missed being a mommy. Though I was burying myself in the demands of grueling 12-hour catching-up-at-work days, I knew I would soon carve out time to confront the questions occupying my head and heart.

Near the top of the list was this nagging question about where my yearnings came from. Was it biological? Nature or nurture? Did I long to be a mommy because something at the core of my being cried out to be filled this way, or because my key role models were all mommies? Was it due to peer pressure, or something more insidious, like manipulative anti-feminist advertising? As these questions cycled back to me on repeat mode, I acknowledged I had to ask myself, whose dream was I dreaming?

Stepping outside of myself for a bit, I began a bit of online research during a break between deadlines. My first discovery was shocking: According to the 2010 U.S. Census Report, one in five women of childbearing age (15 to 44) were childless, and an article in *Time* magazine reported the same figures for women in their mid-forties in the UK, Ireland, Canada, and Australia.

One in five. That's twenty *f-ing* percent! That flew in the face of what I had accepted as the "norm" in the society in which I had grown up, as well as the one I was now part of as an adult. I had grown up with this very clear life plan, one that was measured and orderly, one in which love led to marriage, which then led to a baby in a baby carriage. In my young and developing mind, Wife+Mother=Grownup, and as a not-so-young running-out-of time adult, I still held on to that belief that I was not yet a grownup until I achieved those statuses. But, with such a significant percentage of modern women not following the directions, where do we, as a society, get the idea that *womanhood* is defined as *motherhood*?

What was I missing?

Since my emotions were still too keyed-up for me to trust any directions from my gut, I decided to take a detour into the more rational approach. To make informed decisions about my future, I reasoned, I first needed to understand my past, to get clear on the *whys* driving my desires. I don't think I've ever been more grateful for my research skills—creative and analytical—than I was at that moment. The key, I knew, was to gather everything I could find *without* expecting a specific outcome, without asking questions that would lead me in only one preordained direction. I would read, interview, listen, document.

Concurrently, I knew I would employ journaling and long meditative walks, established practices that I knew would allow me to free my mind. I would talk through the pros and cons with friends, confidantes who knew me well and would advise appropriately, as well as friends who had walked different paths.

Once I had everything in place, I could shift, shuffle, and evaluate to determine which answers felt true for me. Or, as I had discovered writing feature articles, my job was to do the research, then I'd let the facts tell the story they wanted to tell. For this wasn't just an exercise in logic. The answers had to feel equally right in my head and my heart.

I pulled out old scrapbooks, opened up the search page for Google, turned to a new page in my journal, and dug in.

"You're the aunt, right?"

My sister-in-law's eight-year-old niece stood before me, dressed in Christmas Eve finery, her eyes squinted in confusion.

"That's right. I'm Chloe and Ellie's Aunt Kath."

"So where's the uncle?"

21

ALL IN THE FAMILY EXPECTATIONS

*W*hen and where I grew up, aunts came with uncles, mommies came with daddies, and it never entered my mind that my adult life would look any different. Certainly my parents and grandparents had expectations that I would carry on the family genes. My friends came from families that had the same expectations, and together we made up neighorhoods and an extended community of like-minded people. But I didn't choose the path of parenthood simply to fulfill others' expectations or out of a need to belong. I wanted what was presented to me on every level as the "good" life.

My nuclear family was traditional, conservative, WASP-y, Republican. We practiced a Christian-based religion and Reagonomics. I've joked that I didn't know any Democrats until I went to college, but in all seriousness, I cannot recall one from my childhood. Dad commuted to work as the family's sole breadwinner, while Mom stayed home with the kids, managing us and the household and leading several volunteer organizations. Like the other moms we knew in our neighborhood, she was there to greet us and ask about our days when we got home from school. Our "set" frowned upon the concept of "latchkey kids," meaning kids who let themselves into their own homes and were on their own—totally without adult supervision—until both parents got home from work sometime in the evening. This was my sphere; I didn't know any different realities.

I had very few friends who grew up in single-parent homes, and only two of my close friends had parents who were divorced. Homosexuality didn't exist in our world. Other than hearing the insult hurled at some poor kid who was different, I hadn't the faintest idea what "gay" meant. And I can't think of even one adult from my childhood who was childfree. It wasn't in my realm of possibility, because our family socialized with other families that looked like ours.

There's an old joke that the worst thing that can happen to a writer is a happy childhood, but I embraced mine. Our parents loved their children and were actively engaged in our lives and our community, in roles including Girl Scout leader, basketball coach, and PTA president (both of them, in separate terms). My siblings and I were surrounded by neighbors and extended family members who loved and protected us. As insular as it was, it was also a great place to grow up: upper-middle class, secure, comfortable. Our neighbors liked us, we liked them, and our front doors were rarely locked during the day.

As I began my research into my mommy motivations, I pulled out some mementos from those formative years. Tucked into a trunk of keepsakes, I found my dog-eared Girl Scout Handbook, which contained evidence of my epic badge-earning years. A flip through the pages reminded me of the skills (and by extension, values) I had been taught: cooking, sewing, needlepoint. We also learned how to ice skate and explored the local tide pools, but included among the memories that had left the biggest impressions on me was going to a friend's house where her mom taught us how to clean a refrigerator with baking soda. (Not a bad skill to have, certainly, but I was relieved and thrilled to learn recently that modern-day Scouts get to experience things like career mentorship and stress management.) I was being groomed for two related roles: homemaking and wifery. Like my peers, I was frequently asked how many children I wanted. "Two. A boy and a girl. Plus a dog." No one ever asked, "Do you want children?" Had I been asked that, I would have answered, "Of course." It's what everyone wanted. Marriage and family was everything I wanted.

Painfully shy, I lived much of my childhood buried in books. I deeply admired, and was absorbed by, Laura Ingalls Wilders' stories of family surviving together, finding joy in life's simplest pleasures. I day-dreamed about being Nancy Drew, going on daring adventures with my best friends, George and Bess, and thwarting the bad guy's evil plans. Naturally, I assumed Nancy would one day marry her dashing boyfriend, Ned, and they'd settle down and give her kind father a bunch of cute and smart grandchildren to dote on. Many of my imaginary games were based on *Little House on the Prairie*, or enacting Barbie and Ken's wedding and setting up their Dream Home.

Couples—Caroline and Charles Ingalls, Nancy and Ned, Barbie and Ken—were normal, and old maid, spinster, and maiden aunt were derogatory terms still in circulation. Mary Poppins, Auntie Mame, Mother Teresa, and Joan of Arc were among the single women who crossed my path via books and movies, but they were considered oddities. Not one of their lifestyles appealed to me. In the real world, up till adulthood, I viewed a single woman as someone who was on the brink, waiting for her life to begin, because her goal was to eventually become a helpmate to her husband and children. The message I got was full of *shoulds*: I should have a husband, should have children, should be an adult. I know. Just writing that is creepy.

A lot of interesting stuff was brewing out in the big, wide world beyond our cozy neighborhood culs-de-sac. The National Organization of Women (NOW) was founded in 1966, the year I was born. Betty Friedan was breaking down assumptions in *The Feminine Mystique* (1963), which would later help me feel compassion for my mother and her Baby Boomer peers. (After reading Friedan's work in my 30s, I better understood their frustrations at feeling stifled creatively and professionally and what they rightly perceived to be limited options.) Title IX, enacted in 1972, demanded no one could "be excluded from participation in, be denied the benefits of, or be subjected to discrimination under any education program or activity receiving federal financial assistance" based solely on gender. Meanwhile, the fight for equal pay and equal rights, first introduced to Congress in 1923, took form as the Equal Rights Amendment (ERA) in 1972. (It was designed to help protect women in the middle and working class, but Phyllis Schlafly mobilized conservative women in opposition, arguing it would be devastating for unskilled middle-aged housewives. The amendment died.) In 1973, *Roe v. Wade* brought out of the shadows the topic of elected abortion and a woman's right to make her own decisions about reproduction.

Naturally, as a budding young trophy wife, I didn't pay much attention, feeling none of this applied to me. I planned on working at a job (not a "career") that would keep me busy till I got married, then I'd stay at home and raise my kids. The timeline I envisioned for myself was modeled on my mother's, and I certainly felt the need to measure up. College-educated, she married ("late") at 24 and had her first child (me) at 28, at which point she stopped working as a teacher to stay at home. She had her last child at 32. My favorite aunt was a stewardess, which I thought was quite daring and glamorous; she also left her profession to become a full-time, stay-at-home mom. That was how their era worked. "If I had two lives, I would have loved teaching, but I chose to be home with the children," my mother once told me. "It was so much more interesting being out in the world versus staying home, but I never would have left you."

At least she'd had a choice. Her own mother, like many women of her generation, had a clause in her contract that stated she had to resign from her secretarial position when she became pregnant. In 1938, my grandmother shared the happy news that she was expecting her first child with a few friends, only to have one of those coworkers rat her out to their supervisor. My grandmother was fired on the spot, and she remained unemployed while she raised her children, supported by my grandfather as he pursued his professional career.

Although I recognized how my situation differed greatly from that of my mom and grandmother, I also saw how their values, and their life experiences, still colored my worldview. I was raised with their expectations.

It's interesting that once I entered college and started to see other possible paths—including academic, athletic, political, and career achievement—I could no longer consider my mother's generation's romanticized path to earning an "MRS" degree the norm, even though it was the "norm" that I wanted. My classmates were intelligent and ambitious high-achievers, and I admired and often envied them. So I watched with some dismay as many became sidetracked professionals post-graduation. These women had competed to get into prestigious graduate schools, began promising careers in fields they loved, then traded everything they'd earned to be full-time wives and mothers. Why had they worked so hard to achieve goals they would never claim? While I couldn't exactly judge them, as they had gone after the roles I wanted for myself, I felt disappointed that they hadn't continued on their paths to reaching their full potential.

I sometimes wondered how my life would have been different if my mom had used her education and her gifts in a profession. When I asked her if she ever considered getting back into the work force, my mom responded, "Not to the detriment of my children." She was adamant she'd made the right choice. "But at times I was bothered that staying at home was downplayed," she added, "that the importance of that role was downplayed."

If she had worked, would it really have been detrimental to our lives? Or would I, my sister, and friends of our generation have been better equipped to figure out work-life balance, so that today's young women could better see their options and maybe—for real—have it all?

When I didn't earn my MRS along with my BA, I felt a strong sense of failure—to myself, my family, my gender, my society. I had worked hard, played by the rules, behaved myself, done everything "right," so it came as a hard shock that I had not been rewarded with what I wanted in life, had not achieved what had been modeled for me as The American Dream. Marriage+Motherhood was the path I'd been trained for, and as my 20s and 30s flew by and I stood on the sidelines as the perennial bridesmaid—smile frozen in place, swathed in taffeta, toes crushed in dyed-to-match shoes—I dreaded hearing friends assure me "You're next!" Thinly veiled behind that promise was the not always unspoken question "Why aren't you married yet?" The longer I waited, the more unnatural I felt, and the more I wondered, "Why, God? Why not *me*?"

But I suppose I was lucky that Fate didn't deal me another hand. At college, I ran into a girl who looked familiar. We got to chatting, discovered some things in common, and I remembered we'd gone to the same high school but she had moved away midterm. Or so I'd been led to believe. Turned out she'd gotten pregnant and—and this makes my flesh crawl— was informed she would have to transfer to another school district. Her mom helped her raise the baby, she'd finished high school in a different community (while still living in mine, but pretty much invisibly), and earned her way to college. She gave me a glimpse at the underbelly of unspoken values that had made their way into my veins, for even though I was not an active player in her excommunication, I had been subconsciously taught that single, unwed mothers were immoral and should be removed from view.

Was this how I would be judged? I mean, I would be overreacting if I embroidered my maternity clothes with scarlet letters, but I had to anticipate that a subtle form of social outcasting was a real possibility.

As much as I wanted to believe my hometown had evolved with the times, that we were above shunning people for perceived moral transgressions, I knew I would be facing new levels of shaming if I bucked the traditional world order and became a single mommy—with sperm from an anonymous donor—by choice. Was I strong enough to handle that? It wasn't like I was some TV character who could fight the big machine of societal expectations and win over all of her silent and in-her-face naysayers.

And how would this affect my parents? In bearing their longed-for grandchild, would I also have to bear their discomfort at being seen as having raised a nonconformist?

So many of the old values felt absurd to me, but like deep wounds from abuse, they still held power over me. I felt funny talking about the expectations placed on me by my family and society, knowing how women in other cultures, classes, and economic statuses had to work to support their families. Just bringing this up made for uncomfortable conversations, and I knew I would sound disconnected, irrelevant. And yet, there was something in me still operating with this mindset. "Our friends who now have kids in their 20s and 30s have encouraged their daughters to get educated and have careers, and they're proud of their daughters' successes," my friend Lisa emailed me after I'd shared some of my background with her and how it had influenced me. Initially she had felt my experiences were isolated. "And yet," she said, as she thought more about our conversation, "they are thrilled and excited when a marriage and babies happen. There's still a disconnect between what we're told and what really happens."

I experienced this disconnect when I went to holiday parties and caught up with old family friends. There were a few tales about career achievements, but I mostly heard exuberant stories about grandbabies. Holiday cards included photos of weddings and family members, not images of awards and corner offices. As the daughters of my peers came of age, I occasionally heard proud mentions of graduations and job offers, but their mothers became absolutely giddy when they got in touch to share engagement and pregnancy announcements.

Taking this all into consideration, I didn't think we'd made much progress for women. And as I was still single, I continued to feel like my parents' great disappointment.

22

OUTSIDE SOURCES & EXTERNAL FORCES

*B*ack in my formative years (1970s–1980s), family life looked an awful lot like what we saw idealized on TV—or at least on the "wholesome" shows we were allowed to watch. My siblings and I learned we were part of the normal, traditional, nuclear family model—and we aspired to the same —based on what we saw on *The Waltons, Family Ties, The Brady Bunch,* and *Eight Is Enough*. Hell, even the alien on *Mork & Mindy* fell in love and had an offspring.

Certainly there were exceptions. *Charlie's Angels* (1976–81) featured strong, independent, unmarried, and childfree women detectives, and my friends and I spent hours in the front yard creating our own dramatic adventures inspired by their exploits. *Cagney & Lacey* (1981–88) were a couple of tough nontraditional policewomen. *The Mary Tyler Moore Show*'s Mary Richards (1970–77) and *That Girl*'s Ann Marie (1966–71), though a bit ahead of my time, both modeled paths for bright young women who prioritized their professional over their personal lives. *Murphy Brown* (1988–1998) offered a different take on a fiercely independent and successful woman, who struggled as a single working mother. That show gained notoriety in 1992 when then-Vice President Dan Quayle criticized the fictional character for going against family values by glorifying single motherhood. She was, he claimed, "mocking the importance of fathers by bearing a child alone and calling it another lifestyle choice." In a follow-up episode, a disheveled Murphy watched his televised rant and responded by stating, "Whether by choice or circumstance, families come in all shapes and sizes, and ultimately what really defines a family is commitment, caring, and love."

Although I admired these characters for their boldness and independent thinking, they weren't role models for me at the time. They weren't modeling the expectations *in the air around me*. I couldn't relate to them, couldn't emulate them, because, of course, I would be married with children, like any other normal woman.

And for me that normal woman looked a lot like Marion "Mrs. C" Cunningham, the traditional homemaker and mother on *Happy Days* (1974–84), the hugely popular TV sitcom that depicted and idealized family life of the mid-1950s to early '60s. The show was goofy and at times so canned, that it seemed to be a depiction of the earlier everyone-is-happy-and-attractive sitcoms that came to us as reruns, including *The Donna Reed Show, Leave It to Beaver, Ozzie and Harriet,* and *Father Knows Best.* Surely there were troubles lurking behind the scripted stories —like repression of women—with expectations for perfection that were impossible to achieve, but this was what I was encouraged to emulate. (To learn more about how those myths were busted, I recommend reading *The Way We Never Were: American Families and the Nostalgia Trap* by Stephanie Coontz © 1992 BasicBooks, division of HarperCollins Publishers, Inc.)

But I couldn't just dismiss these influences. I needed to take a look at the models created in the late 1940s and 1950s because it felt like many of the values with which I was raised, which I continued to carry at a cellular level, originated there—in the post–World War II era. When Rosie the Riveter and her gal pals were sent packing as men returned from the front and wanted their jobs back, where did Rosie go? Home. To populate suburbia (thanks to government-subsidized home loans), to make babies, to live "the dream." Merriam-Webster's *Dictionary* says the term "nuclear family," meaning married parents plus their children in one household, originated in 1947. As the Baby Boom began and the nuclear family became the norm, women were encouraged to "find" themselves in keeping homes and raising children in what was becoming a child-centric society. Motherhood became glamorous, sentimentalized, and young women were encouraged to aspire to be stay-at-home moms. A google search brought up sexist and jaw-droppingly offensive (to my 21st-century perspective) print ads from that period that encouraged and reinforced the stereotypes of the hard-working (and often hard-playing) husband and the perfectly pulled together (and quite sexy) and supportive happy little homemaker.

The movement toward this was also rooted in economics. "Many women who began their families in the 1940s and 1950s associated their mother's employment during the 1930s with economic hardship and family failure," writes Coontz in *The Way We Never Were*. "They looked forward to establishing a different pattern in their own marriages." In the 1950s, employment rose for single women (40% of women over age 16 held jobs), but these jobs were meant to be held only until marriage, not to build résumés and climb ladders to the corner offices.

Significant gender wage discrimination also made marriage the more appealing path. In 1959, the average cost of a new car was $2,200; a new house went for $12,400. The average working man might have been able to afford these niceties—plus major appliances and the latest fashions—on his annual income of $5,010, but the average women made 59 cents to a man's dollar. True financial security, therefore, was possible only by being married to a gainfully employed man.

Beyond financial considerations, this new model came at a great cost to women. A stay-at-home wife and mother was taught to put her needs second (or third or...) behind that of her husband and children, even behind the needs of keeping up a house. While displayed in the media of the time to be thrilled with the time-saving gadgets available to her to fulfill her duties, by the early 1960s, we now know, thanks to Betty Friedan, these women were feeling trapped. The college graduates she interviewed for *The Feminine Mystique* "resented the wide disparity between the idealized image society held for them as housewives and mothers and the realities of their daily routines."

Think for a moment about the images of women in the popular media. On TV, all the normal families (white) moved to the suburbs. Middle-class (white) men boasted mild-mannered, submissive, and pretty wives, while working-class and minority men couldn't control theirs. Joan Crawford, who excelled at portraying strong-willed women in films from the mid-1920s to the 1970s, was photographed mopping floors and interviewed about raising children for features in popular magazines. (In 1978, Crawford's adopted daughter Christina released a book, *Mommie Dearest*, in which she dispelled the perfect motherhood myth and revealed a horribly abusive family life.) The myths these images promoted are not all that different from what we see today: baby bumps, celebrities' children's milestones, what's in a female celebrity's pantry.

In a 1955 study, "less than 10% of Americans believed an unmarried person could be happy." Marriage and motherhood equaled stability, security, and, most important, happiness. That's the message that got passed down to me. Yes, yes, I know this is a skewed vision of the real world, the one in which people struggle to meet basic needs. But it wasn't unrealistic based on my upbringing. It was what I was born into, it was what I knew, so it was what I aspired to.

And it was that "reality" I still had to grapple with as I made my own way into the future.

OTHER WOMEN'S STORIES: LIZ, CAREER WOMAN AND LATE-IN-LIFE MOM

Although she is older than I am, Liz came from a similar socioeconomic and cultural background. I was interested in hearing if she had experienced the same influences growing up that made motherhood a desired or expected benchmark for her. She confirmed my assumption in part when she told me motherhood wasn't discussed much as she was growing up, because everyone assumed she and her peers would have kids. Period.

The other reason I wanted to talk with her is that she came to motherhood after the age of 40. She had already built a solid career for herself, one in which she was respected and in demand. Although she was married and wasn't wholly dependent upon her income for financial security, I wanted to hear from her how she handled the tradeoffs that came from sacrificing career momentum for mommydom.

The moms from her childhood reflected the role of the model housewife that I had seen in my neighborhood: they stayed home, cooked, cleaned house, and raised their families. "None had a career that I remember," Liz said, until the "massive societal shifts" of the 1970s took place with respect to motherhood, and women—including her own mother—went back to work. "All of a sudden, we women were supposed to 'do it all': have a family and a career, and do it all well," she said. *"It was a confusing time for a young girl, but of course, also a significant opportunity for the empowerment and independence of women."*

A family friend's divorce—which left the wife to raise three young children on a low-skilled, minimum-wage job—was a watershed moment for Liz's parents, who then set about encouraging Liz and her sister to get educations, pursue careers, and have a foundation to make their way in the world independently. *"This was something that was discussed at length in our household: what my sister and I would do to make a living,"* Liz told me. Her brother, she says, was left out of the conversations because of course he would have a career. *"When my sister declared that her ambition was to 'marry a doctor and have kids,' we would make fun of her, saying, 'You're supposed to pick out a career, and that doesn't count!'"* Liz said. To appease their parents, Liz's sister enrolled in medical school —long enough to meet and marry a successful doctor. She is now a full-time stay-at-home mom.

Liz supposes one of the reasons she came to motherhood later in life was because the importance of making a living was the primary focus of her formative years. She was 42 when she had her son, and coming to motherhood late was hard. *"The sudden lifestyle shift was difficult. It was almost like starting a new job in a field you have never worked in, and where you have absolutely no training or experience."* She felt incredibly insecure for the first couple of years, when she found herself surrounded by much younger and much more experienced mothers who made her feel like she was in over her head.

For example, when her son, Dylan, was six weeks old, she signed up for a Mommy and Me class. *"On the first day of class, one young mom asked me if I had Dylan signed up for preschool yet. When I answered 'no,' she gave me a look of horror. Apparently in order to get into a 'good' preschool, you had to add your name to a waiting list once you became pregnant. Who knew?!"* Liz remembers leaving that *class feeling like a failure as a mother. Good grief, I thought, commiserating with Liz over the not-so-subtle dissing she had received, do women ever stop judging each other? "Plus, these young ladies had the outward appearance of motherhood down: efficiently packed diaper bags, complete with the right snacks and baby wipes," she said. "I was just a thrown-together mess."*

In time, she was able to mentally take on the role of mother with less mess and more confidence, though she admitted it wasn't an easy path, especially when it came to making hard choices about her career. "I'm not a big believer in 'doing it all,'" she told me, "and the only real regret that I do have is the missed opportunities with my career." She decided to quit working full-time soon after Dylan's first birthday, to be able to commit time and energy to him while she had the chance. She cobbled together a home-based business that has worked out well so far, especially in that it has allowed her to set her own schedule. "You do have to make sacrifices," she said. "I avoid any potential clients that would ask me to work evenings and weekends consistently. I can't take out-of-town jobs, either."

Turning down work—and lucrative rush and weekend fees—was hard for me to imagine and stomach. The impact of losing those sources of freelance income could be significant, and I wondered if shifting to a corporate job had appealed to her. As Dylan got older, and more independent, she said she briefly considered trying to get a full-time job. She was quickly discouraged as she realized no one would want to hire a woman in her 50s. "Plus, I'd have to find a company that would let me leave at 5 PM to pick up Dylan from school (until he can drive himself), which is unlikely," she said. She's talked to other mothers who have found ways to balance working and raising children. "Some job-share, some freelance, others work part-time," she said. "It's not an easy thing to do, and there is no sure path to follow." I felt somewhat encouraged that other women had done it, so I could too.

As I anticipated my own choices, I wondered if being a mom was worth the sacrifices she had made. "When I reflect back on the first decade of motherhood, I cannot imagine what life would be like without my son," she said. "At times, it is definitely not easy, but you live for the good moments."

I reflected on the moments I'd shared with Jake, the challenges of trying to wrestle my way through a meltdown with grace followed by a sweet and tender moment of deep connection and affection. I could relate—from experience—to what she was expressing.

But would the tradeoffs be enough for me?

23

INTERVIEW QUESTIONS FOR THE WORLD'S HARDEST JOB

*P*arenting is the hardest job in the world. That's what I have been told over and over again in popular media and by friends and family members. If that's the case, then why would I or any reasonable adult—want the job?

My research revealed and confirmed that mommy propaganda was not a new construct. In the 19th century, a childless woman was at a "social disadvantage," and by the 1950s she was considered a "quasi-perversion" and "unnatural" (See *Madwives* by Carol Warren, © 1987). Only by being a married mother of legitimate children, according to the prevailing sentiment, could a woman find true fulfillment.

In a survey taken in the 1970s, 78% of married women under 45 said it was better for wives to be homemakers and for husbands to do the breadwinning. In the 1980s, at the height of the Reagan years, we also saw some serious backlash to the Feminist Movement with the push to a return to conservative family values. *Time* magazine in 1991 wrote "Americans are rediscovering the joys of home life, basic values, and things that last." I was skeptical about the "joys" bit, especially when I discovered the rate of divorce tripled between 1900 and 1982.

And who was it who did the bulk of the work to support that joyful home life? I sensed decades of repressed resentment from generations of women.

I imagined having a conversation with my own on-the-brink-of-adulthood daughter (should I be so lucky), as she grappled with the pressures (assuming we hadn't made much progress from where I now stood) and tried to make choices for her own best interests. What would I want most for her? That she be true to and happy with herself. I wouldn't want her growing up trying desperately to keep up with the Joneses or the Kardashians (don't *even* get me started)! I'd want her to experience and risk and explore and try! And I'd want her to, as much as possible, benefit from what I'd learned on my journey.

I'd encourage her to ask the questions I wished someone had asked me much earlier in life; job interview questions, if you will, part of my own life-planning survey. The list would include:

- Do I really want to have and raise a child/children? Why?
- Am I pursuing motherhood for any other reason other than my own desires (i.e., parental and/or societal pressure)?
- How might I make enjoying a career and raising a family coexist?
- If I do have children, who are my role models for parenting? What did they do that I want to replicate or avoid like the plague?
- Can I conceive of a life without children? What might it look like? Could I find fulfillment in doing other things with my life?
- If I don't have a child, what might I regret?
- Who are my role models for living a great life? What about them do I want to emulate?

- Most important, how do I define my worth right now? What do I envision a "successful" life will look like for me?

These were among the questions I was now asking about myself, for myself. Not "What is expected of me?" But what did *I* truly *want* for myself? I was able to give informed answers, based on my experience and interviews to date, but the sum of my responses didn't leave me convinced. I still wasn't ready to accept the job offer.

Here was the big mother of all questions: What would make me happy?

"Once, at an event at church, I overheard a guy say about a childfree man, 'If he was a real man, he could have had a baby.'"

—*Jill, who is a childless stepmom*

"I don't want to adopt, and it makes me feel guilty. I'm well-off, I'm capable of doing it. But a lot of it is because I chose not to have a child as a single mom. I explored that option in half-hearted ways because my mother wouldn't shut up about it, but then I witnessed a not-by-choice single mom. She had an unhealthy relationship with her son, in which he had to be the son and her partner. It scared me."

—*Kim, who has given up on having children but still hopes to find love*

24

DAMNED IF WE DON'T, DAMNED IF WE DO

*B*eyond the financial anxieties, I took stock of my emotional anxieties. My feminist fore-mothers had promised that I could have it all, but in light of the realities that were being revealed, I was starting to think of this as the grand lie. What I suspected I feared most was the very real possibility of *self*-sacrifice.

My concerns went so much deeper than losing the respect —and business—of my clients. I thought back to my chat with Lori several months earlier when—after rushing into marriage, giving up her career, and having two children in rapid succession—she'd told me, "I hate it. If I'd known what I was getting into, I wouldn't have done it."

At the time, I could barely allow her words to seep into me beyond what I needed to do to be supportive, but I thought hard about this now. One of the great *dis*advantages of becoming a late-in-life mommy, she confided, is you are well aware of what you are giving up. You've had time to experience the pride that comes from succeeding, of overcoming failures, of carving out an identity that's all your own. You experience the strength that comes from gaining and improving upon skills and talents. You are pursuing your passions. You learn to love being appreciated for your contributions. You are a *you*, not someone else's someone.

Lori had been on track for a prestigious job with perks she'd worked hard to earn. Two back-to-back pregnancies and maternity leaves, and she was sure she couldn't reenter the work force at the same level. She also didn't have the energy she used to have, energy she would need to keep up—and remain competitive—with her colleagues.

"You've been building this identity for yourself," Lori said to me, as she gazed into the iced tea she was slowly stirring. "Suddenly it all goes away and you're just someone's wife, someone's mother, and you no longer exist. You don't even recognize yourself."

She looked at me for support, encouragement, maybe an "Oh, you so haven't lost yourself!" But I couldn't give it to her. I was too caught up in contemplating this scary scenario for myself. All I could offer her was "I'm so sorry."

A girls night out with my much-younger friend Beth gave me another glimpse at the pressures we put on women to choose. She was on the fast track in her career, way ahead of the pack in terms of getting to the CEO's corner office, which was what she had always wanted. She was bright, beyond capable, open to learning the ropes, ethical. She was our future, our great feminist hope. She loved her work and was passionate about her chosen vocation.

But there was a roadblock: Her husband wanted kids. Now. He wasn't capable of bearing and popping out babies, and he certainly had no intention of getting off his own exciting career ascent to raise children (evidence that we haven't yet fully evolved from 1950s gender roles), so it fell to Beth—who wanted kids someday—to "choose" to make the sacrifices for their family.

These were not insignificant sacrifices. Her long-time

mentor, a woman who faced incredible societal obstacles, was blunt with her early on. "Do one or the other," she advised Beth. "If you try to do both, both will suffer, and it's always your career that suffers most," she said, because your role as a mom will always take priority over your responsibilities to your career. Beth's mentor, by the way, had chosen to stay single and childfree in order to succeed in a career she loved, and she had no regrets about her choices.

Beth was also contending with the biases against women who choose careers over children. In "What Hurts Working Women Most, Going Childless or Having Kids?" (Fortune.com, December 4, 2015), writer Erik Sherman cited a National Bureau of Economic Research study that showed "having a child costs the average high-skilled woman $230,000 in *lost* [emphasis mine] lifetime wages relative to similar women who never gave birth." Those costs sometimes come in the form of passed-over promotions. "Yet," he wrote, "our society remains suspicious of childless women—and especially those who make the conscious decision not to have kids. Those prejudices, too, can hurt women in the workplace." How? "Employers often have less respect for their non-work responsibilities and may even expect them to pick up some of the slack for their parent coworkers."

I couldn't advise Beth beyond the need to follow her heart and her dreams, which felt trite, and I worried she would give in to her husband's desire for a family right now and sacrifice herself. Modern-day polls indicate that working mothers are still wearing themselves out trying to balance two full-time jobs, one at the office, another "after hours" at home. You'd think we, as a society, would have figured this out by now.

My friend Lynn, who grew up with the examples of "Gloria Steinem and crew" a generation ahead of me, echoed my thoughts. "In my 20s and 30s, we were raised with the cultural message that bearing children is not the fullness of your identity, but years—and decades—later, we still haven't fully embraced that," she said to me. She expressed dismay over the conversations we're having about freezing eggs, one more example of the pressure placed on young women to make certain they would become mothers. "There's a million and one ways to shame women," she said, citing direct and indirect methods of fertility and general body shaming. "I saw something recently about how you can tell a woman's age by looking at her hands, so now there's botox for hands!" she said, with shock clear in her voice. She and I both are confounded by the mixed messages women continue to receive.

Let's be clear: I am not criticizing anyone's choice or her path. I celebrate that the Women's Liberation Movement gave us options to be a mom or not, to be a single mom or not, to be a working mom or not. That each choice is more socially acceptable than just a couple of generations ago, I think, is extraordinary progress.

However, it's not enough. Women's choices are never clear-cut and simple, and there are, I feel, too many "ors" and not enough "ands." Whatever roles we might choose for ourselves, there's still a sense of lack or sacrifice, there are still unrealistic expectations about what we should want and what we can have. I want us to demonstrate and explain—without bias—all options to our younger generations. I want all of us to have the tools, information, and self-confidence we need to be able to evaluate all of our options and make the right decisions for ourselves. And then I want us to place value on each path, not just glorify the mommy path as the ideal. We all are contributors to the world. We all have something to offer.

Having not had any mentors or single gal role models, I now had to self-mentor. I acknowledged what was becoming clear through self-counseling and what had been revealed to me through my single mommy internship. I didn't want to give up my career, a business I'd worked hard to build and loved. I wasn't convinced that being a mom would be all-fulfilling. I didn't want childcare and family responsibilities to consume me.

Furthermore, I couldn't give up my career. As a single parent, I would need that income; not working was not an option.

I wanted to do it all, and do it well, but I no longer believed without reservation that I could. I didn't want to sacrifice myself. I wanted to embrace fully whichever life path I chose, and I didn't want to have any regrets.

———

I'd looked back at the 1950s, '60s, '70s, and even '80s to see where my influences originated, and there was indeed more clarity as to why there were still external pressures in my world of today to comply with "social norms" and "traditional roles." I got that women of childbearing ages today have been programmed for a must-be-a-mommy mindset, but what else was going on?

Look no further than economics. *Time* magazine reported in August 2013 that moms in the United States account for a $2.4 trillion market. That was twice the annual defense budget. Put into terms I could somewhat better understand, $2.4 trillion would provide four years of undergraduate tuition, room, and board at a public university for 39,941,419 students.[1] That, my friends, is Big Business, and Big Business needs a steady stream of consumers.

But it can't be all about the money. Why are we coerced to become mothers? Why are all of us pushed toward this expectation when obviously many of us don't want it? Why do we never stop to ask ourselves "Why do I want to be a mom?" If it's "the hardest job in the world," why would/should I want it?

Because it's assumed we *can* become mothers (through IVF, adoption, test tubes), and because we're judged more harshly when we don't. My friend Jill, who is a devoted stepmom, was once told "You've missed out on the biggest thing in life" because she didn't have children of her own. As much as she values her contributions to her family, this condemnation still undermined her self-worth. And my friend Kim, who feels she has the "heart of a mother," demonstrated in how she is "motherly" with many people in her life, told me she still feels "marginalized" by friends and family members who unintentionally (we hope) shame her for being single and childless.

Look at the negative stereotypes and influencers in our popular media. I was really excited to watch the TV sitcom *Modern Family* (2009), with its gay couple raising a child and mixed-race families. But I couldn't get through the first season when the only single women portrayed were an overly sexy divorcée and another woman who hated children. Single people in movies and on TV are regularly portrayed as flakey, obsessed with sex, noncommittal, desperate for love, and a little scary. Great for the laughs, but not so great when you consider the messages these types convey.

On the worldwide political stage in the first two decades of the 21st century, the mommy card figured large. First Lady Michelle Obama relished and promoted her role as First Mom. Hillary Rodham Clinton, in her bid to become the first female U.S. president, frequently talked about being a grandmother. On the flip side, in 2007 it was suggested Julia Gillard was unfit for leadership because she was "deliberately barren," and Andrea Leadsom claimed that "being a mum" made her more worthy of people's votes than Theresa May, who was childless.

(I felt a slight sense of relief, and even triumph, when Ms. Gillard became the Prime Minister of Australia and Ms. May became the Prime Minister of Britain.)

Throughout 2020, we heard repeatedly about Vice President Kamala Harris's blended family and how her adult stepkids call her "Momala" (which I love, by the way). It stung, though, as I wondered what was wrong with recognizing her as an intelligent, hardworking, overachieving woman and leaving her maternity out of the conversation. Haven't former Secretary of State Condoleezza Rice and Supreme Court Justices Elena Kagan and Sonia Sotomayor proven that not having given birth is not a job requirement? I applaud all the long-overdue wins women get in politics, but how is it that shaming someone for being childless is not abhorrent? I believe all women deserve a voice in legislation that affects them.

In her article "The Mother of All Questions" in *Harper's Magazine* (October 2015), author Rebecca Solnit talked about being repeatedly asked why she's not a mother. On tour to promote her latest work, and anticipating questions about the books she'd written, she was frustrated when one man who was interviewing her—onstage, before a live audience—"hounded" her about why she was childless. "No answer I gave could satisfy him," she wrote. She labeled his line of questioning "indecent, because it presumed that women should have children, and...assumed that there was only one proper way for a woman to live."

Why should anyone decide what is the proper way for me to live my life? If I become a single mom, I'm not contributing to the decline of the American family. If, after evaluating my options and choosing to not become a mom, I'm not attacking anyone's values system. I'm simply trying to make the best choices for my best life.

At least I was finding bits of encouragement along the way.

Statistics continue to show more women are having kids at later ages. They are establishing and embracing their own worth first, versus having their worth determined solely on how many children they produce.

[1]National Center for Education Statistics.

25

WHAT'S GOD GOT TO DO WITH IT?

On that topic of feeling damned....

Why is it, when faith is supposed to lift us up from our human troubles, so many religious practices instead judge, shame, persecute, and condemn women? We receive conflicting information from sacred texts and contemporary leaders, and we are measured against impossible role models. We are instructed to be moral, pure, to protect our "virtue" until sanctified by (heterosexual) marriage. Then, of course, a sure sign of being "blessed" by God is becoming a mother. We are called upon to bear fruit, to be co-creators, to fulfill our purpose before God by bringing children into the world. What if...what if we fail to fulfill those expectations and obligations?

In my Christian-based faith, we're encouraged to emulate Sarah (who gave over Hagar, her handmaid, to her husband, to bear his first son) and Hannah (who, "although the Lord had closed her womb," held the position of her husband's beloved first wife while his second wife, Peninnah, gave him seven children). In the bible stories, both women agonized over and were ashamed of their barrenness, and ultimately both were rewarded for their faithfulness to God with late-in-life pregnancies and the delivery of sons.

We're taught that if we displease God, he might rebuke us by making us childless (II Samuel, 6, 23), but if we please him, he'll bless us with sons (II Kings, 4, 14-16; Psalm 113, 9). In the same breath, we're taught that we are made in God's image, that we are perfect in the sight of God. How in the world are we supposed to reconcile these mixed messages?

"Part of the challenge is the text," Lynn, a retired Presbyterian pastor, shared with me when I asked for her perspective. "They're ancient, ancient stories. Somehow, we got the line it's not descriptive, it's *prescriptive,* and those messages haven't yet translated into any faith tradition," she said, commiserating with me.

Friends of mine who are Catholic or Jewish report feeling pressured by their parents and in-laws to produce offspring to propagate their religions, and I've been to countless wedding ceremonies in which the vows included the promise to reproduce and raise those children in the family's faith. I'm not as familiar with the tenets of other world religions, but I have learned that in Hinduism, if a wife fails in her duty to bear sons —whether she is barren, has children who die young, or bears only girls—her husband has the right to marry another woman. And "May you be the mother of a hundred sons" is a traditional blessing in India. The pressure on women has been and continues to be intense.

As I struggled to clarify my place in humanity as a so-far single and childless woman, I ached to find the solace my faith promised to me. I reached out to a handful of female pastors for insights and guidance. The first two with whom I spoke quoted scripture and summed up with: "It is God's will." I felt like I'd been slapped in the face. I felt judged and dismissed; I might as well have been accused of being faith-less. I needed to know "Where is God in all of this pain?" and "How will I survive this crisis with my faith intact?"

I got answers in my third call, with Lynn, someone I respect as a leader, a scholar, and a woman of genuine 21st-century faith. Her responses were a relief to me in that they were thoughtful, candid, and mercifully not preachy. Our conversation was also grounded in compassion, for she, too, is a woman who is childless.

"At all the churches I've attended in my lifetime," I said in a lengthy phone interview, "Mother's Day, the weekly *family* service, and the annual *family* picnic were heavily promoted and lauded events. Family family family all the time!" (I did a poor job of concealing pent-up slights and frustrations.) The narrow focus on family I endured was incredibly annoying at one church in particular, I told her, because demographics continued to show that over half of the adult congregants were single, either unmarried or divorced, and we had a large population of childless women. "We—the childless, single gals —used to talk about it off-campus, quietly, secretly. We felt ignored, if not unwanted," I confessed to Lynn, "but we never would have complained to anyone, because we feared coming across as haters."

"We have to figure out how to not do that anymore," Lynn said, taking a deep breath, and I was encouraged to learn her last church, where she had been senior pastor to a large congregation, did things differently. "I didn't do—and my church doesn't do—the whole Mother's Day shtick anymore. Single women don't feel alone." I wanted to believe that could be true, not just lip service, and she did qualify that she has served in pretty progressive Presbyterian churches. "Yes, there are parts that are conservative, and there's a sense you must bear children or you are less of a person," she conceded, noting that traditional messages still resonate. But she felt change was possible. "We need to own our own identities, free and clear of being a mom," she said. "And officially, there is no 'have to'; you are not the fertility of your womb."

I am not the fertility of my womb. I was so stealing that line.

But I needed to dig deeper. I needed to hear from God—through Lynn—how to recover after I hear someone say "You aren't faithful enough" or some other condemnation for why good people are not blessed with children. Whether it has been directed at me or someone else, it's a punch to the gut, one that leaves me speechless and feeling diminished. Maybe it's well-intentioned—encouragement, not admonishment, to work on becoming more faithful—but when delivered as a statement, it's judgmental and cruel. I know in my head it's not true—I know I am faithful—but in my heart, I still feel twinges of doubt, of unworthiness. How, I asked, has she counseled women who found themselves childless-not-by-choice and in despair?

"Several women came to me after miscarriages, and they asked 'Where is God in this? I've prayed and prayed! How has God let this happen?' I tried to shift the emphasis," she said. "I told them God is not upstairs doling out 'You get a baby...you don't.' God is not playing favorites." Instead, she emphasized, "Life happens, there's randomness."

But...but.... She could tell where I was going, sensing that what still needed to be addressed was the deep grief. How do we survive a crisis of faith? As she engaged with her parishioners, Lynn said, she reminded them every life has grief in it. "We must ask ourselves, 'What decisions will I make?'" She told me about one of her aunts who was desperate for marriage and children, and, when she didn't get what she wanted, "She curled into a ball and stopped living." It was a story she had shared in counseling sessions, to remind women of their options. "You *do* have choices," she said. "Life comes with grief, so make choices for your own good when faced with it."

Resilience is an interesting notion, she continued. "We have these expectations of perfection, then life happens. We need to talk about our issues, to be in them together, and trust that God is in it with us." I saw her point, that resilience is possible when we find the strength to ask for help, for guidance, and accept it.

"We need to reshape what God is in our lives," she said, "God is present, and we get God through community, through one another, friends, family."

"Look," she continued, "life hands everyone great stuff and crappy stuff, and God experiences pain with us," she said. "Our job, as best we can, is to make sense of that, to determine who we are, and to figure out how we can carve out a future."

I took a deep breath as I let her words sink into me. She's right. Every person is presented with challenges and hardships in life. For some, it takes the form of involuntary childlessness. "You get through it," she said, repeating words of encouragement she had offered in innumerable counseling sessions. "This isn't your forever, and there is a great gift in this."

I needed to reevaluate what my faith meant to me. It's not that God is here to answer my demands, although that pretty much was what I was hoping for. Faith, I was learning, was more about having complete trust and confidence that God would be *with* me no matter what, even in the times I railed against what I perceived to be unfairness in my life. I wasn't being judged. I wasn't being abandoned or condemned. I was being given the promise of a lifetime of care and comfort.

"We get *God*; we don't get *fixed*," Lynn said, to summarize her point.

I let out a long breath, relaxed my tight shoulders, and felt my burden lighten. It had been lifted, because God was sharing it with me.

26

PROS, MEET THE CONS

*D*on't cry at work. Act as if. If things go south, suck it up.
There are so many odd rules for being a grownup, and I seemed to be breaking them all. I think what bothered me most was that I used to be so on top of everything. I made plans! I achieved goals! I was self-sufficient, independent, and strong!

But somehow, on the most basic to-do list for what I wanted in life, I couldn't help feeling that I had managed to seriously, maybe irrevocably, mess things up. As I tried to bury my frustrations, disappointments, and confusions with work, friends and family members emailed and called to check up on me, ask about my experiences from my internship with Jakey, and weigh in with their own perspectives and suggestions.

"Are you glad you're home?" my sister-in-law Molly asked in a phone call, and I had to think about it. "Not really," I said. I missed getting hugged, being part of a family. Other than work and Beau, I wasn't sure what I had come home to.

"I just spent a day with my friend and her three brats, and I'm soooo glad I made the right choice to never have kids of my own," my long-time friend Denise said to me. "Did you make the right choice?" I wasn't ready to answer her question, to myself or anyone else.

Lisa told me about a single woman who decided that she really didn't want kids, then later adopted an 11-year-old. Another friend suggested I could end up as the world's greatest stepmom. Or I could become a preschool teacher or volunteer at a shelter where I'd help "mother" OPCs (other people's children). *Aaarrgghhhh!*

I knew they were trying to be helpful, to help me think outside the box, to offer encouragement for whatever path I chose for myself, but I wasn't ready to hear it.

"I loved every moment with Jake, even during the kicking-the-furniture tantrums," I confided to my close friend Dominique, who had three teenagers at home. "I'm not at all surprised," she said. "You're such a loving and nurturing person, I knew you'd do well." She was right. I was the friend who remembered birthdays with cards and calls, I organized get-togethers and reached out to check on people when I hadn't heard from them in a while. I was the grownup who talked to her friends' children as if they were adults, who was genuinely interested in hearing their own ideas and opinions and gems of wisdom. I was the first to give a hug, even to friends of friends I was meeting in person for the first time. On dog walks, I would stop to let small children meet and pet Beau, my gentle giant.

It was encouraging to be reminded of this. I was great with my nieces, my dog, my friends, their children. I possessed deep wells of love and nurturing, and I wanted to share.

Part of me was tempted to take the easy way out, to let biology seal my fate, to put off any decision-making until a doctor told me "No babies for you!" Then I could allow myself to wallow in bitterness over the unfairness of life, grieve the loss of my dreams and drown my sorrows in Prosecco, then maybe, eventually, I could release it all and figure out how to get on with things.

But that wasn't how I was wired. I knew I needed to take charge, to do the work that would force the answers I sought to bubble up from my subconscious and reveal themselves. No more "maybes" or "what ifs" or "it will happen when you least expect its"; no more hoping, waiting, longing fors. *I wanted an answer*: To be or not to be a mommy?

———

Since the Universe wasn't going to make this easy on me, I knew I must soldier on by looking more critically at my internal and external research and trying to make the best choices for my best life. Feeling a surge of empowerment and determination, I grabbed pen and paper and (deep breath) began to list the positive things I'd learned about mommyhood during my time with Jake (pros) and the negative things that scared the bejeezus out of me (cons):

PROs

It had been easier than I thought. Jake and I managed to get into a routine, I didn't burn the house down or kill the kid, and I was semi-confident I'd eventually figure out how to get more sleep, be the breadwinner and bread-maker, and keep myself and my little person happy.

I loved feeling part of a family. And I wanted this for myself, whether it was with a child of my own or with a great guy + kids + dogs + hamsters + fish. Meanwhile, I loved being closer to my extended family, my siblings and their kids. I wanted to be with them for future holidays and normal days.

I felt more "complete" when I was with Jake. As clichéd as this sounds (How many celebrity moms tell *People* magazine that having children made them feel more complete?), I loved how he reached out to me with a look or a movement when he needed comfort or calming or just plain ol' love. I loved that he trusted I could give him what he needed, and I loved the feeling

I got when I realized I had reserves of love I never knew existed. It felt natural to be meeting his needs. And, let's face it: I loved my dog, but he was never going to call me "mama."

I wanted to have kids of my own. I loved being with Jakey. He is a light in the world, and I'm so grateful he's in *my* world. But with all selfishness, I also realized that I'd love to have a mini-me, not a sibling's child or an adopted child, but a blue-eyed imp who would mirror back to me my genetics, my expressions, and a few endearing personality quirks.

CONs

Unpredictable income. I could not do this on my own, relying on a single, erratic, freelance salary. No trust fund was going to bail me out. No lottery ticket was going to save the day. If I got sick or injured and couldn't work, and became financially insolvent, I was screwed.

Undesirable, but necessary career change. I couldn't do the work I loved at a rate that would provide the money needed to support me plus one or more children. The thought of taking a higher-paying job doing something I didn't love to support a full-time nanny who would essentially raise my child made my stomach churn. I know women do it, but I couldn't bring myself to choose it.

Unsuitable home environment. An un-insulated, cramped, one-bedroom apartment with a colicky newborn? Not so much. Maybe I could put up with the cramped quarters for a short period of time, but what if that "temporary" living situation was where we got stuck for 18 years?

My aging body. Let's see, if I meet a man (or buy some sperm) in October, get knocked up by December, give birth in August, that would make me...47 years old when the kid hits kindergarten, 60 when he finally heads off to college. I got wiped out chasing after a 15-month-old now; I'd be a train wreck if I tried to do it in three or four years with a full house, a full-time job, and the onset of menopause. There are women who do it, and I applaud them if it's really what they want, but I can honestly say I don't envy them.

My dating & social life would suffer. This circled back to the 24/7 reality of single parenting. I wanted and needed friends, and friendships took nurturing too. I also wanted to keep the door open to a fulfilling adult relationship, not just with the donor/father figure of my future offspring, but with a true companion for me.

Parenting without a partner: The thought of traveling from conception through pregnancy to delivery to raising a child through to graduation all by my lonesome self depressed me. Not only did I want to share the experiences of exploding diapers and first words and baby steps with someone else who wanted to be there as much as I did, but on a very basic level, I felt it was unfair to the child to deny him or her two parents. Many people do it, and do it well, but, again, it was not something I felt I could *choose*.

Also, I'd been living an adult lifestyle for a long time. I was comfortable with my responsibilities, my social schedule, my to-do lists. Could I give it up? Did I really want to?

I stared at my list, wanting to make sense of it, wanting to see a simple, rational solution. But "life is not a math equation," my wise friend Lisa said to me. Fate, timing, chemistry, feelings, biology, emotions, values, temperament, and more are part of the complex calculations. Even if one column was more heavily weighted than the other, "wanting to be part of a family" might trump "can't afford vacations," Not all units are equal.

I mean, if I were to get pregnant, by accident or on purpose, I'd figure out how to see it through, and I believed I would do an admirable job as a mom. I wasn't lazy, I wasn't selfish. I wasn't afraid of hard work. I'd find the reserves in myself, and I'd make the necessary sacrifices. But a deliberate "accidental" pregnancy was kind of cheating. I knew I had to work my way through my issues to get to the answer that was right for me, to take ownership of my choice.

But...but...there were so many valid reasons *not* to become a solo parent. I know most people don't take the time or make the effort to ask the tough questions and think through the tough answers before deciding whether or not to have kids, and I was choosing to ask and answer honestly for myself. Over and again I hear that parenting is the hardest job in the world, so why did I want it?

Because I still really wanted it.

I still wanted to feel love for and from a child. I still wanted someone to hold close while they slept. It wasn't all programming or targeted marketing. It was in my DNA.

The answers would come, I told myself. Surely, they would come. Surely I would find that my life had meaning as a mommy or as...well, just a woman. Yes, I needed to answer the big question about the value of my life to others, but I also needed something to *do*, someone to *be*.

———

The composition of this longing wasn't just nature or nurture, it was a complex mix of both. Every fall, I am struck by reminders of family rituals. Autumn always felt more like the start of a new year to me than January 1st. It was when we bought new shoes—dressy, school, and tennis shoes (as we called all versions of athletics shoes). We made the annual trek to Longs Drug Store, where I was given my own basket and set free in the aisles to select colorful pens, pencils, binders, packets of crisp notebook paper, and those zippy pockets to hold supplies. The brown paper bags that carried home our loot were later used to create book covers, decorated to fit subjects and personalities. I dreamed about finding my area of expertise and being a teacher's shining star pupil, achieving new goals in my various extracurricular activities, maybe making new friends and getting a do-over in my social life. As the summer days and nights cooled off, everything took on a more serious tone, and I vowed that *this* would be the year I'd get up early and not rush in the mornings.

The first day of school was electric with excitement and potential, often captured in the traditional First Day of School photo taken with siblings and/or carpool mates. Naturally, on those first days, I was decked out in a whole new ensemble, including shoes that would inevitably give me blisters before the day's end. Selecting and shopping for new clothes to replace those we'd outgrown and worn to threads was a whole ritual in itself. My family was not into brands or labels; Mom found plenty of cute and well-made things at trusty ol' Sears.

There was an important ritual that we practiced for years. About two weeks before the first day of school, all the neighborhood moms set their alarm clocks for early-dark-something. We were roused from our beds, tucked into warm layers of clothing, and led in a too-tired-to-be-cranky shuffle to the car. At the Peninsula Center, we made our way to the queue with the other moms with half-asleep kids in front of Little Folks Shop. The moms at the front of the line had been there at least since 3 AM. We never quite got there that early, although we had visited the shop earlier in the week to scope out the offerings and plan our attack. As the clock ticked down the last few minutes to the 6:00 opening, a current of nervous excitement and anticipation rippled through the crowd. The volume of chit-chat rose from muffled and subdued to a crisp, sharp, unspoken directive to *Look alive!*

The doors opened and a horde of determined bargain-hunters and their slightly terrified offspring surged through. Normally calm moms drew from reserves of adrenaline and found their inner aggressiveness as they grabbed pants from tables, ripped shirts from hangers, yanked piles of neatly folded sweaters off shelves. As an older kid, my attention was torn between keeping an eye on younger, more vulnerable-to-being-trampled siblings, always keeping Mom within sight, and hoping to grab the cute jeans in my size without losing an arm to one of the crazed mothers who wanted those same pants. The lines for checkout grew quickly, but the adrenaline didn't stop. You'd see mothers' eyes darting to the tables around them, making sure they hadn't missed any great deals, occasionally sending a small fleet-footed kid to navigate through the melee to pick up that one almost-missed item.

At home, we dumped out our bags and examined our haul. From the skirts and sweaters and socks, we mixed and matched outfits, oohing and ahhing. We considered what might be First Day of School worthy. Mom took it all in and calculated her savings, deciding it had to be worth it.

I wanted this. I wanted all this craziness. And autumn was coming.

OTHER WOMEN'S STORIES: JILL, CHILDLESS STEPMOM

Well-intentioned friends and more than a few acquaintances tried to convince me the answer to my mommy dilemma was to settle for what I considered to be a consolation prize. "Become a teacher and parent other people's children...just tutor in the library's reading program...volunteer in a children's hospital." (I resisted telling them about a friend who reasoned that by holding babies in the NICU while she was undergoing fertility treatments, she would speed up manifesting her own; she ended up permanently childless and completely traumatized.) Every time someone tried to "fix" me with these alternatives to what I wanted, I was left feeling hollow—when I wasn't fighting the temptation to rage at their insensitivity.

But there was a small corner of my heart that wondered if I could love someone else's children and find the solace I needed in receiving a portion of their affection. I reached out to Jill, a woman from my generation with a similar background who, like me, had dreamed of marrying for love and creating a family. She held out for Mr. Right, and by the time she found Marc and married him, her age and related health issues meant it was too late for her to realize her dream of being a mother. However...he came with two teenagers, and Jill found herself in the position of being a stepmom, but not a mom. I was curious about her journey, her experiences, and how she had grown to accept her role.

She offered a healthy perspective, recognizing that timing and necessary personal growth played roles in earlier relationships not leading to marriage. "My dad said I was a free spirit," she said, "and he was right. In high school, I tried to be another version of my mom; then through my 20s, I was trying to find myself, trying out different professions. I still struggle with my identity."

Jill felt tremendous pressure from her "very conventional" *parents to get married and settle into a lifestyle that mirrored their own.* "My mom clipped out my classmates' wedding announcements from the local paper. It made me feel like she was saying, 'You're not keeping up!' but I thought, 'I've tried everything, I'm not in control of this!'" *Feeling frustrated and depressed, Jill wondered why life had been unfair to her, or worse, what was wrong with her. She finally asked her mom to stop forwarding the announcements, but still she struggled as younger family friends and cousins beat her to the altar.*

Her sister relieved some of the parental pressure when she married and quickly produced two grandchildren, but in some ways the silence amplified the negative voice in Jill's head. "This was especially hard on me. She was experiencing something I was so far away from, and I was jealous because, in my head, she was more of a woman," *Jill said.* "I remember crying in her driveway. I cried a lot. I was happy for her, but I didn't understand why she got to find her Prince Charming so much sooner than me."

Like me, Jill grew to feel like an outsider at family gatherings. "My cousins brought their kids, so one Christmas I brought my dog," *she said,* "my way of saying 'I'm not alone!'" *Meanwhile, she gave herself pep talks*—"I'm a good person. I'm going to be happy, no matter what!"—*and tried to find answers through her faith*—"It's God's will. I wasn't meant to have kids." *Finally,* "I just gave up...then I met Marc."

The fact that her stepkids have their mother in their lives—albeit on a limited basis—has pros and cons for Jill. "I do things to help them not because I'm expected to, but because I want to." At the same time, she knows that no matter how much she does for them, she'll never be #1 with them. "On good days, I feel like I have a purpose in running the day-to-day operations and serving as the center of the family," she said. "On bad days, like a lot of stepmoms, I feel lonely, isolated, despairing, and unappreciated, not quite a 'real' parent." Even though she is raising these kids, often treating them as her own, she said, "I feel like I missed out on life's big moments, and the grief often surprises me. Like on Mother's Day, when the kids do something with their mom and I get really, really sad."

She refused to languish in self-pity and called out the wins, like the moments when she finally felt part of the family unit. "This year, we—me, Marc, the kids—took a family vacation together. I felt like the oldest son was finally warming up to me when he put his arm around me in a photo. It took ten years! I'm guessing allegiance issues maybe?" Just last year, she added, the kids gave her a Mother's Day card with "Mom" on it. "They did it on their own—i.e., Marc didn't push them—and this was fucking huge! (excuse my French)."

I laughed out loud with her at her spontaneous outburst, while acknowledging that our laughter masked a wound that ran deep in both of us. If I did make it into the mommy club, I'd hoped I'd remember how brutal this holiday is for so many women, women with all kinds of hurts and losses. There's a real possibility, I thought, that I could carry some guilt for getting my unfair share of happiness while so many others—like the women Jill and I have been—suffer.

I was encouraged to hear that she had found a level of comfort in how she, Marc, and their kids had defined family for themselves. I also wondered how things worked in their community and circle of friends. She shared with me that at times it's easier to let other people assume she's their mom, but it leaves her secretly feeling like a fraud whenever she is invited to activities such as Moms' Night Out. "When we moved to our current neighborhood, I quickly discovered it is Mommyville. I tried a stepmoms' group, but honestly, I didn't get a lot out of it."

She continues to seek out broader social events and friendships with more depth and intimacy, but it's a challenge in a family-centered community. "I was at a group event, and I was trying to somehow fit in with the wives of my husband's friends. All they talked about were their kids and the teachers and other kids I didn't know. I was soooo bored and wanted to escape, or at least have a conversation about some current event or travel or anything except their boring lives! I know I probably sound like a hater, but it's how I felt!" she said, again laughing at herself. "A single dad finally came over and said, 'God this is boring. Where are the cocktails?' I loved him for saying that."

As her stepkids get ready to head out into the world, Jill is optimistic about the next chapters in her life. "I'm looking forward to travel with my hubby, and I'm looking ahead to grandkids one day." That surprised me. Does "grandmother" need to come with an asterisk, I wondered? Will she be "stepgrandma"? She gave herself a moment to think, then explained that because she was so present in her stepkids' lives, she felt they would evolve into a new definition of "family," one in which she would eventually play a grandmotherly role. What they might call her remains to be seen.

Jill shared with me the best advice she'd received was to "look at the advantages," and she admitted she was relieved she didn't have to go through pregnancies and births. As someone who looked forward to experiencing those miracles, I couldn't share her perspective on that, but I did appreciate her response when I asked what advice she wished she could have given her younger self.

"'Trust that you are exactly where you are supposed to be.' This is where my faith comes in," she said, "because the person I will spend most of my time with in my life is me. Me and God."

She was thoughtful for another moment, then added, "And happiness is an inside job. I would tell myself, 'If it's meant to be, it will happen. If not, you're going to be okay.'"

My conversation with Jill stayed with me long after we'd said our goodbyes. I admired her for her courage, I ached for the losses she still *carried, and I wondered how I'd fare in a step-family situation. Listening to my gut, I sensed that I would give and give and give of myself, hoping that I would get a morsel of love, affection, and appreciation in return—and that I would still carry resentments for what I did not get in life. Geez, what a yucky future. I didn't want to be bitter and resentful. I didn't want regrets.*

I reminded myself of Jill's last words of advice, that if the life I was hoping for did not happen, I would, somehow, be okay.

What, I wondered, would it take for me to be okay?

"It was getting to be pretty expensive, easily $400 a month in the 1990s. Although I was making good money, I wasn't saving anything for the future. Everything went to this endeavor."

—Joanna, who spent six years enduring fertility drugs, inseminations, miscarriages, and surgeries before finally achieving her dream of becoming a mother

"My pregnancy certainly did present economic challenges. I wound up having a cesarean section with a hospital bill of over $40,000, so health coverage was much appreciated."

—Alicia, who struggled to keep up with the hours and demands of a management position during her pregnancy and in the first few months of her son's life

"Life is not a math equation."

Lisa, who pursued motherhood for years before resigning herself to being childless-not-by-choice

27

DOLLARS & SENSE

I have plenty of friends who grew up in single-parent households and turned out just fine. I understand that there are no lives without regrets, that no life path is perfect, and every choice requires sacrifices. I also am well aware that women of all colors, cultures, and backgrounds have served in hard and menial labor positions in the workforce while raising and often sole-supporting their families on meager incomes. For reasons of pure luck of birth and upbringing, this was not my lot. This was also not part of my story, for while I had multiple advantages, the questions that continued to nag me were *could* I choose a single-parent lifestyle—for me and for my potential child—and *would* I do so with my whole heart and head?

Alongside the social and emotional research I was doing, I needed to explore and analyze potential financial challenges and prepare for them. I needed to look at the numbers, the dollars, the economic realities of single motherhood. I needed to gather hard evidence so that I could make the choices that were best for me and then be able to embrace those choices—and plan accordingly.

I put on my investigative journalist hat and dug in.

I started by taking a hard look at my current financial status. The previous year, I'd grossed $75,000 as a freelance copywriter and editor. It was a healthy take; not my most profitable year and, fortunately, more than double my leanest year. It was also hard-fought. I can tell you where every one of those dollars came from, because they each connected to my time and talents, and each was billed to a specific job. I wasn't paid for sick days or vacation days, nor was there any mention in my contracts of a possible future maternity leave. I clocked out for lunch. If a client was running behind getting feedback to me, I wasn't paid to sit in my office reading a magazine or surfing the Internet while I waited. I was comfortably well off, I'd say, and confident about being the sole generator of my income.

For expenses, keep in mind I lived in Southern California where a dollar didn't go quite as far as in, say, a suburb of Omaha. I paid $1,600 a month to rent a one-bedroom apartment, which included one parking space—not always a given. Public transportation wasn't viable, so I made monthly car payments ($220), paid my own auto insurance ($100), covered maintenance and gas, which seemed to go up in cost on a daily basis. I paid my own renters' insurance and health insurance ($300), plus any co-payments and incidentals. I'd never had dental insurance as an adult and paid out-of-pocket for twice-yearly checkups and the incidental repairs when a filling had to be replaced or I broke a tooth on a gumball.

I purchased groceries at the supermarket (not a gourmet specialty food store) and made almost all of my meals; dining out was an occasional luxury, and even then I made frugal choices. I maintained a simple hairstyle and stretched out trims as long as I could bear it. I did my own facials and mani-pedis, and on rare occasions when I shopped for clothing and shoes, I looked for sales on classic styles and good quality so that the items would last for years. I saved up for occasional travel, much of which was in-state to see family. Utilities, business expenses, and taxes, which were levied at a high rate since I was self-employed, also chipped away at the balance in my checking account. Each April, after having made certain quarterly tax payments to cover the year's bill, I scraped together enough cash to contribute to a small retirement savings fund. I lived a modest life, and I was doing okay.

With a kid, the pressures on me to produce additional income would be substantial. At some point, I'd need to provide a second bedroom. My little two-door economy car would need to be upgraded to a four-door to provide ease of installing a car seat—and getting my little passenger in and out. My health insurance costs would increase, and I'd need to add life insurance. I might be able to wear my clothes and shoes for years, but a growing child would need new items with every new season. In addition to day care for an infant, I'd need to one day cover after-school care. I'd also want to enroll my child in sports programs, dance classes, and music lessons. School supplies and savings for college tuition would take a bite out of the monthly income. According to the Institute of Education Sciences[1], in 2012–2013 the cost for one year of undergraduate tuition, room, and board ran just over $15,000 for a public university. If my kid got into a tony private school, I'd be looking at $39,000—for one year! With that hanging over me, I'd likely need to increase my self-care budget to cover more-frequent dye jobs to color all the new gray hairs I'd sprout.

These issues were not insurmountable. I still believed I could do anything I set my mind to. However, if the bottom fell out of the economy or all my work got outsourced to India or I broke all my fingers in a freak accident or, like women on both branches of my family tree, I produced twins, I would be screwed. Just thinking about this potential for financial disaster amped up production of stomach acid. Right: ulcers. Add that to the list.

I knew a few other single working mothers, but they had the financial support of former husbands who provided alimony and child support and contributed to mortgages, health insurance, and college tuition. Joanna, my friend who had purchased donor sperm, was a full-time working single mother for the first few years of her son's life. Family money and a high-salaried job made it possible for her to hire full-time live-in help. I didn't have the securities in place that these women had.

Therefore, I needed to get a picture of what options were available to me if, God forbid, I fell into dire circumstances.

CalWORKs (California Work Opportunity and Responsibility to Kids), California's welfare program, provided short-term aid to needy families. To be eligible, I would need to have a gross income that was a maximum of 130% of the Federal Poverty Level (FPL). According to the U.S. Department of Health and Human Services' Poverty Guidelines, that would be $13,690, or $20,650 for a family of four.

I spent $19,200 on rent alone.

Ohmygod. I couldn't imagine being that destitute. Furthermore, I knew I wouldn't be eligible simply because I had money in savings, I had work, and I had pride that wouldn't allow me to take services away from families—who had fallen on difficult times—so that the system could support a slacker (because that's how I would see myself) who had *chosen* her lifestyle. The spirit of the program was designed for families who had lost one parent, been victims of domestic violence, or lost jobs, not for a woman who opted out of having a second wage-earning parent in the household in the first place. For the same prideful reasons, I could never expect or ask my parents to step in with room and board or financial support. It would be one thing if I'd gotten into "trouble"—I know they would help me—but quite another for them to withdraw money from their retirement savings to fund their grown daughter's pipe dream.

I thought perhaps I would be eligible for assistance with day care options, but the numbers for that were sobering too. "Cheap and affordable does not equate to good and safe," one mother wrote on a support site for new parents looking into their options. In the San Fernando Valley, a suburb of LA that had some more affordable housing options, day care costs ranged from $1,000 to $1,500 month ($12,000 to $18,000 a year) versus $2,500 a month in LA. For an infant, I saw rates quoted at $174 to $194 a week ($9,048 to $10,888 for a 52-week year) with a footnote that rates went down once a kid turned two. I felt a bubble of hopefulness for half a second, then completely deflated when I found another note that there was a two-year waiting list. The California Department of Education (CDE) provided financial assistance to low-income families, but first you had to complete paperwork and interviews to prove eligibility, then there was a waiting period, then you had to hope there was space available for your child, and then you had to pray that funding would be available. Lordy!

I could keep the kid at home with me, but after having had Jake underfoot during my internship, I had no illusions about the "convenience" of being a full-time work-from-home business owner and full-time mommy at the same time. One responsibility was going to suffer. Perhaps, I thought, I could have someone watch him while I worked. I looked into the costs of a full-time nanny ($25,000 to $50,000 a year), which led to my discovering information about an au pair arrangement. Offering a young woman a "cultural exchange" would cost me a place in my home and $250 (if the kids were in school) to $500 in spending money each month in exchange for childcare. Since I wouldn't technically be employing this person, I could save some money on taxes and medical insurance, but I would have to come up with extra rent money to provide a private room for this person. One room for me, one for the kid, one for the au pair, two bathrooms; I found apartment listings in the $4,000 range. I felt my first ulcer take up residence in my stomach.

Okay, okay, I had options. Hire the au pair, move to the suburbs, buy baby gear from consignment shops, get aggressive about lining the kid up with scholarships. I wasn't expecting some lavish lifestyle of the rich and famous. I could do this!

When I ran this past a couple of girlfriends, the obvious question was, "You have the skills. Why don't you just get some mindless corporate job? You know, two weeks paid vacation, sick days, benefits, family leave, maybe even paid childcare...." It sounded so simple, but I reminded myself of why I left the corporate track in the first place. It wasn't (and this may come as a surprise) because a freelance lifestyle affords me lax hours and allows me to work in my PJs (something I don't ever do).

The most compelling reason is I never felt in sync with being a corporate drone, I wasn't wired for it. If I had to write the same press release day after day, I would quickly go bonkers. I needed to be creative, not stuck in a cycle of productive drudgery. And creativity, I knew from years of experience, happens when it happens; not just in a 9 to 5 framework. I also loved that my current work fed my brain and curious nature by pushing me to learn something new every day.

From my years in corporate settings I'd grown to loathe mind-numbing meetings in which wannabes talked to hear their own voices, the mandatory team-building events that everyone dreaded ("You *must* have fun!"), the efficiency consultants who had no experience with the realities of creative and production processes, and the hours wasted while I waited for other people to make decisions or get components back to me. When I work from home, I can juggle projects as needed, or I can fill the space by taking a ten-minute break to switch over a load of laundry. Not only was that more productive than playing some brain cell–killing online game while sitting in my office, but it kept me from spending my Saturdays trying to cram in all those household tasks and errands. And commuting sucked the life out of me. My last one was 90 minutes each way to travel a mere 14 miles. Once I gave that up, I was able to end my day relatively calmer and had the energy left over to put together a balanced home-cooked meal. Being a solopreneur who worked from home was a healthier choice in so many ways.

At one office where I worked as a contractor, a full-time staffer said to me, "I could never do what you do. I need job security." But I've seen colleagues who have been loyal to their companies for decades, then laid off weeks before they would have been fully vested in their retirement plans. Sometimes they were rehired as cheaper contractors, sans benefits. I knew I could land on my feet and find other sources of income if one client pulled all their projects from me (which I saw happen to a whole generation of graphic designers at one job). In a corporate environment, I was a number, a statistic, a cost that could be excised in a "re-org." My job security, for me and my family, would come only from me.

Ultimately, having a flexible schedule and being able to have balance in my life was a hard-won perk. I wouldn't even really say "perk" because it feels to me more like a necessity. Twice in my adult life, at 19 and then 34, I battled and overcame serious, but not chronic, illnesses. One friend called the second illness a "Holy Kick in the Butt," as in "Wake up! You haven't been listening to your body, it's exhausted, so now it's going to shut down until you learn to take care of yourself!"

During a lengthy recovery, I finally got the message that deliberate self-care needed to be a priority. I took a close look at how I lived my life and reevaluated my priorities and life plans.

Sleep, stress, what and when I ate (yogurt at 11 PM did not count as dinner), where and how I worked all were factored in as I made drastic lifestyle changes to regain and continuously support good health and well-being. As part of my doctor-ordered recovery, I left the 14-hours-a-day, 7-days-a-week job that had worn me out, and pursued work I could do from home.

That's how I became a full-time freelancer.

And a freelancer I would stay because my ticking clock would not allow me to go back to school and train for a more child-rearing-friendly job, such as teaching elementary school. I also couldn't go back in time to start over as a corporate attorney who worked 90-hour weeks for the first 10 years of my career, saved my big paychecks, and funded this next chapter of my life. I was going to have to work with what I had.

I can figure this out, I can do anything I put my mind to.

So. It was settled. I *could* and *would* work from home while raising a small child. It wouldn't be easy, but it would be possible, and that's all I needed. Possible. I revisited the challenges I'd experienced with Jake and felt I was prepared to anticipate the stumbling blocks. I felt armed with information. I would employ discipline, determination, and order to manage my beautifully creative chaos and find my own rhythm.

For no matter how I rationalized all the reasons why being a single mom didn't make *sense* for me, there were still aspects of parenting that I longed for in my life. Sure, I wanted the cuddly baby love. But I also wanted to observe as a little human discovered the world around him, that moment when he mastered the art of walking and realized what he'd done. When he read his first book on his own, signed his name, scored a goal, got a 100% on a test, went on his first date, performed a random act of kindness, demonstrated he was better at something than I was, stood up for himself, stood up for someone else. You don't get that from a partner or a nephew or the child of a good friend.

Yes, parenting is a gamble: I could end up with a severely handicapped child or a totally Zen child or a musical prodigy or the Devil incarnate. There was no way this path would be easy for me, but I still wanted it, I still felt all warm and tingly when I day-dreamed about it.

And one aspect of single parenting that was abundantly clear to me as I did all this evaluating was I wanted—passionately—to be the person raising my child. If I was going to bring someone into this world, I wanted to be the person guiding him, enjoying him. How many working women drop their kids off at day care before the sun comes up, and only have time to feed them and hustle them into bed at night; who hope to have play time with them on the weekends, but instead cart them around to sports and social events; who try to do all the laundry and grocery shopping, and when given a few minutes to themselves spend it napping? I also wanted to be engaged with my child, not That Parent who palmed her kid off on Sunday School teachers to get a few hours of relief, who missed school events because she had to catch up on emails, who planted her kid in front of the TV all day because she could barely get herself dressed and out the door. I knew I was being unrealistic, but what kind of mommyhood would I be choosing if I had to work so hard just to be able to financially support myself and that child? To any naysayers, who will accuse me of waffling on this decision because I must not want to be a mommy bad enough, you're right—and you're wrong. I wanted to be a mommy in every sense of the word, not just be the person who gave birth to a child.

As I imagined the possible scenarios, my blood began to boil with anger and resentment. How many couples or individuals think through all of the challenges of parenting before becoming pregnant? How many budget, plan, prepare, or seriously consider if this is a reasonable and right choice for them and the children they may bring into the world? My guess is not many, and news stories backed me up with daily accounts of neglected, abused, and unwanted children around the world. It pissed me off that I was one who was being responsible, was asking myself the tough questions, and that it was still possible I'd come to the conclusion that it wasn't a good choice.

And wouldn't this kind of responsible behavior indicate that I was an excellent candidate for being an excellent parent? I'd like to think yes, but not really. There was no test, no checklist or set of requirements or tasks to complete to demonstrate my suitableness for being a great parent. And I'd have to figure it all out once I got into the real world. What makes a great parent? Wow. There are so many possible answers. One who is present for their child without losing themselves in that role. One who provides for that child's comfort and safety. One who raises that child with good values. One who celebrates that child for who he is, not who the parent wants him to be. One who shows up, every damn day, and as much as possible for every celebration, every emergency, and most of the small events in between. But again, I feel the fact that I was considering all of this first, was asking myself the tough questions and considering how I might handle the possible scenarios, put me ahead of the pack in fitness. Is that egotistical? Perhaps. But also responsible. And the result was feeling my teeth clench in frustration and my gut reacting to the potential discouragement ahead. I wanted to hit something, pound my fists until the angst turned to rage turned to disappointment and allowed tears to clear away all the uncertainties.

I shook myself out of my negative headspace and, in a desperate burst of optimism, thought about Anne Lamott, another one of my writer/mom idols, who had done it with support from her family, her church family, and a loyal village of friends. She famously turned her first year as a struggling single mother into a best-selling book, *Operating Instructions*, and launched a stellar writing career.

And Toni Morrison gave birth to her second son *after* her husband left her. A single mom supporting two children, she worked as an editor for 19 years at Random House (in an industry that paid notoriously low salaries) and managed to carve out time to create her own glorious works.

If Anne and Toni could do it, maybe I could too.

[1]For the 2012–13 academic year, annual current dollar prices for undergraduate tuition, room, and board were estimated to be $15,022 at public institutions, $39,173 at private nonprofit institutions, and $23,158 at private for-profit institutions.

"The first challenge I encountered was the first fertility specialist I saw. He refused to help me with insemination with an unknown donor because I did not have a partner. He actually suggested I go to a bar and have unprotected sex with a stranger! Once I was pregnant, he said, he'd be happy to deliver the baby. (My second doctor was a woman, by the way.)"

—Joanna, who became a single mom with donor sperm

28

GOT SPERM?

*D*eep thinking went on the back burner as I returned to my normal work routine. I was at my desk, scanning emails, when one subject line jumped out:

"You are invited to the Egg Meets Sperm Networking Mixer!"

Was it a sign? Was this my neon light from God, pointing me in the direction of my next step toward single parenthood?! I took a deep breath and opened the email. Turned out it was an event being hosted by one of the many nonprofit LGBTQ organizations I support, and it was intended for gay couples who are exploring their options in adoption, surrogacy, and IVF. I had to laugh at myself for thinking it was a personal message. Not everything is all about me!

At the same time, it served to remind me that, while I had dollars and sense dancing in my subconscious, I had yet to pursue the final, practical, and purely physical steps toward making a baby for myself. My curiosity piqued, and with my project deadline safely days away, I decided to google sperm banks. Just for fun, just to explore the what ifs. I sat at my desk, typed "los angeles sperm banks"...took a deep breath, and tapped SEARCH.

329,000 results popped up, including "Quality Sperm Bank!," "Lesbian-Owned Sperm Bank!," and "Got Sperm?"

An ad labeled "Seeking a sperm donor?" caught my eye, so I clicked it open to discover a privately owned site featuring a "tall, fit, handsome, and Ivy League–educated donor." It reeked of B.S., along the lines of the sleezeball who posts a model's photo on his online dating site profile. The large clinics were too impersonal (probably true), he wrote, so out of the goodness of his heart (really?), he was offering a more direct route to parenthood (interesting). My B.S. meter calmed down a little as I continued to read the guy's bio, for he actually sounded like a decent human—albeit one who wanted to dominate the world with his DNA.

Other links led not to banks but to clinics offering miracle cures for infertility. I skipped past those, but then I hit the mother lode and found the Big Businesses. I learned a lot.

Each year, according to one site, 75,000 children are born in the United States as the result of donor insemination (DI). Fees were fairly reasonable, I thought, with one site offering a "unit" of sperm for about $500 plus $200 for shipping. If I picked the unit up directly, no shipping costs were charged, and I would have to pay only $50 plus a deposit for the storage tank. Assuming I only needed one go-around to get knocked up, this was surprisingly affordable. I was also pleased to note that they accepted American Express, which meant I could score some rewards points in the process.

One site described their services as a way to help lesbian couples and other women hoping to "form alternative families." Except for the lesbian part, I figured I qualified for that one. Some banks, I learned, required that the mommy candidate be under a doctor's care (i.e., I couldn't just pick up the unit and impregnate myself at home). Another offered an "identity disclosure" for when the resulting child turned 18, but information provided about the donor was limited. The site stressed that they didn't want the children conceived with the donor sperm to grow up with "unrealistic expectations of future contact." I hadn't much thought about that possibility, and it gave me pause. I knew I had no expectations, but would I be setting my child up for some serious therapy costs to address 21st century abandonment issues?

I perused FAQs pages and learned about the rigorous screening processes for the sperm donors. Men must be between the ages of 18 and 38, with, as recommended by the American Society for Reproductive Medicine, a "retirement" age of 40. (I found that ironic since most of the *women* I knew who considered this option were north of 40.) Prospective donors might be evaluated on medical, genetic, psychological, and social criteria. Test results and bios were available for review, as well as photos from childhood and adulthood and audio interviews (for an additional fee, of course).

I was reminded of a list a friend once gave me of things to look for in a potential husband. It included:

- Play tennis with him. (Is he a competitive jerk?)
- Observe how he treats his mother. (This is how he will treat you.)
- Pay attention to how he drives when you're in the car with him. (Does he value your safety?)

The data gained from the above observations gives a preview of the man, and while I'm not sure how much I believe in the power of nature over nurture, I thought these were things I'd also want to know about the possibly innate personality and character of the child I might be bringing into my life.

Giving in to my curiosity, I decided to shop the catalogues. I scanned the first and noticed a large number of students, I assumed in it for the cash. I wondered if everyone went for the drop-dead gorgeous model/actors, but skimmed past them as I narrowed my search for someone kinda like me, with blonde hair, blue eyes, and fair skin. Students, doctors, an accountant, and a firefighter/EMT popped up. *Ooo, firefighter/EMT.* I toyed with the idea of getting jiggy with the hunky-doo, which made absolutely no sense since I would never have any direct contact with him.

I hopped over to another site and entered my preferences: 6' to 6'4", brown hair, blue eyes, open to all races and ethnicities. A whopping 113 candidates appeared before me, and I was given the opportunity to evaluate them by face shape (never thought of that as an option), body build, education & occupation, interests & personality descriptions. I thought it was weird that one guy listed as his career goal "Have a happy, healthy family" and even weirder that a number of men listed "family" in their interests and "family man" in their descriptions. I thought it was totally creepy that these men might already be fathers, that they might be putting their children in the position of one day discovering secret siblings on Ancestry.com. I wondered how their wives felt about their "contributions" to society, knowing that, if I were the wife, I would no-freakin'-way be cool with this.

"It's so easy," these sites seemed to purr to me, luring single women into the fantasy that they can shop for and purchase their perfect children, their perfect lives. But dancing in the back of my mind remained the doubts about getting pregnant and sustaining a healthy pregnancy at my ripe ol' age, then raising a child with unforeseen challenges—even more so since I would have only half of a complete family medical history. The purchasing donor sperm part could happen with the click of a button and typing in my credit card info, but the thought of

18-plus years of tremendous sacrifice held me back from taking the leap.

Ah...but then I met Donor 1011. My Mr. Right was 14 years younger than I, born to a French and Scottish father and a German mother. (Would she be a challenging mother-in-law?) He stood 6'2" with an athletic build, had light brown hair and blue eyes. He was an only child (that could be an issue, especially if my child was going to be my mother-in-law's sole grandchild), and worked in a creative career (like me!). He loved to travel (like me!). It was a match made in heaven...except...oh, wait. I wasn't searching for my soul mate, my other half, my life partner, I was shopping for sperm.

I switched gears and started reading Yelp reviews of the various banks. Not surprisingly, the lengthy and glowing reviews came from women who had delivered healthy babies. The scathing reviews came from women—and men—who were unsuccessful in their quests for parenthood. I read horror stories about poor customer service and appalling bedside manners from cold, clinical doctors. I discovered that men who wanted to be donors were lied to about their fertility or the quality of their sperm when they were part of ethnicities that aren't much in demand. Geezus! And I learned about ginormous invoices and billing headaches that came about because clients were filed with partially anonymous codes (so Ann Baker could end up paying for Ann Brown's procedure because they were both filed as "Ann B.").

I learned about "premium donors" who were made available for higher rates, and I read a Q&A that discussed the possibility of two half-siblings, later, unwittingly, hooking up and becoming parents together. Um...ick! It sounded like a great premise for a future horror movie.

I knew I needed to wrap up my research in a happy place, so I returned to one of the sites to read the success stories. It was these stories that drew me in because so many of the women sounded like me: approaching 40, no mate in sight, longing to be a mother. They described their searches, with several women sharing that they'd selected two possible donors with equal attributes and followed their hearts to the right choice. One mentioned how important it was that her donor be a Christian, and I wondered *How would you know? Will the child be born already saved?* I silenced my inner snarky voice and acknowledged how amazing it is that potential parents can be that choosy about the attributes of their future children.

These mothers spoke of miracle babies, finding the loves of their lives in those babies, and how fulfilled they felt. One woman wrote, "I know my life would have been empty without it, and I didn't want to risk being 80 years old and childless, just sitting in a rocking chair, alone." There, in one sentence, was my greatest fear. If I didn't do everything within my power to become a mom right now, I certainly would find myself alone, unwanted, unmissed, unloved, and left to look back at the waste of my years on Earth. I couldn't choose that life path either.

But the same woman offered this advice: "If you can financially support being a single mother, go for it." And there was the flip side of my fear. As affordable as buying the sperm might have been, I still doubted I could support myself through a pregnancy and then support myself and child through everyday life and the challenges that might come.

I exited the site and took inventory of what I had just experienced. As much as I'd been telling myself I was looking for a child, I'd ended up shopping for attributes I really wanted in a mate. I shivered involuntarily as I acknowledged I might be looking for a child to fill that role in my life, that companion place, that empty space in my heart.

Maybe, just maybe I was going about this all wrong. Did I really, truly, from the depths of my soul want a child? Or did I want a partner, a loving companion?

I wanted to experience closeness, a bond, as well as pride (yes, pride), joy, heart-expanding love—all those emotions we're told we only get to experience as a mom. I didn't want to live a less-than life. It wasn't simply the feeling that I was less worthy, it was that horrible fear that I was missing out, that I would continue to miss out on major life milestones, that I would not live up to my full potential as a human being, as a woman, as a creator and giver of life. I mean, holy cow! I had the body parts to create A Life. Who wouldn't want to experience that miracle?

But (this was a Big But), did I want to do everything I possibly could to have a child or...could I build a life—*my* life—without children?

"If it's not definitely 'yes,' it's a 'no,'" a wise friend once said to me when I was faced with a career choice years earlier. There was no right or wrong answer to my mother of all dilemmas. No one was forcing my hand, but my body did have an expiration date, or "Best if used by" date, and I was feeling the pressure. Baby, no baby, maybe baby. Whichever path I chose, I would face challenges and possibly regrets. Only I could make the choice, and it had to be made soon.

A choice. A *choice!* How could I choose?

I reached out to my friend Joanna. If she had a do-over, I wondered, knowing the years and expenses and stress involved in becoming a single mom by choice, would she do anything different? "It was an emotionally difficult time, for sure, but it was what I wanted," she said. "Would I do it again? Probably, yeah. It's a very difficult thing, and each woman has to determine how far she's willing to go."

Just how far was I willing to go?

"There are shifting dynamics in my friendships as we drift into groupings of parents/nonparents/not-in-relationships. I want to feel happy for my friends, but I'm also bummed for myself. I sometimes feel really alone. I still have hope, but if that door [marriage and family] closes, it will be really hard for me to accept."

—*Chelsea, on the hard reality of being 33, single, childless, and still hopeful*

29

SELF-PITY, PARTY OF ONE

I missed the cuddles and the conversations over meals, but, in all honesty, I was relieved to no longer be at anyone else's beck and call. There was a lovely freedom in being able to go to sleep when I wanted, go to the bathroom when I wanted, go to the bathroom alone, and go to the grocery store without feeling I needed to rush home to feed a hungry kid.

When I finally caught up with work and had some free time, I trudged off to the market to restock my kitchen. The usuals, *my* usuals, were on my shopping list: salad makings, roast chicken, cans of tuna, chocolate chip ice cream, and a bottle of Prosecco. No frozen blueberries or Os made the cut, although I was tempted to pick up some Puffins to feed my newest addiction. While I unloaded everything from my cart onto the check stand, the cashier informed me he needed to see my ID.

"Really?" Excellent!

Maybe I looked like a teenager because I was wearing shorts and hadn't put on mascara. Or maybe I appeared younger than my years because I hadn't developed the frown lines and gray hairs that come with parenting. Surely he wouldn't have asked if I was accessorized with barf on my shirt and a baby on my hip. But it was possible that he made his assumption simply because I was hot and he seriously thought I was underage. Who cares! I GOT CARDED!

I got carded and I still got it! I congratulated myself as I sashayed across the parking lot. *I'm hot! I'm a hot not-mama!*

I loaded my grown-up groceries into my family-unfriendly car, turned up the volume on some rockin' '80s tunes, and pulled out of my parking space.

The high was short-lived. As I waited to turn left out of my lane, I watched as a small child wandered one direction into oncoming traffic while his mother (I assumed), pushing a baby in a stroller, walked in the other direction, totally oblivious because she was texting on her phone.

By some miracle, no children, mommies, or motorists got hurt. I, on the other hand, was boiling with indignation. And that's when I started to lose it. I wanted to scream: *Pay attention, you dumbass! Don't you know how blessed you are?*

Why why *why* did I have to pay for a (business) license to work as a writer on my oh-so-dangerous laptop while this idiot was given the responsibility for two precious lives, with no vetting whatsoever, just because she could reproduce? Why did someone have the right to verify the year of my birth and right to purchase alcohol, but no one questioned this gal's maturity for raising children? Why did this LOSER get to be a mother, and I got jack?!? And what about all the drug-abusing, child-neglecting, child-abandoning parents I heard about on the news? How come people who clearly don't want anything to do with children get to overpopulate the world while my dreams, desires, and all I had to give to my children seemed destined to rot with me? I wouldn't be a perfect mother, but I knew I would be better than so many other women I saw and read about.

IT WAS NOT FAIR! Did you know that a mama flea can lay

2,000 eggs during her lifetime? Even my great-great grandmother produced 16 babies (my grandfather was number 11), the last one when she was 42. I always thought I was capable of having at least a half-dozen of my own. But *nooooo!*

As much as I wanted to believe or deny, I was *not* a late bloomer. Some random cashier at the market thought I was under 21? Big whoop! My ovaries were not, far from it, and coming face to face with how *cheated* I felt allowed the confusions, contradictions, longings, and fears to roar from the depths of my subconscious to broad daylight. I thought I was strong, but they were stronger.

I felt frantic on the short drive home, my eyes darting for something I could (mostly safely) ram into. I wanted to throw back my head and scream, pound my fists on the steering wheel, stomp my feet through the floor. I hoped (just a little) that some asshole would cut me off so that I could fly out of my car and take my rage out on him. I wanted to physicalize the hurt that came from the emotional acid burning inside me, the searing, toxic spew that threatened to erupt and destroy every good thing in my radius.

I made it home without criminal incident, but my demons were just getting warmed up. My heart threatened to pound out of my chest, my skin itched. I lost the chance to build a thick, protective wall around myself as the questions, the dings and slights, the pity, the humiliations, and the fears began their mocking parade before me.

Why have I been unsuccessful in finding love? (Because the right guy isn't yet ready for me? Or am I truly, profoundly broken?) Why has no one wanted to marry me? Am I not good enough? God, do you feel I am unworthy of marriage? Do you feel I am unworthy of motherhood? Why have I been robbed of the beauty and privileges of becoming a mother? Is it my destiny to remain lonely, miserable, and broken in spirit? Will I never achieve adulthood? Am I destined to grow old and die alone? Oh, God, I am so alone!

Fueled by ice cream and bubbly, I let my heart and mind process while angry tears burned on my cheeks and strangled sobs choked from my throat. *Maybe,* I thought, *the answer to all this is to actively choose to be single.* Maybe what I needed to do was embrace my aloneness.

Emotionally ragged, I let my mind take over. I knew I didn't want to be left out anymore, but I didn't want to force myself on family or friends with families either. Maybe I needed to think outside the box to find a solution to my situation. Maybe I needed to go to another extreme.

I felt very protective of myself. *I'll be home alone for Christmas this year,* I vowed. I'd rather be alone by choice or with friends who are also "orphaned" for the holidays, I thought. Or maybe I'd just spend the day working, reading, watching movies, and pretending it was another single-gal-over-a-certain-age Sunday. I could hang out with my dog and save the $200 I'd normally spend on airfare plus the costs of boarding that dog while I was away. I could catch up on sleep. I could be a Scrooge and forego hanging lights and putting up decorations and sending fake-cheery greeting cards and simply pass the time between December 23 and January 2 distracting myself by going to movies.

Or...I could get serious about moving to Northern California and making myself more a part of the lives of my siblings and their kids. I could become the most devoted maiden aunt ever. There were money-saving benefits in that plan as well, since I was already spending a mint and most of my vacation time traveling back and forth for family events. If I lived closer, at least I could drive over for an hour or a day for a holiday gathering or birthday celebration without having to sacrifice a whole weekend for one big meal. That might also mean I could put that time and money into taking real vacations, like to Hawaii or Ireland or...heck, Madagascar.

But what if I made the big move, got myself settled, then

Kevin announced he was being transferred to London? Carrie and Kathy, having caught the international travel bug, might decide to teach abroad for a few years while Jake was young. In which case, I'd be screwed. I would have left my friends, deserted my network, hauled my stuff across state, and then I'd be stuck in unfamiliar surroundings. And since I wouldn't know anyone other than my family, I'd end up even more alone than I already was.

Part of me wanted to ditch it all and go on the road as a backup singer with, like, Sheryl Crow or Katy Perry. In this new fantasy, I'd be the sexy, mysterious woman in the background, plus I'd be the cool aunt that the kids would brag about to their school friends: "My Aunt Kath is a rock star, like, for real." I could drop in whenever I felt like it, or not. I could have a fling after every gig and never form another attachment of the heart. I'd be safe. I'd be strong. *I'd be Teflon.* I could be like my brave friend Christine who, whenever asked why she'd never been married would answer, "Lucky, I guess." I'd be the sassy spinster aunt, not the one defined by *Oxford American Dictionary* as "...unmarried, childless, prissy, and repressed." (I took offense with "and.") No, I'd be the woman "koolcharm" defined on *Urban Dictionary* as the "attractive lady who can spin dreams of her own, has the freedom to make them true." Furthermore, koolcharm wrote, "Men often spin around her for marriage proposals, [however] it depends entirely on her to accept or reject proposals. Married ladies often envy spinsters." Could I live up to that?

I wished...I wished I could have a do-over. I wished I could have more time to find my Mr. Right. I wished the divine plan for my life came with more specific instructions, like with a neon sign that spelled out a message so clear that said either "You will have children, so stick it out!" or "You aren't going to have children. Get on with your life, woman!" I wished I could embrace whatever path I'd been given and find purpose in my life.

I wanted a second act, one in which the princess's dreams all come true, and I begged and pleaded God and all my fairy grandmothers to make it happen before my clock struck done. If I really thought about it, the upswing was that I didn't have to include anyone else's wants or needs in my decision-making, as I carved out a path for my life. The cruel irony was, I *wanted* to have someone else in my life with whom I could dream and plan. I wanted the family experience. I wanted *all* of it, the messy and the funny and the good. The stay-up-all-nights and the messy diapers and the worrying and the team-parenting. The first steps and the big achievements that meant something to the child, so it meant something to me. The stories, the memories, and the summer vacations, and the dogs, cats, hamsters, goldfish, and rescued baby birds that fell out of their nests and we would nurse with eye droppers until they passed and I'd have to lie to my kids and tell them the bird got all better and flew away (until they got older and I got braver and used it as a life lesson). And delighting in the different personalities, talents, skills, gifts that revealed themselves over time. And the funny family photos and the traditions that we'd pass down and create. The teaching and modeling values, like the importance of informed voting and honoring our veterans. The launching of good humans out into the world.

Aargh, I was so sick of my life sucking! Twenty-plus years possibly wasted in a crazy dance between longing and hoping, praying and wishing, denial, regret, jealousy, dreaming and despairing, having faith and losing faith. My journey felt like the quiet drip-drip of a faucet; it's imperceptible, so no one calls in the plumber, but over time it causes the same amount of catastrophic damage as a flood. I *needed* something to live for, something or someone for whom to get out of bed in the morning, some reason to be. Otherwise, really, why bother?

I grabbed my hair with sticky fingers, launched my grief-exhausted body off the couch, and willed the negative thoughts to SHUT IT! I had so much to be grateful for: my health, my friends, my dog, my life that put me in a position of even being able to consider options. "You're 41—you're not *dead!*" I yelled at myself, only slightly concerned that my neighbor might be home and be rattled by my outburst. Whatever. I didn't care. This was about me and finding my way, thinking my way to the next steps on my path.

I had to have faith. I had to own that I'd felt love and joy in the past, and now that I knew what it felt like, I had to trust and believe that it would find me again and I would recognize it. I could continue to reach out to others. Maybe I wouldn't find a romantic till-death-do-us-part relationship, but that didn't mean I had to accept growing old and dying alone. "You can be a good and loyal friend, Kath," I told myself. "You can show kindness to others, you can be thoughtful and encouraging." I could start with facing the truth about my present and being kind to myself.

I knew there were no guarantees that either—or any—path would make me happy. It has to be my choice to be happy with the hand I'm dealt. But dang, this one was hard.

The summer sky darkened into night as I allowed the emotions I'd stirred into a fury to wind down. I was fully aware that I was going to have a killer Prosecco-and-sugar hangover in the morning, and I figured I might as well beat myself up a little longer. Blech. I was so tired of the broken record that replayed my whines over and over and over. I was so sick of myself, sick of my yearnings, sick of the uncertainties and my own indecisiveness.

As I curled up in my calm and quiet bedroom, I realized I'd achieved a high point in something: complete self-loathing. And, that perhaps, became my greatest motivation. For despite the aging ovaries and limited options and wasted years, I couldn't accept that it was too late for me to have happiness.

So, I became determined to change. I felt ready, finally, to do something—anything—else.

OTHER WOMEN'S STORIES: VALERIE, SINGLE MOM OF A TODDLER

Valerie had always wanted children. "I wanted to be a mother, a teacher, a den mother," she told me, and as a teenager she dreamed— like me—of one day being a stay-at-home mom while her husband brought home the bacon. Priorities shifted in her late 20s, when she discovered she loved having a career, loved having her independence, and thrived in a community of friends.

A brief marriage in her 30s rekindled her desire for a family, but when that ended in divorce because her husband decided he didn't really want kids, she suddenly found herself facing a loudly ticking biological clock. "As I got older, I developed a big motivation to live with no regrets, and I asked myself, 'Will I regret not having kids?'" Although she had family with her mother, grandmother, sisters, and nieces and nephews, she sensed the answer to her question was "yes." She started exploring her options.

She looked into artificial insemination, but never had the guts to do it. "I think you must have balls of steel to make that decision," she said, and so she stalled before committing. Meanwhile, the realities of being an older mother hit hard. "Doctors began telling me getting pregnant was becoming more dangerous," she said. Financial realities also deterred her. "I looked at day care, and there was no way I could afford it on my own," she said, "so I chickened out."

But not entirely. She gave herself until 42 to make a final decision. "I went out and had a lot of fun. If I trusted someone, we hooked up; I was kind of haphazard about protection. There's always the thought: If you're having sex, what if...?" Her mother had gone into early menopause, so when she skipped a couple of periods, she assumed she was following the same schedule. But Fate had intervened, and at 43, Valerie became pregnant as the result of a casual relationship. "When I saw the result of the home pregnancy test, I looked at myself in the mirror and said out loud 'Holy shit.' I was totally excited, but talked myself down in case it was a false positive or there were problems." She called her doctor, who told her the chances of having a viable pregnancy were a sobering 50/50, and an ultrasound was scheduled. "The waiting was brutal, because I couldn't talk to anyone," she said, "and I was freaked out thinking I was either pregnant or my body was doing something funky that may require a procedure."

She was pregnant, and the baby was healthy.

At the time I interviewed her, Valerie was a single mom of a toddler, Mara. She was living the life I had tried to replicate in my brief internship with Jake, and, as I continued to struggle to make my own decisions, I reached out to her for some more reality checks and, I hoped, guidance.

I jumped right into one of my biggest fears: that I couldn't do it—from getting pregnant to raising a child—alone. Valerie was candid about her experience. Mara's father's absence was not a disappointment; he didn't want to be part of their child's life, but there was no animosity in their agreement to go separate ways. What was surprising was the lack of support from Valerie's inner circle. "My family could not get on board until the third trimester," she said, reflecting back to challenges in the early stages of her motherhood journey. "They felt I was too old, that being an older mother was physically dangerous. They worried I'd have a child with special needs, and they were scared for me." She was also hurt by the lack of support from long-time friends. Granted they were scattered across the country, as Valerie had moved around a lot with her job and during her marriage, but only one flew out to help for a week after Mara was born. "Otherwise, I was really floundering," she said.

The most supportive of all were co-workers—all parents—even though she was then a recent hire in her department. One woman brought over formula when Valerie had trouble with breast-feeding. Another, an experienced mom, cut Mara's fingernails for the first time, showed Valerie how to do it, and boosted Valerie's confidence that she could do it on her own. A male colleague brought over a ready-to-reheat meal and rocked Mara to sleep, giving Valerie time for a much-needed nap of her own. "Through day care I've met other moms, and we help each other with breaks to do laundry, go grocery shopping, or run errands without having a kid in tow," she said. And Facebook, to her surprise, has proven to be a great source of information. "I post parenting questions and solve issues. When Mara was colicky, I got 50 responses." Hearing about how she found her new tribe gave me a shot of encouragement as I imagined my possible future.

Her job became a lifeline for other reasons. "I go to work for adult time. I'm very lucky." She's also lucky that her boss, who has a toddler of her own, understands the needs of a single parent and offers some leeway. The support runs up the chain of command, and their company recently introduced new time-off policies to provide for personal sick days as well as for caring for a sick pet, child, or parent. Additionally, Valerie has a flexible work schedule that will allow her to attend Mara's future school and play activities. I admit, I was envious of her professional situation, as it allowed her freedoms I didn't and wouldn't have.

I wondered if she ever got any flak for being a single—by choice —parent. "My therapist helped me navigate this," she told me. "A child at day care asked Mara, 'Where's your daddy?', and I was able to respond, 'I am Mara's mommy and daddy. We are a family. Families come in all sizes and shapes, and this is our family.'" I loved how simple this answer was, and Valerie didn't bring up any negative comments from adults, so I assumed it wasn't an issue. What a relief to not have to worry about any social stigma.

The best parts of being a single parent, she told me, included not having to negotiate decisions like picking her child's name, setting the household rules, and disciplining. "She's my buddy, and we go everywhere together," she said. "I am the sun and moon in her life," which, in all honesty, she says, is a blessing and a curse, because "sometimes I'd like to sit on the toilet by myself." We both laughed at that. The hardest part, she said in a more serious tone, is "the sheer terror that you can lose this little being," to accident or illness or worse. We didn't entertain possible scenarios, as a quiet understanding passed between us. Certainly for me, one of the "worse" possibilities was that something would happen to me, the sole caregiver of my child, leaving us both at risk. My chest constricted, a bit of bile rose in my throat as my overactive imagination threatened to send me into a panic attack. But I closed my eyes, pushed down the fear, and pressed on with my final questions. I wanted her advice on how I—and anyone else who was in the middle of this dilemma of whether or not to have a child on her own—might move forward.

The discussion of hard realities behind us, Valerie offered encouragement and motivation. "Don't listen to the naysayers who tell you how hard it is to raise a child, how expensive it is, etcetera, etcetera," she said. "Yes, it's all true, but you can't let that stop you from doing something you really want to do, or at least trying to do something you really want to do. I guess that goes for life as well as wanting to have a child."

She wasn't finished with me. "Be brave," she said, and she recommended I take the next steps, to check with my doctor to see if I could conceive on my own. "If you let your fear take over, you'll *never do it," she said. "Gather those people who are supportive of you, and let them bolster you through it. You'll make it work."*

She'd done it; I could do it. This wasn't anything new to me. I knew I would find support if I asked for it, and that I could, indeed, make it all work—if I really really wanted it.

30

GETTING OUTSIDE (& INSIDE) ADVICE

I needed an objective opinion as I began my for-real plans for the future. I needed the perspective of someone who knew me well, who knew all the players in my game, but who didn't have an emotional investment in my decisions. That meant I couldn't call my mom. Our life paths were too different. I wasn't sure she could relate to my struggles, I felt certain her own expectations would muddy the waters, and, frankly, I didn't want to hear "advice" that would leave me feeling judged as a total social loser.

So I called Joan, a family friend my parents' age to whom I had grown close as an adult. Although she was long married and all of her children were married with children of their own, she never came at me with one of those thinly veiled "So why aren't you *settled* yet?" questions that other family friends asked me. I never felt I had to be on the defensive with her. Most of our conversations revolved around great books and art, and through these exchanges I knew her to be open-minded and supportive of people with "different" lifestyles, including my sister's gay almost-marriage. She might have been born to and raised by The

Greatest Generation, but she had a viewpoint that had evolved with the times. Every time I saw her I felt at ease, like I could introduce any topic and she would take it seriously without making it too important or precious. I knew she could look at my situation with a clear eye and render an opinion with compassion. I respected her, I trusted her, and I was eager to know what she saw in me and what she thought about my pursuing motherhood, specifically single-motherhood.

"It used to be an ethical question," she mused, thinking back to a friend who had chosen to have a child on her own a generation ago and was deemed "immoral" for making that choice. These days, she felt, the question was more about how hard it is, how it is a demanding, all-consuming, 24/7 job. "Babies are cute, toddlers are cute," she said, "but then they become teenagers." I.e., not so cute. "You think you know what you're getting into, but parenting is full of surprises."

She mirrored back to me all of the potential difficulties I had been examining on my own, forcing me to deal with them on a more conscious level. "Are you ready for a child to rule your world?" Joan asked. Was I willing and able to sacrifice everything else in my life to raise a child? How would I juggle work and soccer practices and dental checkups? What if the child was sickly, or autistic, or otherwise incapacitated? How would I handle taking care of a special needs child on my own with the toll on my finances, time, and energy? "It takes strong people to be single parents," she concluded, "because even garden variety kids can be a pain."

Dang, she was a wise woman. But I was a strong person. Of course I could do this if I wanted, I argued, and she agreed, but she had more for me to consider.

"There's also the fact that you've been living an adult lifestyle for a long time, and that would be hard to give up." I thought back to what Lori had told me, about the pain of sacrificing her identity to be "someone's mom," and I knew this would be a sticking point for me.

"If you end up going for it, I'm sure you'll work it out," Joan said, with characteristic grace and encouragement. "But I wonder...maybe it's better to borrow kids occasionally, instead."

Would that, could that, be enough for me?

I couldn't answer that yet. But over the next several days, while I let our conversation percolate, I sat myself down, turned up the volume on my head and heart, and asked myself the key questions. Then I paid attention to my brutally honest answers, and made note of the ones I identified as the most influential for me.

Why do I want to be a mom?

- To not be lonely.
- To not miss out on what I believe will give me a fully human, fully female life experience.
- To experience the miracles my body was designed to create: pregnancy, birth, nurturing.
- To feel loved and to give love; to experience the love of a child.
- To hold a tiny being, flesh of my flesh, in my arms.
- To enjoy "family" stuff—sports, holidays, vacations, daily and special occasion meals, Scouts, music recitals, carpooling, road trips.
- To feel part of the "club" with my sister, sisters-in-law, and friends. To finally be seen as someone who belongs.
- To be part of and contribute to a legacy; to have someone to whom I can teach and pass on family lore, traditions, treasures, and traits.
- To not be pitied or ignored, seen as suspect or,

worse, to grow more and more invisible (what I, to my shame, presume childfree people are like).

My answers to the next question repeated much of the above, so I had to look a little deeper at why I might *want* to pursue this path.

Why would I want single mommyhood?

- It's my last chance to be a mom.
- I don't want to miss out on Life.
- I wouldn't have to worry about neglecting a husband because I'd be too busy caring for the child.
- I'd get to form and enforce all of the good parenting rules without compromise with a co-parent.
- I would finally gain access to the "clubs" and be acknowledged as an adult. (Even if I did feel like sort of an associate member, I'd still be able to vote.)
- To feel that I was contributing at least one thing of value to my time on Earth.
- To pass down good genes and family traits.

Now for the tricky-sticky one. To be fair to myself, I had to consider all the options. What if...?

Why might I consider *not* becoming a mommy (at all, like forever)?

- Shouldering the financial strains and concerns.
- Having to do it all alone. Ironically, being lonely in parenting.
- Fear of doing it and realizing (too late) I can't do it.

- Bearing the stigma of having a fatherless child.
- Enduring the hardships of being a single parent.
- Due to my advanced age, risking my health and that of my baby.
- My absolute terror about what might happen to my kid, should something happen to me.
- Because my head, my heart, my gut were *not* telling me to do it.

Ah. Hah.

That last thing.

Having listened to my Intellect, having reviewed my research and weighed the gambles as well as the potential and known sacrifices, my Intuition was finally standing up and demanding to be heard. It wasn't enough that I wanted a child of my own. My desire to be a mom in this lifetime, for all the reasons I'd considered, wasn't something that absolutely compelled me to risk everything to have it. There wasn't this huge "YES, by any means!" push coming from the core of my being. It wasn't "light," therefore it wasn't right...for me.

Well, shit.

———

This is when I reveal that my Miracle happened, the "When you least expect it, it will come" bit.

Or...this is when I report that I ignored everything my head and heart were telling me, and threw myself into making my mommy happily ever after dreams come true at any cost.

Or...this is when I divulge that once I got that message from the Universe, I embraced that clarity and began an inspired and intentional journey toward my Plan D (or is it E? F?).

When has Life ever been that easy?

I still wanted the magic, the miracles. As weeks and months

passed, I continued to tread water and float in denial, waiting for my "real" life to be revealed to me. I continued to annoy myself with my indecision, bouncing between rationality and emotionality. I would still be there if I hadn't made a conscious decision, a choice, to stay open, breathe, and live in each moment.

And in those moments, I expanded my view, pixel by tiny pixel. I took note of celebrities who were role models for successful childfree living: Jennifer Aniston, Helen Mirren, Marlo Thomas, and Elizabeth Gilbert. Hello! *Elizabeth Gilbert!* And Oprah, for God's sake, Oprah! If they could make their marks on the world and thrive without children, maybe, just maybe, I could too.

I got back online and googled "childfree"...and got nothing. Nothing? I tried again, searching for "childless" and got a ton of articles and reports. (Perhaps this is just me splitting hairs, but I think there's a gulf of meaning between the two terms and how they are applied to women, one implying "choice, look at the bright side" and the other "lack, failure.") Among the links I visited I discovered this quote from a book, written in 1915, called *Herland* by Charlotte Perkins Gilman:

"We soon grew to see that mother-love has more than one channel of expression."

I flipped back through my notes and revisited the statistics from the 2006 Pew Research Center report that indicated 20% of women ages 40 to 44 in the U.S. did not have children. Their lives couldn't all be miserable; maybe my future could be not entirely miserable too.

It was time I started exploring what those other channels might look like for me. I had a handful of friends who were quite comfortably childfree-by-choice. When I talked with them, the answer consistently was "I was just not born with that gene." There was no angst, sadness, guilt, shame, or longing. No amount of prodding by well-intentioned adults ("You'll regret it some day...you'll love them once you have them...you'll change your mind when you get older") would change their minds. As much as I'd known since I was a child that I wanted to be a mom, they knew, to their cores, that they didn't. I admit, I was envious. And when I probed, trying to figure out how I could get what they had, I didn't get anywhere. There was nothing they could offer me, nothing they could teach me. Other than they were content with their lives in the here and now. They were confident in their choices and their lives' paths. That was something I could work on.

For, more than ever before, I needed to find meaning and value in my life. I needed a purpose. It was more than the vague dream of being "happy," in large part because "happiness," by my own long-held definition, prominently featured the fairy tale ending with husband, babies, home, and dog. I was starting to accept—on a conscious level, finally—that not everyone who got all those things was happy, and there were plenty of people who didn't have the socially expected trappings and were.

Furthermore, I didn't, couldn't, accept that I needed a child to be complete, fully human, fully a woman. It just didn't compute with my feeling that I had a right to be on this planet, me, as I was.

For far too long, I'd been buying into the traditional mindset, accepting the sentence that I was unworthy as a single and childless woman. What total BS. I was starting to see—and maybe even believe—that there was another way. I didn't need to breed to be a better and less selfish human, more of a woman, or a legitimate grownup.

Though my wounds still felt raw, and my wrestling with all my dilemmas, both internal and external, was, I suspected, far from finished, I was ready to start exploring my options.

OTHER WOMEN'S STORIES: CHELSEA, 33
AND STILL DECIDING

Was it just me? Was I stuck in this limbo because I was paralyzed by the mixed messages I got from previous generations and legions of marketing executives? I looked around and took note of women a decade or more younger than me, and marveled at their apparent confidence. They took on big jobs because they were smart and capable, because they had been educated and encouraged. Some chose to marry, some chose to commit to partnerships, some chose to embrace their independence. I knew I was glorifying and simplifying what I saw, but I still sensed a level of fierceness about life I didn't possess. I was open to learning from them how to better navigate the pressures and expectations placed on me, on all women, although I also fought the envy nagging me just under my surface that they had more time to figure out—and maybe revise—their plans.

I met Chelsea through mutual work friends and was impressed by how bold she was. At 33, she held a challenging job, one with power and prestige. She was bright and fun, with a positive attitude. I saw some of my younger self in her, and I admired her. I knew she was divorced, I knew she had close relationships with her friend's kids (she'd recently gone to a Taylor Swift concert with a gaggle of preteen girls), and I wondered how she was faring in the wrestling match with her own dilemma of motherhood options. Was she panicked about running out of time to find a spouse and create a family? Could she see herself having a child on her own? Were she and her peers freezing their eggs, praying they would have more time to have the "all" our feminist foremothers had promised? She seemed to love kids, to thrive in their company, so it was hard for me to imagine she'd choose to be childfree, but it was a possibility.

I didn't want to make assumptions about how much easier things were for her generation, so I invited her to lunch, fully transparent about my intention to ask some deeply personal and sensitive questions. I wouldn't be judging, I assured her; I hoped to learn from her, maybe even be emboldened by her. What I didn't say out loud, though, was that as I listened to her answers, I'd be imagining how I might have done things differently if I were in her Italian leather loafers in this day and age.

Chelsea was an only child with parents who loved her, but her childhood was rough as both her mother and father struggled with addictions. "I was often the parent in my own home," she told me, and she longed for what she thought was "normal" family life. That, to her, meant people in close-knit neighborhoods, who put up traditional Christmas decorations and took vacations together, who lived like the family in TV sit-coms like Full House. "I saw those images of kids being a priority," she said. "They seemed to have it all together."

She pursued that dream life, which seemed to be fulfilled when she met her husband in her freshman year of college. "I married his family," she said. "They had a tract house in the suburbs, three kids, and a Golden Retriever. It was everything I thought I wanted." Following their fairy tale wedding, it was "box-checking time." Both Chelsea and her husband launched their careers, bought a starter house, and got started trying to make babies. Chelsea, to her surprise, was having doubts—which led to massive anxiety attacks. "I was traumatized," she said. "I had finally got my happiness, but I still felt totally screwed up." She sensed that their relationship wasn't truly the right fit, while at the same time felt pressured to stay the course. "I had participated in creating this life, I essentially pushed us down that path," she said, "so how could I abandon it?"

Should she stay in the marriage to have the children she wanted and likely face divorce and single parenting later on? Or should she leave and face an unknown future—basically kicking all her carefully laid-out plans to the curb? When Chelsea and her husband finally addressed their issues, one became a clear deal-breaker: She didn't want to co-parent with him.

As her marriage dissolved, she found herself leaning on the advice of women who had carved career paths ahead of her. Two of her early professional mentors chose to devote themselves to thriving in their careers over having families, and they had been wildly successful and fulfilled. "I wanted that same level of satisfaction in my job," Chelsea said, "and I plotted my (post-divorce) life to look like theirs."

I wondered, though, if they had regrets, if they felt they'd missed out on something important. Did she think it was possible, I asked, to have a fulfilling career and be a good parent? "I believe you can have it all, but not cohesive and balanced," Chelsea said, "and I don't have a romanticized picture of having kids. I see the total grind that is parenthood." She mentioned a friend whose full-time job is raising two kids, who complains to Chelsea about having to wear mom jeans and live up to the expectations of being a super-parent while she sees Chelsea's life as "free and glamorous." There was the either/or dilemma again. "The issue for stay-at-home moms is loaded. My friends say they think it's best for kids, but there's also the loss of the mom's identity," Chelsea said. This reminded me about what my own mom had said about making the choice to stay home because it was best for the kids, and my friend Lori's regrets about losing her hard-won identity when she gave up her career for motherhood. "We all have a desire to have everything, what others have." And we still haven't found a happy middle ground.

Chelsea makes an extra effort to be kind, thoughtful, sensitive, and respectful in her interactions with other women. "It's not fair to put moms on a pedestal or say 'You're so lucky you have a husband and two kids,'" she said. "Everyone's fighting a battle you know nothing about."

As the pendulum swings, as she tries to make balanced choices for herself, she feels in her heart she still wants kids, a family. Social pressure is a component as well, as most of her college friends are married and already have kids or are on the path to having kids. Among her friends who are single and in their early to mid-thirties, the anxiety is building. "None of them conclusively doesn't want kids," she said, "but we're facing the Big birthdays and...shit!" I took in that not much had changed from my peer group to hers, though I didn't feel any pleasure that I had confirmed this.

"Do you discuss your options? What are they?" I asked. One friend, she told me, suggested they "tribe it out," meaning if they hit 40 without spouses, they would have kids on their own and raise them together in a modern-day tribe or village of their own design. Another friend, a man who is gay, fathered two kids with a lesbian couple, and they co-parent in an arrangement they put together with counseling and legal advice.

A tribe, I thought, what a great idea! (I felt a twinge of envy, wishing I could have been part of a tribe. But then I thought, hell, I can't even get one person to join me in marriage-plus-kids, how would I find a group of like-minded and likeable people to join me in a whole communal arrangement?)

Several of her single professional colleagues froze their eggs, but none had taken the leap to using any of them yet. One met her husband shortly after going through the procedure, then got pregnant not using those frozen eggs. Another woman had planned a future with her long-term girlfriend, but they broke up when her girlfriend decided she didn't really want kids; Chelsea's friend is now dating men.

I was reminded of a one-line message I received on my home answering machine shortly before my 40th birthday:

"You need to freeze your eggs."

Oh, sweet God.

Love you too, Mom.

Chelsea and I laughed at the all-too-familiar well-intentioned advice. My mom wanted me to have what she thought would make me happy, a someday baby. But the promise of maybe wasn't enough for me. I didn't believe banking my eggs would "buy" me time, would guarantee me an extended window of time for a viable pregnancy. Plus, I didn't trust the gamble with my health that was part of the process for extracting the eggs, and I didn't later want to be the medical miracle who gave birth at 60 then was unable to get on the floor to play with blocks with her toddler. (Well, getting on the floor might have worked, but getting back up would have been the challenge.) So much of the process felt sci-fi and creepy and experimental not in a good way. I couldn't bring myself to trust the companies that were making money off the hopes of desperate woman. But maybe I was being unjustifiably paranoid. Was this just me being a big chicken who fears new science and technology? It seemed to me younger women were more open to it. Was Chelsea?

"I grapple with this, but I do not want to freeze my eggs," Chelsea confessed, in part because she still was not on board with being a single mother. "If I get pregnant by accident, I'll have that baby," she said. "But I want to share it with someone. I want my baby to have two parents, I want to have 'our' kids." Echoing some of my concerns about freezing eggs, she said she'd be more open to adopting a child, but she wasn't ready to dive in. "The decision to have kids is selfish," she said, "and I suppose it would fill a need in me." She mentioned a couple of friends who were single moms by choice, but they were supported by extended family, something she didn't have. "While I have great friends," she said, "it's not the same as family."

As I had done, she continued to look for a partner to share the journey with her. "I want to meet a guy who wants kids or has kids," she said, but if pushed, she would choose having a partner over kids. "I look at guys and wonder would they be good, kind, caring. Would they make me laugh, would they be positive even when bad things happen," she said, wistfully acknowledging these were characteristics she looked for in both a partner and a co-parent. She was grateful she has the time—sort of—and freedom to get to know herself, believing self-awareness will help her identify the right relationship for her.

Meanwhile, she got her kid fix with the children of friends, one set in particular that she has known their whole lives. "I am part of their family," she said, sitting up a bit straighter to support her conviction. And she had a dog.

Still, she said, the holidays are an assault. "I have to take social media breaks," she said, "All the happy photos of husbands and babies—it's too much." Having had my share of lonely holidays, I could commiserate.

"You're not alone, you know," I said to her, as we acknowledged each other through our tears.

"There's this quote," she said, sniffling and wiping her eyes with a tissue, "something like 'you don't have to be perfect, you can just be good.' And I try to live into that. I just want to be here, *versus wasting energy wanting my life to be something else."*

Me, too.

31

PASSPORT TO SOMEWHERE

$\mathcal{A}$ s I reflected upon my journey thus far, and prepared myself to sail off in a new, uncharted direction, I felt a quiet sense of gratitude. I am so grateful that I was provided the luxury of trying the mommy business without the pressure of having to also produce a paycheck. Not only did I have the opportunity to see if I could juggle and balance a home life with a child and a professional life, but I gained tremendous appreciation for women—and men—who make it work.

As for me, I was still a work in progress. Using all my analytical and creative thinking skills, I worked my process on my own complex problem. I took in all the information, let it stew. I revised and polished, then edited out the scenarios that didn't work for me. My deadline wasn't imminent, but it was looming, and I felt I was on the right track—or at least one that would get me closer to my right track.

But there continued to be moments of doubt and wishful thinking. Natural, I suppose, but still so frustrating. I thought back to a few years previous, when, in a moment of epic self-pity, as I bemoaned the sad fact that I hadn't yet found someone to marry me and was no closer to having the children I longed for, an older friend offered another path. "Maybe you're not supposed to be married or be a mother," she said. "Maybe you're supposed to, I don't know, birth a book."

On one level, I appreciated her rationale. There is more to life than the mommy path, and I just had to find the path for me. But "birth a book"? C'mon! It was so cold. Yes, I get that crafting perfectly polished copy is an achievement that gives me great satisfaction, I know that I take pride in the work that I create and deliver on a regular basis, but something else I now knew was true: It will never kiss me on the back of the leg.

It will never kiss me on the back of the leg.

No matter how I rationalized all the reasons why being a single mom didn't make sense for me, there were still aspects of parenting that I wanted in my life. I knew, that for me to be able to thrive in this life, I would need to figure out how to nurture someone or many someones. I needed to be able to express that part of me. Even more than that, I needed to discard the "truths" I'd been modeled and taught about a woman's roles, and discover and embrace another way to *be*.

The next phase of my journey would take years, years filled with emotional triggers including baby showers from hell; Facebook photos depicting Christmases, graduations, and Fourth of July gatherings, all the family celebrations and milestones I was missing; encounters with sweet darlings I'd meet on the street and imagine were mine; the frightening anticipation of growing old and dying alone; bouts of extreme envy; and slights from friends, family members, and strangers. Would I ever make peace with my childless status? I often thought I couldn't possibly, but I put one foot in front of the other, trying so very hard to find a way to take full advantage of this one precious life of mine.

Despite the struggles, losses, regrets, and other ugly old emotional baggage, I also felt like I had a crisp new passport.

What adventure was coming next? Who and what might I become?

As I look back, I wish I could go back in time, pull that broken young woman into a bear hug, and tell her what was coming. "You'll have help and support from places and people you can't even begin to imagine," I would say to her. "You'll make friends who will inspire and challenge you and expand your heart, friends you never would have met had you stayed on your chosen path." I would offer her encouragement and hope and the promise of real joy.

Her path would not be better or less than or the same as getting kisses on the leg, but it would be different and purposeful in new ways.

But she would have to open up to those possibilities and live it herself.

OTHER WOMEN'S STORIES: KIM, 50, SINGLE, AND MOVING ON

Kim never thought she wouldn't be a mom, and she always figured she'd easily check falling in love, getting married, and raising a family off her list. "Everyone does it," she said, echoing what I had been programmed to expect. But as the years passed, and relationships came and went, she had to take stock of what her life path was and might become. Now 50, and six months out of her last serious relationship (which lasted three years), she has taken stock of her journey so far, paid attention to what's been happening with her friends, and is making conscious choices about how to embrace a childless future.

"But...but...we have options! It's never too late! You can do this if you really want to!" I said, parroting the well-meaning people who offered not-always-supportive advice. She laughed, familiar with the lines, then grew thoughtful. "Although more and more women are waiting to have children, I really believe that I'm too old," she said. "I believe it's not fair to the child when their mom is 49 or 50. You can't possibly run after a kid like when you're 20." She mentioned a recent get-together with a friend. "I thought it was just the two of us, but then she oh-so-casually mentioned that she was bringing along her nine-year-old son, and my first thought was, 'Oh,

god, I'm tired.' I spend 10 to 12 hours a day in a stressful job environment, and I don't want to be around a kid." I totally got that, and I appreciated that she'd worked hard to earn her quiet time; it wasn't right for her to have to sacrifice for the high-energy sucking needs of a kid.

She wonders why people still try to talk her into attempting the miracle pregnancy, though she has friends who wanted kids so badly they did in vitro, egg harvesting, and surrogacy. But it wasn't something she wanted—or wants—to do. "I think having a child at 65 is not a good thing, even if science makes it possible. I believe biology takes away the longing," and at 50, she was ready to let the subject drop. But not everyone has given up. "I have an insanely Jewish mother—who is a daily pressure," she told me. "Now that I'm too old, she'll say, 'It's such a shame you didn't have kids'—yes, she uses the word 'shame.'"

When Kim was in her early forties, her mother tried the Darwinian argument to convince her to freeze her eggs. "You're smart, you have an obligation to create children! It's a shame"—there's that word again—"that you have not left your genetic signature on the planet! You need to procreate because so many people who don't have your gifts are procreating!" To get her mom to stop bullying her, Kim agreed to get tested at a fertility clinic. "Bottom line, I was told I had a zero to three percent chance of having a healthy live birth," she said. Even though she was deemed healthy enough to carry a pregnancy, her eggs were shot. "They told me I'd be a great candidate for a donor egg, but I didn't want anyone else's stuff in me," she said. "It just felt oogie."

She thought perhaps she'd found an alternative when she dated someone who had a middle-schooler. "My mom hit the roof," she said with a shrug. "She didn't want me to have to financially support someone else's kid."

Sometimes she feels wistful that she's missed her chances; other times she feels relief that she's no longer looking at parenting in the future. "I won't torment myself with every 'what if?'," she said, "but there are moments when I see families and think I'm going to be alone without that."

Still healing from her last breakup, she shared with me she was more concerned about how she'd handle being alone in life than being childless. The "Do you have kids?" question didn't make her feel as badly about herself as the "Are you married?" question. "When you're younger, all things are possible," she said. When she turned 49, she admitted she felt like a loser because she had not managed to get married when it seemed like the whole rest of the world was married. "Then when you get the news that you can't have children of your own, it comes as a shock that a whole portion of your life is behind you. It's a weird, sobering moment," she said. "The shock was not so much that I was going to be childless, but that I was aging."

Aging for women, she observed, comes with all sorts of challenges. "There is a sad group of women who try to put on a brave face about it," she said. "Well-intentioned people offer up solutions, all kinds of stuff to try to make you feel better, but there's this whole stigma around 'single women of a certain age,'" she said

I asked her for an example. "A while back, I had a friend who had had a baby, and I hadn't heard from her in a while. Then I got a call: 'Are you free Friday night?' 'Yes!' 'Great, because Brian and I want to go out and we want you to babysit.'" I wanted to believe her friend hadn't meant to be hurtful, but I ached for Kim. Her take on the exchange was that some people assume single women of a certain age are (1) available for babysitting or (2) feel the need to babysit, to be able to express their nurturing onto other people's kids, because they don't have their own. "I'm happy to help," she said, "but don't take advantage. Be a friend first." It was good advice, I thought, for any women trying to honor their friends' needs, whatever path they were on.

Hoping to gain some more insights for myself, I asked her what advice she would give her younger self. "Honestly," she said, "I wouldn't have taken any advice. But I guess something like 'Don't live your life in waiting. Do what makes you happy, and what *happens, happens. Be kind to yourself, and no matter what happens, make sure it's your choice."*

She was again thoughtful for a moment before adding, "But I came to these conclusions because of the path I'm on and have been on."

How much easier our lives would be, I thought, if we were better at listening to our elders and learning from their lives. But maybe it wasn't too late for me to find my way with the guidance of contemporary mentors and wise women like Kim.

"You're still going to grieve, but you're also still fully who God created you to be, not less than. You will find life on the other side of this."

—*words of encouragement from Lynn, a senior pastor (who is also childless)*

32

SEASONS OF LOVE

"*W*hat would you think…?"

A couple of months after the mommy internship, my sister was on the phone with another babysitting opportunity, this time to cover a brief gap in childcare when Kathy's back-to-school week overlapped with Jake's nanny's vacation. It was a no-brainer.

"I need to move there," I responded, thinking at first that I'd said it to myself. But I actually said it out loud, and Carrie heard me.

"You do. You really do."

If I did move to Northern California to be closer to my extended family, I wasn't worried that my siblings and their spouses would take unfair advantage by calling on me too often to babysit at a moment's notice. To the contrary, knowing I would be where I was needed and wanted warmed my heart. Plus, I wanted to attend soccer games and ballet recitals and every event that involved cake and ice cream. I wanted to be able to say "OKAY!" when Ellie called and asked, "Can you come over and play with me *right now*?" I wanted to be a close spectator and participant as my little loves grew up, and I wanted to grow older and wiser alongside my sister and brother.

I knew I could network in Northern California, and much like I'd done in Southern California, I knew I could build a life for myself. It wouldn't be easy; change never is. But I could do it. I could make new friends and add to my list of clients and form closer bonds with my nieces and nephew.

I asked my brother for his thoughts. "A lot of lives would benefit," Kevin said.

Mine especially, I thought.

So, with all this in mind, I accepted my sister's invitation and returned to Alameda for a little more Aunt-Kath-and-Me time with Jake.

As the seasons changed, the answers I sought were still unclear, but oddly, I was okay with the uncertainties. I didn't feel a panicked urgency to make decisions or make a big move, but subtle shifts were taking place.

Fall breezed by, and as I looked around me with a new perspective, evaluating the life I had carved out for myself, I started to sense that I was "done" with LA, with the traffic and the smog and constant arrivals of Hollywood hopefuls. Four close friends had moved out of state over the summer, each in search of affordable homes, backyards for their kids, stronger links to extended family, and improved quality of life. My village was breaking up. I had little keeping me there, and much to pull me north, but I still wasn't ready to take the leap.

A quiet, simple holiday season was merrily interrupted by the arrival of Kevin and his family for Christmas at our parents' home. I joined them for a couple of days, taking my spot in a sleeping bag on the living room couch and soaking up the festivities as I watched and played with my nieces. The tug to move closer to them grew stronger, and I felt myself heading emotionally in their direction.

Then, on the drive home from my parents' house on Christmas Day, my cell phone rang. Braden! We hadn't talked in a couple of months, so it was a nice surprise to see his name appear in the caller ID box. We talked for 45 minutes, caught up on jobs, families, and life. It was fun. It was easy and friendly. It was warm and comfortable. As soon as I hung up, I thought, *Something has changed.*

He came down to LA a month later, and over lunch he said, oh-so-casually, "You need to come up for a weekend so I can take you dancing." *Hello...what?* "I have a guest room," he added quickly. *Okaaay.*

By April, I was seeing the world through rose-colored glasses. By May, we were planning weekend-long visits to each other's cities. I allowed myself to hope and to enjoy being someone special's someone special. With my heart opened to new possibilities and fueled by the news that Carrie was expecting a baby in September—another nephew!—I started doing research for a major move.

One year after my vacation mommy adventure, over the Fourth of July weekend, I found an apartment in Alameda that would accommodate both me and my dog. It was a 25-minute drive over the bridge to Braden's and two and a half blocks from my sister and her family. I would be able to move in a month before Carrie's due date. I signed the lease and confirmed with Kathy and Carrie that I would be there to babysit Jake while they were in the hospital welcoming son #2, then I accepted an invitation from Braden to spend a romantic weekend with him in wine country.

A romantic weekend in wine country with Braden. How dramatically—and wonderfully—my life had changed in just a few seasons!

I spent the morning of the Fourth with Kevin, Molly, and

the girls watching the hot dog eating competition, then, inexplicably, ate a hot dog for lunch. But my traditional experience ended there. Braden and I enjoyed two quiet days filled with wine tastings, long walks, leisurely swims, and dining al fresco for two. No parade, no boisterous picnic with extended family, no sugar-amped kids, no fireworks—except for the ones sparkling between us. It wasn't the embodiment of my long-held fantasies, nor was it lonely or sad.

It was...different. And it was good. I was opening up to the possibility that there were other possibilities, other avenues to my dream life, and I started to feel that those other options could be good, maybe even better than what I had imagined for myself. I could see that future Fourths could be a variety of experiences, with different players, different locations. I felt the bonds to my long-held dreams begin to loosen.

"I'd like to be known as your boyfriend," Braden informed me as we strolled from the pool to our room to get ready for a very grown up holiday dinner of oysters and mojitos. It was so easy, so effortless. I'd released all expectations, and what rushed in to fill my open heart was love.

"Works for me," I said as nonchalantly as I could manage. But then I burst out in a silly dance of joy, which made him laugh.

Over the weekend, we talked about our expectations of commitment, whether or not marriage was something we each wanted or needed. We shared stories about our families, our role models, what we'd learned in previous relationships. We talked a little bit about the plans for my upcoming move to Northern California. Although it had been a year in the making, it felt like all of a sudden I had a new plan for my future, my new and improved future.

Back in Southern California, I scrambled to let clients know about the move, and everyone was supportive; they all moved with me. Gotta love the Internet. I ran around to make last-minute visits to favorite restaurants and stores, and spent some quality time with long-time friends. I cried after I sold my beloved washer and dryer, my first real grown-up purchase, but otherwise, there were no tears. I had no misgivings, no regrets. I knew good friends would keep in touch, and I was excited about the adventures ahead of me.

On August 18, I sent off the movers, loaded Beau and my computer in the car, and never looked back.

It was the best move I ever made.

I settled in just in time to help Carrie during the final weeks of her pregnancy, and was with Jake the day his brother, Emmett, arrived. I helped out as best I could while the family transitioned from zone parenting to one mommy per kid. Several times a week, I bumped into them around town. Sometimes Carrie would call and tell me to go to my balcony, where I'd look down to the street to see Jake's little face as he peeked out of a car window, his tiny hand enthusiastically waving to me as they passed by. My heart miraculously expanded again as it made room for Emmett—flirtatious, shy, cuddly, clingy, tough, adorable Emmett. I became a regular at family dinners and birthday celebrations, and I accepted last-minute invitations to go to Peet's for coffees and scones.

It started to feel like Northern California had always been "home."

––––––

My dad had a theory about love: "It will happen when you least expect it." He was right.

Having given up on the perfect family-making timeline for myself, having accepted that my revised definition of family might be nontraditional, I found myself easing into a real, adult relationship. As Braden and I grew closer, as the layers peeled back, I discovered a man who was respectful, funny, generous, compassionate, and, in my Aunt Sharon's words, "smokin'." It was a revelation and a delight. There was no point comparing him to my previous relationships because he was in a completely different class. Maybe it was because he had been married before, had known what true love looked and felt like. Maybe because of the loss of his beloved first wife, he better appreciated the value of commitment.

When I took the leap of faith and moved to Northern California, I told myself it wasn't for him. And it was true. "You are the icing on my cake," I told him, as I made clear to him I didn't want my move to put any undue pressures on the development of our relationship. I never wanted to be in a position in an argument where I could lay blame on anyone else, as in "I gave up everything for you!" My decision to move was about me, making the right choices for me.

But on my first day in town, I knew deep in my soul that Alameda was going to be a temporary stopover. As the seasons changed again, Braden and I moved forward swiftly, effortlessly, lovingly. We flowed into each other's lives. We made plans for me and Beau to move in with Braden and his dog, Scout, once my 12-month apartment lease ran out. We looked ahead to a largely unknown and interesting future.

When I stopped to survey my feelings, I was surprised to discover I didn't feel the need or desire to rush the process in order to get back on track with baby-making. Maybe I should have. There was still time. But in my heart, I felt that this relationship deserved more. I respected it more, I honored it more. Our coming together, at this time, at this place, felt so right, and I wanted to let it grow organically.

As I became more a part of "we," I felt less and less urgency to pursue the answers to my mommy questions. I think in no small part it helped that I had my research and experience to back this up because I was aware of the pitfalls of rushing into parenthood. I liked my life just as it was. I was grateful that I had the time and resources to take care of myself and to nurture this relationship. I liked that we could take off for a spontaneous romantic weekend, that our holiday celebrations would not be predetermined, that we could go to the gym in the morning before work, take our bikes out for long rides on Saturday mornings, and watch marathon sessions of *Law & Order* (if we so chose) on Sundays.

We could stay in bed when we had head colds, we could work late when we needed, we could eat dinner and carry on conversations without interruption. Somehow it had slipped past me that I considered me + a great guy a form of family, too. Yet here we were. Being childfree gave us options, gave us possibilities, and I didn't feel the need to move beyond our two-ness. What I felt was a strange-to-me sense of contentment. It was lovely, and I embraced it.

———

With the whirlwind of the speedy move, the adapting to the new neighborhood, new climate, and new lifestyle, I didn't allow myself time to sit down and think or even feel all that deeply. I had thought I wanted the lightning bolt moment, the neon sign that pointed me in the direction I was supposed to go, but when that didn't happen, it was really okay. My life simply progressed. Because I had put in the time for deep self-reflection and understanding, I had all the information I needed, and I was aware that on some level, I had been processing this information for myself all along. I trusted that the answers were already inside of me and that they would reveal themselves in their right time.

As time passed, what I noticed most was the absence of longing. It was a subtle shift, lacking drama. I no longer had that drive, that panic, that desperation (or what I'd once called "eagerness") to figure out what I wanted, or to strive for what I thought I wanted. I was happy, content. I felt in my right place at the right time, and on a quiet level, I knew things would work out the way they were meant to. *Huh*, I thought. *This must be what it feels like to be a spiritual grownup!* Do the work, get out of the way, and let it come.

It was like working on a complicated 1,000-piece jigsaw puzzle. I could stare and obsess over it, stress over it, bang my head against the wall, trying to cram pieces into sections that didn't quite fit. Then I'd finally give up and walk away, or maybe sleep on it for the night. When I returned to it from a fresh angle, I'd see instantly how shifting a large section just a tad to the left would make it link up with another section. The picture revealed itself, different from what I'd envisioned, but with every piece in its proper place.

I knew that I was moving toward acceptance of my not being a single mother, of maybe not being a mother at all, and I was feeling more and more comfortable with my decision. I started practicing the words: "No, I don't have children. I'm not a mother." It was scary, and I couldn't yet say it with conviction, but I continued inching toward that direction.

But.

When I forced myself to be completely honest with myself, I knew there was one part of me that was holding back, one chamber of my heart that remained sealed shut as a means of protecting myself from future pain. As Braden revealed his feelings and intentions, I was the one hesitating, trying to read my own heart, trying to interpret his, trying to see into the future. Because I still had decisions to make, and now those decisions no longer impacted just me. I wanted to return Braden's promises and commit myself fully to our relationship. I needed to feel free to open my heart—all of it—and give myself completely over to the love that Braden was offering me. And to do that, I needed to know *his* definition of family. Soon.

We had talked briefly about children earlier in our getting-acquainted phase, and I understood him to say that his late wife had not wanted kids, but he had. Now, here I was, approaching 43, and I had to be realistic that this was not something I could promise him. I feared not only that I couldn't get pregnant, but, worse, that if I did, I might deliver a special needs child with physical or mental challenges.

Plus, if we started having children now, in our 40s, our remaining active years would revolve around raising children. Selfishly, I wanted to enjoy all that time with Braden. I wanted to devote myself to taking care of him and nurturing our relationship. I didn't want to be cheated out of our play time. There were places I wanted to go and things I wanted to do and experiences I wanted to share with him.

I didn't seek his answer earlier in the relationship because I didn't want to scare him off ("She was cute and nice, but her biological clock was like a time bomb!"). But there's that tipping point, when you still haven't fully 100% given your heart over to someone, when you're still playing it a little bit safe, because you fear the answer, whatever the outcome may mean to you, is a deal-breaker. This is a harsh reality for single women trying to date to mate in their early 40s. Because I had given up my dream, I knew, with all my heart, that if being a father was his dream, I wouldn't and couldn't ask him to do the same for me. I wanted to honor his choice.

As I prepared myself to ask him the Big Question and (gulp) accept his answer, I experienced a buildup of familiar emotions and fears. I was terrified. I knew his answer had the potential to cast the final, crushing end to my dreams of family in any form, and I visualized transitioning back to a life of loneliness and isolation. I expected to get an answer that would confirm my worst fears and condemn me once again and forever more to growing old alone, to being one of society's outcasts.

It had taken me decades to meet a great guy, the first guy I truly wanted to marry. I didn't think I had it in me to go back to square one and try again to build a new relationship. This was it. And I couldn't put it off any longer. I needed to know before I invested any more of my heart, before I allowed myself to enjoy any more of what I had and would have to sacrifice.

It was a late afternoon on a warm fall day. Braden and I had returned from a quick trip to Southern California where I had been in a childhood friend's wedding party. We were starving, so had stopped for a snack at a new gourmet hot dog place in Jack London Square in Oakland. We were relaxed, we were in a happy place in our relationship, and this seemed like as good a time as any for me to risk blowing it all.

"I have a big, serious question to ask you."

"What's up?" he asked.

I reached across the café table to wipe a glob of chili off his cheek as I sucked up all my courage and asked,

"Do you want children?"

Oh, God, I loved him so much. I wanted him to have everything he wanted out of life, I wanted him to be happy. And if he wanted kids, I didn't want to be the one holding him back. If becoming a father was at the top of his bucket list, I couldn't provide any guarantees, and I loved him enough to let him go find some young fertile chickie who could. I bit the inside of my lip, almost as if I could call back my question. I held my breath and willed my spine to hold me steady.

He looked deep into my eyes, into my soul. *Oh, God, this is it.*

"No," he answered quietly. "She wanted kids, but I didn't...I don't."

I didn't feel happy, I didn't feel sad. What I felt was relief. And for the first time in my life, I felt that I could, after all, say "no" to being a parent, without regrets.

———

My dance with wanting children was not entirely over, and there would be more moments when I'd think *I still want one.* Over time, I'd learn to simply feel them and then let them go. But from the moment that Braden's answer set me free, I opened my heart wide and began to create new dreams around a vision of a family of two.

I measured my life in love, and one warm spring evening, Braden had a Big Question for me.

"Will you marry me?" he asked

No research, reflection, or pro/con list needed this time.

I said "Yes."

"Don't assume that you know me and my story. There are so many paths to being childfree and single. To stereotype is unfair. It *devalues* whatever experience she (the woman you're stereotyping) did have or didn't have, and it trivializes whatever reasons she may have had for not having children."

—*Kim, when I asked her what she would like to say to other people/moms/well-meaning strangers*

33

THE SISTERHOOD

"*I* want to start a blog."

I'd met Lisa Manterfield in a four-day writing workshop several years earlier, and over time we had started a writers group, edited each other's essays and articles, gone on retreats, and shared our stories. Being childless was one of the many traits we had in common, and Lisa had turned her experience of infertility into an award-winning memoir, *I'm Taking My Eggs and Going Home*.

She approached me about contributing to her blog at an interesting intersection of my journey. I'd pretty much resigned myself to the fact that I was not going to have children, but my heart was still courting the *what ifs*: the miracle, the quickie adoption, the rogue hookup of egg+sperm. *It's still possible, right? It's not too late! I can make it happen!* I'd see a child on the street who could have been mine—my eyes, my husband's smile—and think, *I still want this.*

While I celebrated milestones with my nieces and nephews—which at this point included my fourth niece, Grace, as well as Emmett—I found myself stepping back from the merriment and longing for what I had missed and what I *would* miss. While I was happy for friends when they announced their pregnancies, because I knew it was what they wanted, I still ached over my impending isolation. While I struggled to embrace the life I had "chosen," I continued to be bombarded by baby-centric messages from advertisers, magazines, and celebrities that chipped away at my worth in our society. While I pushed myself to consider new paths for my life, perfect strangers asked personal questions then offered miraculous solutions based on no knowledge of reality whatsoever: "Just adopt!" or "Freeze your eggs!" or "I know a woman who got pregnant with twins at 48!" (Well, bully for her, but no thanks for me.) I needed new perspectives.

Lisa launched *Life Without Baby* and I produced a weekly column titled "It Got Me Thinking..." with a clear sense that I was writing what *I* needed to read. Each week I addressed my challenges, issues, hurts, observations, slights, triumphs, and everything in between that came up as I tried to make peace with my childless status. As I opened up my heart, something amazing happened: other women opened their hearts to me, shared their experiences and hard-won wisdom, and offered me their support. It was humbling to be on the receiving end of unconditional compassion from women I could relate to and who could, it seemed, read my thoughts and finish my sentences. Every time I read "That's exactly how I feel!" in a comment, I wanted to cry with relief.

Furthermore, reader comments indicated there were thousands of women just like me around the world—women who were childless by choice, chance, or circumstance—and many of these women were comforted, encouraged, and empowered by what I wrote. They learned as I told my stories, and I learned from their stories. A couple of years in, I added an "Our Stories" column, in which readers shared answers to my questions, such as "Where are you on your journey?", "How do you answer 'Do you have kids?'", and "What have you learned about yourself?"

Together, Lisa, I, and our readers created a safe space where we could share and lament how we continued to feel slighted, shamed, and outcast by society, our families, our religions, employers, governments, the media. But instead of being a place to just whine, it became a place of support and encouragement, and a catalyst for change. I discovered I was not, in fact, in the minority, not a pariah: I was part of a sisterhood of phenomenal women. I came to believe that "You are not alone" are four of the sweetest words in our language.

As my community expanded, I was introduced to more and more phenomenal women—my trailblazers, really—such as Pamela Mahoney Tsigdinos, who wrote about her journey with infertility in her brilliant memoir *Silent Sorority;* Melanie Notkin, who inspired me with her book and website to embrace being a PANK (Professional Aunt, No Kids) and become a *Savvy Auntie;* and Jody Day, author of *Living the Life Unexpected*, whose journey to being "circumstantially infertile" mirrored my own. (The term refers to a woman who has not had children due to life circumstances: hasn't met the right guy, opted not to be a single parent, ran out of time on her biological clock.) Jody stopped me with one line: "I stand here today astonished that I survived the initiation rite it took to join this tribe." Yes. That.

I became better acquainted with role models, people I dubbed "cheros," for heros who happen to be childfree. The list includes such notables as Julia Child, Julie Taymor, Annie Oakley, Mary Cassatt, Dian Fossey, and Gen. Ann E. Dunwoody (America's first female four-star general). Florence Nightingale, Billie Jean King, Sally Ride, and Stevie Nicks are on the rolls, as are Rosa Parks, Betty White, Beatrix Potter, and German Chancellor Angela Merkel. *He-llo!* I cannot imagine anyone labeling these extraordinarily talented and accomplished overachievers "selfish." Just think of all the gifts that childfree women give to the world as artists, activists, volunteers, and leaders. I'm not saying women who are mothers don't make significant contributions, but I started thinking about how much *more* a woman could do if she is free of the constraints of bearing and raising children. Compassionate and kind, generous with each other and our communities around us, I found my sisters to be among the most unselfish people I'd ever known. The Childfree Women of the World Club seemed pretty cool, somehow more exciting, more adventurous, and even more exclusive than the Mommy Club I'd so long wanted to join.

With the help of my *Life Without Baby* sisters, I gained courage and began to creep out of my comfort zone and into the real world. I gulped down my apprehensions and began to answer honestly when new acquaintances asked if I had children. Sure, some responded with the typical miracle cure suggestions I'd heard in the past, but many more surprised me by responding openly and candidly with stories of their own journeys—from both sides of the mommy fence. By making myself vulnerable, I opened the door for other women to be vulnerable with me, and it was a revelation. I learned about failed IVF treatments, multiple miscarriages (previously treated as shameful secrets), and adoptions gone horribly wrong, including tales of scams breaking the hearts of multiple childless couples, tens of thousands of dollars lost, and terrified babies being pulled from the arms of their devasted adoptive mothers and returned to their birth mothers.

A colleague confided in me that she never wanted children of her own, and that she loved being able to devote all of her energy to being an aunt. "I hate that people label me as a child-hater," she said, based on the first impression people made when they learned she was childfree.

"I'm so sick and tired of being dismissed, and it hurts when I'm not invited to join my old group of friends for catching-up lunches and parties," said another colleague. I'd had no idea she felt like this, and I felt closer to her now that I knew we had this in common.

Having learned about my blogging, even mothers confided in me how much harder parenting was than they had expected, especially when mixed with careers. I found myself cornered in a side office when a full-time executive, who was also the mother of two children under the age of four, said to me, "I wish someone—my mother, my aunt, a mentor—had encouraged me to think about whether or not I really wanted children." *If only*, I thought, realizing how we all would have benefited from more candor in our formative years.

When they heard what I wrote about, strangers and new acquaintances shared their own stories, or those of someone they knew, from across the mommy dilemma spectrum.

"When my daughter finally completed her PhD, she was single and 43. So she went to a sperm bank and had a child on her own," a woman at a wedding reception told me. "She was lucky she had a job that allowed her to support herself and her child."

"I had a coworker who adopted two kids on her own—when she was in her 50s!" I heard from a friend's sister-in-law.

"I didn't have children," a woman in her mid-sixties whispered to me at a baby shower. "I knew I wanted a career."

"I have two kids, both with special needs," a man confided to me as we waited in line to check in for a workshop. "This conference is the first time I've been away from home in 13 years," he said, as I took in the strain and exhaustion in his face. "I wish I hadn't done it. If I'd known what it was going to take...." I reached out to touch his arm, to convey that I understood. "I love my kids, but...."

It was as if I wore a T-shirt that said "This woman will really listen. This woman can be trusted," and I accepted my new role as confidante with a healthy dose of respect, awe, and compassion. It became clear to me that more and more of us were acknowledging and embracing that the "traditional," "normal," cookie cutter lifestyle is an unhealthy delusion. I felt responsible for how I treated each human being, and knew they deserved more than easy answers, useless advice, and platitudes. I became more intuitive about when someone was hurting. I learned when to give a hug, when to say nothing more than "I'm so sorry," when to ask "How can I best support you?", and when to kindly ignore the elephant in the room. I learned this because so many women allowed me into their hearts. And because I allowed them into my heart, I finally began to heal and move forward.

When I look back at the pieces of my life so far, with all the right and seemingly wrong turns, I see how they've come together to reveal an unexpectedly beautiful new picture. My remarkable journey led me to a place I never before imagined. When the walls started closing in on me, as so many friends started to shift into all things pregnancy and mommydom and I felt I was being pushed to the sidelines, I desperately needed allies, and I finally found them in and through *Life Without Baby*. I take tremendous pride in knowing I helped create a safe and nonjudgmental place where childless women can be heard, acknowledged, and accepted. And I am so grateful to be part of a sisterhood of women who inspire, challenge, amaze, and comfort. I feel so blessed to have been granted these opportunities, this wonderful life, and am amazed that I am now able to recognize and appreciate it.

The greatest revelation for me, I realized, is I discovered new depths of compassion for all women, my childfree sisters and my mommy sisters. Hallelujah! For we're not mothers and non-mothers, we're not breeders and infertiles, we're not with child or child-less. One path isn't superior to others, one role doesn't hold more value than others. We can all relate to the challenges of being women. It was so easy for me to obsess over other women's haves versus my have-nots—or to gloat over the freedoms I enjoy that mommies have sacrificed for family life. Enough. You are free to be you, and I'm free to be me, and I think this is something to celebrate. I say let's focus on our common ground and support each other regardless of the paths we follow...or chose. Amen, sisters!

OTHER WOMEN'S STORIES: MEGAN, EMPTY NESTER

Megan and I became friends in college and have stayed in close touch, occasionally traveling to each other's towns to catch up in person. But our lives have been very different. She married soon after graduating, had two kids in quick succession, and has since launched those remarkable humans into the world. I've always liked and admired her, for her outspokenness, her thoughtfulness, her generosity, and yes, for being a great parent to these young adults who I genuinely like and respect.

But there was part of me who always felt like the Last of the Single Girlfriends, the one who had a small part in her life, but only in the fringes. I never got to know her post-college circle of companions because they were all married moms in the suburbs. I wasn't invited to the poker nights or the progressive dinner parties or the other social events that filled her calendar, and at times I was envious because I never had a community like she did. In all fairness, I didn't ever live close enough to do a lot of these activities with her on a regular basis, so I don't hold my being left out against her. But there was something to the mom and non-mom divide that nibbled at my heart, that left me wanting to be included, to be part of her fun life.

And once her kids were away at college, I wondered, had she reconnected with any of her other old friends who didn't have kids?

She was very thoughtful and candid in her answer. She thought about the different groups of friends of which she's a part, and realized all of them came together through their kids' schools or shared activities. "This makes sense," she said, and I agreed. "We're not unwelcoming," she said, "it's what you spend your time doing." So naturally, that's where you're going to meet people and start making connections. Megan was, however, adamant that this didn't mean they were "exclusive" groups. "Some of those friends have introduced other friends into a group," she said, "and now they're all friends."

Maybe, just maybe, I thought, someone like me could renew or begin similar connections. But as we explored this further and she examined the makeup of her groups, she realized that even those "outsiders" were mothers. "Are any of these women childless? Are any of your friends today childless?" I asked. She thought for a moment, then replied, "Just you."

Wow.

She, much to her credit, was willing to unpack this with me. For openers, she shared how even those initial friendships had evolved. "I see some of them; others have moved on," she said. But even when she meets women through new outlets, the common bond is still having children.

"With the women you're still close to, do you continue to just talk about your kids?" I asked.

"No," she said. "We talk about things other than our kids, like our parents, dogs, stuff in our lives. There's still lots to talk about."

I chose to find this encouraging, for certainly I could participate in and contribute to conversations about all these topics. There is still lots to talk about when women get together, and it doesn't all have to be about children.

I started to think about my role in this and other dormant friendships that had once been dear to me, because I am an equal player in them. As my mom girlfriends grow out of the full-time, hands-on mommying stage, as their daily lives open up to things beyond kid-focused issues, we can, I hope, find more commonality. Although the specifics vary, we are all going through some sort of transition or reinvention, so maybe we can support each other in that. We can talk about our roles as daughters, siblings, wives, neighbors, volunteers, professionals, and whatever else we might take on as 21st-century women.

And there's no reason I can't take the initiative. Like this phone call with Megan, maybe it's up to me to reopen the doors. I can send a note or an email, or make a call in which I simply say, "I'd love to catch up with you."

I think it could be the beginning of a beautifully renewed friendship.

"And don't try to console a woman just because she doesn't have kids. Being childfree is *not* the alternative, it's just a different 'normal'."

— *more wisdom from Kim*

34

EMBRACING THE CHILDFREE LIFE

*A*fter my single mommy internship adventure, I started to listen more closely to my friends who were parents, and I started hearing more about the flaws in the myth of picture-perfect contemporary family life: the mind-numbing boredom, how the relationship/marriage with the person you've chosen as your soul mate takes a back seat ("We fight all the time now," my friend Lori confided), chronic sleep deprivation, stress, and crushing financial burdens. "I love our children," my friend Jason told me, "but if I had known what we were getting into, I wouldn't have done it." What a sobering reality.

And these were parents with "normal," healthy children. I also listened with compassion as my friend Dominique cried with despair about her son with special needs. In addition to dealing every day with her son's physical challenges and behavioral issues, she felt isolated and depressed. She was the recipient of stares and insensitive comments from other people, including other parents who treated her as if she had a contagious disease. She did an admirable job of maintaining a happy demeanor and looking for the silver lining in her family's situation, but at her core, she was frightened by her son's limitations and how he would survive when she was no longer around to take care of him. And she and her husband were worn out by the toll their son's needs had taken on their marriage.

These were raw truths about parenthood. Now that I was armed with experience and information, now that I'd discovered that the fantasy I'd held onto for so long could suck in reality, I started to think I'd gotten the better end of the deal.

I was conscious of the many perks of a child-less marriage when, on a gorgeous fall day, I promised to "obey...my heart" and give Braden the best of my love. Family members and friends joined us on a lawn overlooking the San Francisco Bay as the best part of my original dream came true. I would no longer be sleeping or dancing alone. I became part of a family of my own making. And no priest told us how we should raise our children, should we be so "blessed." No guest encouraged us to "get right to work" on baby-making because of my age. No well-meaning mommy told me, "You're next!" We knew the kind of marriage we wanted, and we surrounded ourselves with family and friends who respected our decisions.

"We have dogs," my darling husband says when asked if we have kids, and when we're pressed for details about why we don't, I think about how lucky we are that we can travel during the off-season, zip around town in a two-seater convertible, and turn on the TV or computer without first having to adjust the parental controls. Instead of scrambling in different directions to kids' activities every weekend, we run errands together, go on long bike rides, and enjoy leisurely meals à deux or with friends. I can be available for a chat on the phone with a niece, and I can curse a blue stream when I stub my toe (without having to worry that my words will be repeated in church). We cheer for friends' kids at their dance recitals and sporting events, and we dance until the last song at weddings while other couples rush home to relieve babysitters, feed infants, check on teenagers, or just because they're tired.

In addition to thinking about what I can do, I also think about some of the annoying things I'll *never* do, such as I'll never ruin another couple's romantic dinner because I've let my toddler run amok in a nice restaurant. I'll never saddle a colleague with extra work because I have kids. I'll never tell my husband to go take a cold shower because I'm worn out from taking care of his kids. I'll never, ever con extended family into going on a Disney cruise. And I'll never wound a friend by saying, "How would you know? You're not a mother."

My journey has been one of moving from frustration to acceptance and ultimately to appreciation. For so long, I could only see the woe-is-me side of life, the loss of the family I couldn't have, the experiences I knew I'd miss. Having shifted my perspective, I now see all that I *have*, all that I've been given, all that I didn't lose. We each have the power to curate our life styles, to pick and choose elements and experiences that fit us. We can each define what a "meaningful" life means for ourselves. That we have so many options is a gift of our time!

What now, what next?

I don't know.

And that's okay. I may not have a firm plan in mind, but I find that I'm more open to what may come. I can explore! I can dream! And for all this, I am so grateful.

———

It was early in the morning on a national holiday. I was walking to the gym when I passed one of my neighbors as she loaded kids and gear into a minivan.

"Off to the gym?" she asked, grunting as she hoisted a toddler into his car seat.

"Yep."

"I would give anything to trade places with you."

For a split second I paused, then replied with the only response that seemed appropriate. "I'm sorry."

As I continued down the street, it dawned on me that for the first time in years I wasn't feeling (a) judgmental (she was, after all, dissing her kids) or (b) wistful. So often in the past I would have thought how *I* would have traded anything to have precious kids of my own, but now, not so much. I was pretty happy with the prospect of spending my holiday taking care of myself, maybe even reading a book or taking a nap instead of having to read a book to someone else hoping he would settle down for a nap. I didn't feel sorry for or envious of my neighbor, and I didn't want to trade my grass for her grass. The grass was perfectly green on my side of the street.

The healing process had begun.

Part of that process included acknowledging, grieving, and ultimately releasing my losses. Grieving is a crucial phase of the healing process, but it's a hard one to work through when your losses are invisible, intangible, and, to much of the world, insignificant.

I thought of dreams deferred or lost, all of the things that might have been, all of the milestones I had so long anticipated but will never experience. My great-grandmother used to look at all the sweet souls gathered around the Thanksgiving table and say out loud, "Look what I started." I had to find a way to face the ripple effects of, "Look what I ended." My not having children meant no chance of grandchildren or great-grandchildren, and all the experiences and memories I thought I'd create with them one day, memories I'd planned on sustaining me throughout my life. Yep. Grieving and releasing needed to happen if I had any hope of moving forward.

Packing up my wedding dress and veil gave me the perfect opportunity to unpack some of this accumulated grief one afternoon. I had no reason to preserve my dress for someone else to wear on her big day. Instead, I had the ensemble professionally cleaned and I arranged to donate it to an organization that sold pre-owned gowns at affordable prices and turned the proceeds over to breast cancer–related charities.

I placed the gown in tissue paper, then decided to try on my cathedral-length veil one last time. I placed the comb in my hair, drew the front veil over my face, and floated the sequin-studded train behind me. As I looked at myself in the mirror through the delicate gauzy haze, the tears came as I realized the finality of my experience. There will be no daughter or granddaughter to share this with in years to come. No one will ask to take my gown out of storage, to reminisce, to ooh and ahh. No one will care to find out if it still fits me in 10 or 20 years, and no one will join me a generation from now as we double over laughing that this was considered in style back in my day, like I did when I revisited friends' gowns from the '70s and '80s. No one will slip tiny feet into my shiny red wedding shoes, disappear under yards of tulle, and giggle as she imagines how one day she might walk down the aisle to marry the love of her life. No one will ask to incorporate any part of it as her "something borrowed."

It wasn't so much the veil, the treasured *thing*, that caused me to cry, but the cold, hard giving up on the other anticipated memories I'll never experience. I won't be able to pass along tips for making Gram's Coffee Cake. I won't be the one to introduce holiday traditions to a new generation. I won't take anyone with me to the voting polls to demonstrate the process and impress upon them the sacrifices our ancestors made so that we could enjoy this right. I won't be teaching anyone how to measure flour and even off the top of the measuring cup with a straight-edged knife, or pass along the handy tips my dad taught me about how to fix things around the house.

All of this is compounded by the isolation inherent in my brand of grief. There was no funeral, no public notice, no quiet calls to a chain of friends and family members announcing the news followed by a deluge of cards and casseroles. I would never ever trivialize the pain of my sisters who are childless by infertility. I've held too many friends and sobbed with them over miscarriages, failed IVF treatments, and the loss of their dreams, and I know too well that their paths are filled with heartbreak. But many of them had defining moments when they could let it all out, when they could openly grieve and open themselves up to receiving support. When a close friend went through a series of miscarriages before her first son was born, I was among the friends who supported her through her grief. We were there to listen and cry with her, we did our best to encourage her to keep up her hope and faith. We brought flowers and cookies, things we shared along with her mourning.

But for me, there was nothing tangible. As a woman who was circumstantially infertile, I experienced a different level of anguish. I never had that moment of finality, never experienced that intense period of grief. And so, it was up to me to, over time, welcome in those moments of grief, acknowledge the feelings that bubbled up, then as best I could, feel them fully and let them go.

With my tears dried for the moment, and the dress and veil sealed in their package, I reviewed the past several years and thought about what I'd like to say to 38-year-old Kathleen. I knew I couldn't change the course of events, but perhaps I could have offered her some guidance, wisdom, or encouragement that would have helped her/me get through the journey with a little less self-loathing and a lot more grace.

"Would you have done anything differently?" I imagine her asking me, and my answer, after a moment of reflection, would have to be, "No." Because I couldn't have chosen the obstacles presented to me, I still would have had to work through them. Maybe I could have pushed harder to marry one of the early husband candidates who came before Braden, but the thought of having children with any of them is not a pleasant day-dream. Maybe I could have taken a different career path, invested heavily (if only I'd bought Apple stock at the IPO), and set myself up for financially secure single parenting. But those are all pipe dreams. I don't think I'd do anything differently because, as hard as this journey has been, it has brought me to where I am and made me who I am today. And my life today is better than anything I could have imagined.

When I introduced the "Our Stories" column on *Life Without Baby*, I asked contributors, "What would you like to say to your younger self?" I thought about my own answers, thought about how, if I could reach back into time, I'd share what this journey has taught me. I'd let younger Kath know that the grief still comes, but it gets easier. I'd try to encourage her by promising she'll find ways to rebalance and discover new joys. Here's what I'd try to say to her and what I hope she would hear:

Be gentle with yourself. Change is coming, and it's good. It's so very good. You will be astonished when you look back by how dramatically your life has changed for good in such a short span of time. You will meet new friends who will inspire you with their courage and their generosity. Your worldview, your opinions, and your experiences of people will be broadened. You will be challenged to become a better human. You think you're open-minded now? Just wait. Your capacity for compassion will expand. You will be delighted. You will be awed and inspired, and you will realize that all of it was possible because of what you went through and are going through.

Your journey will get you there. But today you must be brave, because you must face your fears, you must grieve your losses. What you are envisioning right now, that perfect picture of life with baby, isn't going to come out the way you're hoping and praying it will. And I'm so sorry for that. Let your tears fall and your fears rage.

That needs to happen too. But you will, I promise, find happiness, your happiness. It includes wonderfully deep and intimate relationships.

I know this is cheating a little bit, but I want to give you some hope, so know that this is what is coming: You are going to be a dog mama to three of the most loving creatures you'll ever have the privilege to love. You will have close and precious relationships with your nieces, nephews (yes, plural), and godsons (I know—how fun is that?!) And you are going to end up with a husband who is your perfect match in ways you never could have foreseen. Best of all, you will have no regrets. So open your heart wide and go fully live your life.

———

I was beaming with happiness. Braden and I had just stood up as godparents to the sons of two of our dearest friends. To be asked was such a deep honor and compliment, and we took our vows to these precious souls very seriously—and with a tremendous amount of joy.

So I was a little stunned when a woman, one of the guests, ambushed me after the baptism ceremony as we walked to the reception hall.

"So, you're the godmother?"

"Yes! Hi, I'm Kathy."

"How do you know the family?"

"Close family friends."

"And you have kids the same ages as the boys?"

"No." I started to sense there was an edge to her questions.

"You have older kids?"

"No."

"But you have kids?"

"No. Just the two of us."

"If you don't have kids, why are *you* the godmother?"

Whoa.

"That's not actually one of the requirements, you know. You don't have to be parents to be godparents," I said, forcing a smile. "It's more about being there for the kids and their parents."

"But wouldn't it make sense that you'd have to be parents to be good godparents?"

I bit back the "bitch" that was making its way from my brain to my mouth.

"Do you have kids?" I asked her.

"Of course." *Breathe, Kath, breathe.*

"Well...the way I look at it, since we don't have kids of our own, we have more time to be present for these boys. We can attend their events, support them in their faith journeys, be there for them in ways that we couldn't if our time was fully devoted to raising our own."

A man was walking a step and a half behind her—the husband, I assumed. I saw him register the logic.

"Maybe," she allowed. I sensed she wasn't giving in, but I was done.

"See you in the party," I said, with genuine cheerfulness.

I later pointed her out to another guest and learned she was a relative of the family. They did not have a good relationship (shocking), but that didn't stop her from feeling slighted when she was not chosen to be the godmother, something she had felt entitled to. Well, she had her own burdens to deal with.

Meanwhile, it was a revelatory exchange for me. *I win*, I thought. Once again I had been maligned, stigmatized, by my not being a mother in my own right. But I completely stood by the reasoning that I'd expressed on the fly, and I was proud of myself for speaking out. Doors, big doors, had closed to me, then others had opened. I *would* have more time for these boys. I would be able to devote energy and attention to their needs. I would not have been able to do this on the same level had I had kids of my own, and I was, on some very basic level, grateful that I would get to be a significant part in my godsons' lives.

I will never get to experience being a full-fledged, card-carrying, 24/7 mother. I will never be called "mama" or "grandma," but my life is anything but child-less. I am the fun grownup, who gets her hair styled at family get-togethers and encourages the kids to make goofy faces in group photos. I am the loyal cheerleader at amateur theatrical productions and sporting events. I am the person whose lap is rarely empty. I am confidante and friend. By choice, I am "Aunt Kath," the world's greatest aunt.

EPILOGUE

*L*ater that year, Braden and I were having dinner with close friends, their teenage son, and their seven-year-old daughter, Lily. As topics bounced around the table, we engaged various participants in discussing the high school basketball game we'd just attended (they'd won, but strategies were critiqued), shopping for cute shoes, and movies coming soon to theaters. Mid-conversation, Lily leaned across the chips & salsa to say directly to me, "You really should have kids."

It got very quiet, and I could feel the tension in the air as my husband's hand reached for mine under the table. I gave him a squeeze back, acknowledging his support, but I was okay.

I looked into the sweet face of this darling girl. There was no pity or judgment in her pronouncement. Pure love radiated from her, and from me.

"Thank you," I said, with a warm and genuine smile. Then after a moment, "But that ship has pretty much sailed."

Before anyone could jump in with all the usual, and useless, comments ("It's not too late!" "You could adopt!"), I followed up with, "You know, if you think about it, if we had kids, we wouldn't be able to be here. Right?" I looked to her brother and added, "We'd be at *their* basketball games, and their dance recitals, and we wouldn't have the time to hang out with you." I looked back at Lily and added, "and I would miss that."

On the drive home, I reflected on the exchange and how far I'd come in my healing journey since the last time someone said "You really should have kids" to me. I meant what I said to Lily. I would very much miss having these dinners with our friends and their kids. I'd miss not getting to cheer on their endeavors, getting acquainted with different personalities and learning about their unique gifts and passions. I wouldn't be in a position to make Special Dates with my siblings, nieces, and nephews. I would have a lot less time with my husband, a man I married because I love spending time with him.

Life, I've learned, is about constant reinvention. It's never too late to dream a new dream, however, sometimes before we can do that, we have to let go of the bindings of the old, lost dream. I did that. And I came to accept and believe that my life does have meaning, my life does matter.

That's not to say I don't have pings. Even if my body is well past its baby-making expiration date, there are still moments that hurt. At times I do still feel cheated, because I know I, and so many of the women I know, would have been amazing moms. I continue to shut down Facebook and Instagram and all the mommy posts that appear the weeks before and after Mother's Day. Graduation season and Christmas aren't all that fun either. I still avoid baby showers like the plague (always sending a generous gift with my regrets), and am not sure how I'll handle them when it's my nieces' turns to be honored as the mommies-to-be. I'll see how I feel when the time comes.

In the meantime, I honor my feelings, listen to my heart and my gut, and respond accordingly. And I find my value, my purpose, the pieces of my wholeness, in the many roles I play in this life: friend, sister, wife, confidante, godmother, blogger, mentor, and, naturally, auntie.

There's a wisdom that comes only with time and life experience, and yes, hardships. It's the gift of knowing who I am, or rather, being open to becoming who I will be. And if there's one big lesson I've learned about myself in this journey, it's that I'm not, in fact, living a child-less life. Rather, I am surrounded by beloved nieces, nephews, godsons, and young friends.

Acknowledging and embracing this reality about this life of mine has been the best—wait for it—choice I've ever made.

A NOTE TO YOU, IF YOU'RE STILL WRESTLING WITH THIS DILEMMA

I didn't set out to be one of the one in five women who are childless. I never imagined I'd be a voice for childfree women around the world. But here I am. Funny how life works.

Rejecting what I thought was my divine purpose—being a mother—was not easy. But I now see my circuitous journey as a gift, one that has allowed me to embrace change and join the ranks of the many other extraordinary women who are leading happy, fulfilling, and yes, childfree lives.

This path is not right for everyone, and it may not be right for you, but the key point I want to communicate to you is that *only you* can decide what's right for you.

Much of my new-found contentment is possible because I pushed myself to look deep into my heart and explore whether the path I was following was the right one for me. I think this exploration is an essential step for anyone who is making life-altering choices. Do not let anyone tell you you're being selfish. You are being self-aware, and this is a skill you must master to achieve success, however you define it, in every area of your life.

Choose consciously, and make own your choices.

If you are still considering whether or not you want to

pursue motherhood, as part of a couple or as a single parent, I encourage you to start by asking yourself, and honestly answering, the following:

- Ask *why* you want to have children; ask if you have the *desire* to parent, not just the expectation that you will.
- Ask if you are truly willing to compromise—or sacrifice—a career that you love.
- Ask if you are ready and willing to make long-term commitments with your finances, emotions, time, and energy.
- Ask if you can offer a stable and nurturing environment in which to raise a child.
- Ask if you are having a child for the right reasons, not to create someone who will love you, who will take care of you in your old age, who will "save" your marriage, or who will live out your unfulfilled dreams.

If your heart is shouting "Go for it!", go for it. I wish you an easy road to pregnancy and all the joys of motherhood. Please never take for granted how lucky you are. If your answers lead you to choosing a childfree future, I hope you have a community that supports you. Whichever path you choose, I again entreat you to please remember that you are *not* being selfish, you are being conscientious. How lucky we are to live in a time and generation in which we have choices!

You may be at the crossroads in your life where you are beginning to acknowledge that you may not be able (or willing) to have children of your own. If this has been your dream and losing it hurts, I'm so sorry. I know how you feel. I know this is a sad, hard, and painful time, and I know you will feel better someday. I wish you courage as you face the challenges ahead of you, I wish you peace as you grow to accept your new path, and I wish you love, in whatever form it appears.

I also encourage you to look into some of the resources listed at the end of this book. I am proud of my contributions to the alternative motherhood discussions, through my work with *Life Without Baby*, and am grateful to the global sisterhood of childless writers and bloggers who were part of this support system. You may find the support you need through one of the listed websites or publications. Please check out the list.

The answers you seek may be slow to reveal themselves. Healing—and by that I mean going through the stages of grieving the loss of expectations, claiming acceptance, and feeling you can finally move forward and beyond your original dream to a place of appreciation—takes time. That slow pace can be very frustrating. Even now, coming from a place of being mostly at peace with my childfree status, I still don't know what my future holds. The difference is, I am more excited about opening myself up to the possibilities, even the ambiguities.

As I experienced my mommy internship, and as I worked through what I learned and explored what it would mean to share my story, it dawned on me that I was writing the book I needed to read a decade ago. Would I have picked it up? Would I have heeded my advice? Would it have changed anything for me? I don't know. But I hope that by sharing my story I encourage younger women to consider all their options. I want to tell women in their 30s and 40s who are freaking out, "You will be okay," and "Yes, your life matters," for that's what I wish I could have told my younger self.

Women continue to face tremendous challenges. While men gauge their worth on things like job performance, achievement, material goods (that in-your-face red sports car), women are judged by relations: how good she is as a wife and mother, or if she is neither. A childless woman must either hate children or she can't fully understand or demonstrate real love.

Mothers are vilified in the media if they breast feed in public, or if they "choose" to feed their babies formula. A woman leaves a child alone for five minutes, and she's negligent; hovers, and she's a "helicopter mom." A woman without children of her own is lazy, selfish, and predatory, and she shouldn't be allowed inside a playground near other people's children for risk of, well, I don't know what. If a woman who is a mother succeeds in her profession, she might be attacked for shirking parenting duties, but if she "gives up" her career to be a full-time mom, she risks being sidelined and passed over for promotion. But then a childless woman, who has time and energy to devote to service outside the home, runs for public office and is labeled unfit or unworthy of leadership.

Enough.

Let's stop and listen. Let's do away with the mom/non-mom, conservative/liberal, anti/feminist, good/bad, non/traditional labels, and all the other ways we impose judgments. Let's respect each other, celebrate our precious individual paths—forged by choices or circumstances—and acknowledge that each of us is needed to make humankind whole.

Let's change the conversation. Or rather, let's start having the conversations so that things can change. Let's champion a woman's right to choose what is right for her, and let's support each other. Let's value *women*.

RESOURCES AND REFERENCES

If you are struggling with being childless, I encourage you to pick up some of the books listed below and/or check out some of the websites. You'll find forums, groups, workshops & programs, and other resources to help you on your journey toward making peace with—and, I hope, some day embracing—your childless status.

Books

21 Miles: Swimming in Search of the Meaning of Motherhood by Jessica Hepburn

Childless by Marriage by Sue Fagalde Lick

Dealing With Social Landmines by Lisa Manterfield

Do You Have Kids?: Life When the Answer is No by Kate Kaufmann

I'm Taking My Eggs and Going Home: How One Woman Dared to Say No to Motherhood by Lisa Manterfield

Life Without Baby: Holiday Companion by Lisa Manterfield & Kathleen Guthrie Woods

Life Without Baby: Surviving and Thriving When Motherhood Doesn't Happen by Lisa Manterfield

Living the Life Unexpected: 12 Weeks to Your Plan B for a Meaningful and Fulfilling Future Without Children by Jody Day

Love or Children: When You Can't Have Both by Sue Fagalde Lick

Motherhood Missed: Stories from Women Who Are Childless by Circumstance by Lois Tonkin

No Kidding: Women Writers on Bypassing Parenthood edited by Henriette Mantel

Otherhood: Modern Women Finding a New Kind of Happiness by Melanie Notkin

Savvy Auntie: The Ultimate Guide for Cool Aunts, Great-Aunts, Godmothers and All Women Who Love Kids by Melanie Notkin

Selfish, Shallow and Self-Absorbed: Sixteen Writers on the Decision NOT to Have Kids edited by Meghan Daum

Silent Sorority by Pamela Mahoney Tsigdinos

The Next Happy: Let Go of the Life You Planned and Find a New Way Forward by Tracey Cleantis

The Pursuit of Motherhood by Jessica Hepburn

Websites / Blogs

Childless By Marriage: https://childlessbymarriageblog.com/

Gateway Women (international group that is passionate and compassionate about the lives and futures of childless women): https://gateway-women.com/

Infertility Honesty (childless not by choice infertility survivorhood): https://infertilityhonesty.com/

No Kidding in NZ (an infertility survivor's thoughts on life without kids): https://nokiddinginnz.blogspot.com/

The NoMo Book Club (recommends and celebrates books with childless characters): https://thenomobookclub.com/

The Not Mom (dedicated to providing support to women who face challenges dealing with a childless lifestyle, either by choice or chance): https://www.thenotmom.com/

Savvy Auntie (community for cool aunts, great aunts, godmothers, and all women who love kids): http://savvyauntie.com

Silent Sorority (infertility survivors finally heard): https://www.blog.silentsorority.com/

Slow Swimmers & Fried Eggs (married couples share their journeys through fertility treatments): https://www.conceiveivf.com/category/slow-swimmers-and-fried-eggs

ACKNOWLEDGMENTS

Deep appreciation to the many friends and interviewees who shared their stories and wisdom with me. Your candid and honest descriptions of your own experiences helped me make my way, heal, and find peace at my destination. What you have shared with me will also help the readers of this story.

For the successful development and production of this book, I'd like to thank the Sisters of Submission writing group (Jeff Buppert, Shannon Calder, Lisa M. Poole, and Robi Wax) for their early support and feedback; early draft readers Karen Peck and Pamela Mahoney Tsigdinos for thoughtful notes and encouragement; editor Cheryl Woodruff, who saw something bigger in my original story and pushed me out of my comfort zone to tell it; Kelly Mishell, who motivated me to "get it done"; and Nancy Van Iderstine, copyeditor, and Regan Chapman, proofreader, for their eagle eyes and encouragement. It has been a privilege and an honor having you all on my Team.

A handful of very special individuals have been with me as I lived the experiences, and then crafted and published the story that became *The Mother of All Dilemmas*. My sister and biggest fan, Carrie, made this whole experience possible. Lisa

Manterfield, my friend, colleague, and this book's champion, was with me from the first draft, talked me through many seasons of triumph and doubt, and guided me every step of the way. I'm so thankful for Jake, always Jake, for being my companion in this life adventure. And to Braden and our dog, Louie: How I love being a family with you.

ABOUT THE AUTHOR

Kathleen Guthrie Woods is a San Francisco–based freelance copywriter and editor. For eight years she wrote a weekly column for LifeWithoutBaby.com, a website and blog dedicated to giving a voice to women who are childfree by chance, choice, or circumstance. She currently runs her own blog, 52Nudges, in which she takes weekly "risks" to push her out of her sometimes-too-comfortable nest.

With Lisa Manterfield, she co-authored *Life Without Baby: Holiday Companion*, a compilation of humorous, healing, and thought-provoking posts designed to help other childless women get through the holidays and get closer to making peace with being childfree. *The Mother of All Dilemmas* is her second book.

Kathleen's family of choice includes her husband and their

dog, siblings and their spouses, nieces and nephews, godsons, and a wide circle of friends of all ages. She leads a full and interesting life, one that is anything but child-less.

www.kathleen-ink.com

 facebook.com/KathleenInk

Printed in Great Britain
by Amazon